Foundations
for Christian
Education
in an
Era of Change

dited by Marvin J. Taylor

Foundations
for Christian
Education
in an
Era of Change

edited by Marvin J. Taylor

ABINGDON
Nashville

FOUNDATIONS FOR CHRISTIAN EDUCATION IN AN ERA OF CHANGE

Library of Congress Cataloging in Publication Data

Foundations for Christian education in an era of change.
   Supplement to An introduction to Christian education, edited by M. J. Taylor.
   Bibliography: p.
   1. Christian education—Addresses, essays, lectures. I. Taylor, Marvin J., 1921-   II. Taylor, Marvin J., 1921-   An introduction to Christian education.
BV1473.F677   207   75-44185

ISBN 0-687-13329-7

"Education in the World Ecumenical Movement" by William B. Kennedy appeared previously in *Ecumenical Review,* April 1975.

MANUFACTURED BY THE PARTHENON PRESS AT
NASHVILLE, TENNESSEE, UNITED STATES OF AMERICA

CONTENTS

INTRODUCTION

Ten years ago I introduced the predecessor of this volume with this sentence, "One of the most significant characteristics of the contemporary Christian education movement is change." At that writing I hardly recognized the import of those words. In the mid-sixties we were still in the reflected glow of mainline Protestantism's post-World War II "success story." Educational participation was still on the increase, although the curve had begun to flatten out considerably. The profession of religious education still had reasonably clear bench marks for self-analysis. Much of that has been altered in the past decade. Both Protestant and Roman Catholic Christianity here in the States as well as abroad have experienced the pivotal uncertainties accompanying significant change. In many ways this book reflects these new realities.

This volume is preceded by a long series of Abingdon Press publications. *Studies in Religious Education* appeared in 1931, and it was followed by *Orientation in Religious Education* in 1950. Under my editorship, *Religious Education: A Comprehensive Survey* was published in 1960 and *An Introduction to Christian Education* in 1966.

Since the first book, the format has been the same. An editor (or editors) invites educators with special competences to contribute to the symposium. This obviously sacrifices the possibility of a unitary theoretical basis for the volume since multiple authorship will reflect varied philosophies. But I continue to see this as a strength, not a weakness. It introduces readers to representative examples of the several educational perspectives which prevail in the field. It also presents in abbreviated form many authors who have in other publications written much more extensively on these aspects of the religious education movement.

The discerning reader will note a shift of terminology back to *religious education* in this volume. Although the term *Christian education* continues to appear in the title, many authors have quite consistently used the language made standard by the religious education movement in this century. One by-product of the theological renascence, which was best characterized by neo-orthodoxy in American religious thought, was a stress on the distinctly Christian heritage wherein certain theological themes assumed a new dominance in the church's educational thinking. No such clear perspective seems evident today, and the more generic term, *religious education,* has been utilized more frequently.

I have indicated above that many of the authors have here presented an introduction to their work found elsewhere. In this sense our joint effort has been to produce an introductory book whose primary value will be to lead the reader into the broad dimensions of the field. Based on usage given to the previous volumes, this has been planned as an introductory textbook for seminary and college classes conducted on the survey approach. It makes no pretense of detailed treatment of any subject. And, separate courses could be offered in each of the fields identified by chapter headings. For the reader who wants more, I suggest that the chapter bibliographies and notes will be a primary resource. Furthermore, an extensive Selected Bibliography can be found at the end of the volume. This, together with the parallel bibliographies in the previous books, should provide any interested person with adequate suggestions for in-depth research into almost any facet of religious education which may be of interest. In addition to its classroom use, the book should also be of value to church and school libraries, teachers of church education classes, professional leaders—ministers, directors of education, etc. It is to all of these that this volume is hopefully offered.

Persons familiar with the earlier volumes will note that this one is somewhat smaller. The impact of our inflationary times is of course a major reason. Much of the reduction has been in the section on programs, methods, and materials. There are several circumstances which have occasioned this decision. One occasional criticism of the predecessor books was that they were too massive, that they attempted to be too all-encompassing. This has been heard and a response made. Second, this edition has stressed *foundations*. Hence, a lesser emphasis upon programs, methods, and materials seems appropriate. Furthermore, these are the areas of religious education in which the most diversity denominationally occurs, and these books have never sought to describe that widely ranging spectrum of the movement. Finally, readers will find continued treatment of resources in the bibliographies.

As editor, I owe a considerable debt of gratitude to two different groups of persons. Many religious-educator friends responded to my request for their perspectives on a new volume. They are too numerous to mention, but I am nonetheless very grateful for that assistance. It helped materially in planning the symposium. And second, I am also appreciative of the efforts of twenty-one very busy persons who found time in their active lives to contribute chapters for this volume. Each is a specialist in his/her field, and this will be evident in the quality of the writing.

Marvin J. Taylor

Chapter 1

A HISTORICAL PERSPECTIVE ON THE FUTURES OF AMERICAN RELIGIOUS EDUCATION

Robert W. Lynn

On the eve of the Bicentennial, the American people might well heed a warning issued a few years ago by famed English historian J. H. Plumb. "History," he declared, is not to be equated with any one version of the "past." "The past is always a created ideology with a purpose, designed to control individuals, or motivate societies, or inspire classes. Nothing has been so corruptly used as concepts of the past." The work of historians is to cleanse the story of humankind of "these deceiving notions of a purposeful past." [1]

One of the more hopeful developments of recent years has been the renewed assault upon certain entrenched understandings of the American past. After the sixties it is harder for historians to tell only the story of white America. Now we know, albeit belatedly, that an American past without women is, in fact, a "created ideology . . . designed to control individuals."

Yet few historians have explored the multiple uses of expectations about America's future. For if our claims about the past often turn out to be ideological creations, so do those images of the future which have consistently moved successive generations of Americans. We have been a future-chasing nation, possessed and preoccupied by the lure of an imaginary tomorrow. These future concepts have also been employed "to control individuals, or motivate societies, or inspire classes." There has been, indeed, as much American dogma proclaimed about the future as about the past.

But when those images of the future lose their power—as appears now to be the case in this country—then a double-edged challenge of peril and promise is in the making. The peril of the new situation resides in potential loss of motivating power and energy. Make no

Robert W. Lynn is Senior Program Officer for the Lilly Endowment, Inc., Indianapolis, Indiana.

mistake about it: collective convictions about the shape of things to come can unleash incredible strength. To lose that source of energy is to risk anomic drift and inertia. The promise inherent in this loss is the necessity of thinking about the future in new and different ways.

In this essay I suggest that Christian educators in America will be living with both the promise and the peril of this challenge for years to come. The mythic futures which once prompted much of Protestant and Catholic efforts in education have faded in potency and appeal. The apparent decline of these visions coincides (and not accidentally) with an increasing systemic disarray in the ecology of educational institutions. These two developments, in turn, make it possible for educators to ask a fresh set of questions about the shape of Christian education in the coming decades.

First- and Second-Class Citizens in Zion

Out of early nineteenth-century America came two images of the future, both of which have been reflected in the educational activities of the churches in the intervening years. Let us examine each in turn.

Paideia in a Protestant Zion. The first of these visions was entertained by a variety of evangelical Protestants across the denominational spectrum. For many of these folk, the future was lustrous, in fact brilliant, because of America. They could not long speak of their own religious future without also thinking of the United States and its destiny.

In the years between the War of 1812–14 and the firing of the first shot at Fort Sumter in 1861, American Protestants spawned an astonishing number of new educational ventures—Sunday schools, colleges and academies, seminaries, denominational boards, publication societies, etc. What could justify the energy and sacrifices necessary to launch these enterprises? In part the evangelicals appealed to the imperative of accepting their responsibilities as inhabitants of the Protestant Zion. Americans, so they believed, had been delivered out of the Babylonian captivity of the Old World into life in the new New Israel. One of the better selling items in the libraries offered by the American Sunday School Union was a life of George Washington in which the founding father was portrayed as a Moses who had led his people to the land of milk and honey. Moreover the landscape itself was considered to be a reminder of God's providence. The mountains, valleys, and plains—these moral and educational forces constituted an ideal matrix for the nurturing of a new race, open to the Lord's future.

America was not only the beginning of something new; its presence

8

also signified the coming of the final stage of history. These Protestants disagreed among themselves about the imminence of the millennium and, even more important, about whether or not it would come before the Day of Judgment. But whatever their differences, they were largely united in the conviction that they stood on the threshold of an extraordinarily important era. The most decisive future man had ever experienced was about to unfold. It would become evident first in the New World and then in other less favored parts of the world. This meant, among other things, that American Protestantism had a special responsibility as a missionary force both within this nation and to the world. The logic of the mission: Christianize the United States so that it can lead the way in christianizing the world. In this notion—so flatly stated here as to be incomprehensible, much less acceptable, to many Christians living in the last part of the twentieth century—lay the impulse of hope, the source of urgency and quickening expectancy that inspired evangelical educators during those early formative years.

I would not deny for a moment that there were other forces at work in the minds of these innovators. They were also prompted by the ever-present reality of collective self-interest. In the wake of disestablishment after the Revolutionary War, the evangelicals had to develop a new generation of institutions for passing on the Christian faith. Otherwise the Protestant presence in the new nation would have slowly withered away. They were not about to let that happen! A host of other factors—their corrosive hatred of a growing Roman Catholic community, a distrust of the native "infidels" in their midst, and denominational competition—also aroused them to prodigious effort. But none of these motivations, even when cloaked in appropriate ideological disguise, could have provided the requisite rationale and justification for their developing educational strategy. It was their vision of the future, more than anything else, that vindicated the demands they were making upon themselves and others.

The ensuing creation was a marvel of complexity. In the early decades of the nineteenth century these churchmen patched together a new pattern—or ecology—of Protestant educational institutions. By a series of apparent coincidences they devised a variety of ways through which America could be prepared for its future.

a. Foremost among these educational institutions was the revival. That judgment may surprise the latter-day observer whose impressions of this form are largely governed by his reactions to Billy Graham's technetronic spectaculars. In the national period, however, the revival often functioned as the great school of the Protestant public. In that setting, all sorts of educational activity was observable, i.e., the deliberate forming of a community and its self-identity, the shaping of values, attitudes, and beliefs, etc.

b. An allied institution was the Sunday school. As Elliott Wright and I have tried to indicate in *The Big Little School,* this transplanted American version of the English charity school served a variety of disparate purposes. Its foremost function, in the judgment of its evangelical proponents, was to provide a context for conversion so that the next generation could take up the work of a missionary nation. Although these Sunday school pioneers were seldom optimistic enough to think this purpose would ever be fully realized, they still expected that somewhere on every Sunday another recruit would have been enlisted in the army of the Lord.

c. The evangelicals relied upon publications as another educational medium. For example, the American Bible Society and the American Tract Society were among the leading publishers of the time. Meanwhile, the Sunday School Union sold or gave away mini-libraries to thousands of hamlets along the western frontier. The evangelical literature ranged from pocket Bibles and tracts to etiquette books on how to be a Christian gentleman.

d. During the same period the evangelicals took the lead in spawning denominational colleges, a creation that was somewhat different from the colonial college in ethos and purpose.

e. In a parallel move they also developed the confessional seminary. No longer were these churchmen content to rely upon the colleges and the apprentice system for theological training. Andover and Princeton became the models for this new educational venture in the United States.

f. All these schools were encouraged and sustained by benevolent agencies and Sunday school societies which eventually evolved into the first approximation of the denominational board of education as we know it today.

g. Although the emerging public school could not be officially described as part of the Protestant ecology, evangelical leaders often praised it fondly as a Christian outpost in a society which was increasingly besieged by strangers from abroad.

h. Finally, family and congregational life were also counted upon as significant educational contexts.

There, in brief, is the outline form of a potent educational ecology. No self-conscious strategist mapped it out as whole; no committee said, "Now this is what we must do." It came into existence in a haphazard, unplanned manner. Each of its expressions represented an *ad hoc* response to a particular need or opportunity. But what held it together, once it was established in the routines of Protestant church life, was the evangelical spirit, a spirit aroused and enlivened by the conviction that at last in America Christians were on the verge of entering God's future. For here they were planting the seed of the posterity of a new Adam in the virgin soil of Eden, warmed by the Sun of righteousness.

Aliens in Zion. If white evangelicals were at ease in Zion in the last century, the blacks (whether freed or slave) and the Roman Catholics knew they were aliens and strangers in the American Israel. These "outsiders" were fighting for the right to exist. And they had every reason to fear the fate of extinction. Here I will deal just with the Catholic community and its battle for survival in the almost-forgotten past.

The contemporary Catholic church is such a familiar fixture on the American scene that it is difficult to understand sympathetically the terrors and anxieties felt by her leaders in the late 1830s and 1840s. During these years the Irish prelates of the major eastern cities—Fenwick of Boston, Hughes of New York, and Kenrick of Philadelphia—knew full well that their church had barely secured a start in the United States. It was the most fragile of beginnings. In the colonial era more than two hundred thousand Catholics had lost their distinctive religious identity and had vanished into the anonymity of a vaguely Protestant society. That mode of annihilation was still a possibility. Nothing could be taken for granted. It is no wonder, therefore, that these leaders were so intent upon one elemental goal—to keep Catholic Americans Catholic.

Yet how could that future ever be realized when the only "free schools" for the Catholic children crowding into the ghettos of New York were, in fact, Protestant-oriented charity schools? Bishop Hughes suspected—and with good reason—that the sponsors of these benevolent organizations were more interested in the Americanization of Catholics than in providing literacy instruction for the urban poor. The issue at stake in Philadelphia was slightly different. A Pennsylvania law of 1838 made the Bible a required textbook in every public school. Though nothing was said about the version of the Bible to be used, the Protestants insisted upon the King James translation. From that point onward, conflict was inevitable. This dispute over a sacred symbol, somewhat akin to the current arguments about the American flag, eventually culminated in the bloody Philadelphia "Bible riot" of 1844.

This catastrophic experience, as well as Hughes's failure to obtain state aid for parochial schools in New York, convinced the prelates

11

that they could never trust the Protestant establishment. The public schools, according to Bishop Hughes, offered little more than "Socialism, Red Republicanism, Universalism, Infidelity, Deism, Atheism, and Pantheism—anything, everything, except religionism and patriotism."[2]

This all-purpose "swear list" indicates the depth of the bishops' rage and frustration. The only way forward, they concluded, was to strike out on their own and create a system of Catholic schools. In the words of Hughes, "I think the time is almost come when it will be necessary to build the school-house first and the church afterwards."[3]

The school before the church—that is one of the most fateful ideas ever expressed in American history. It became the regulative principle of Catholic educational policy. Even today one can still see its consequences. On any Sunday drive through the suburbs, look closely at the Catholic churches built after World War II. What one often glimpses there is a complex of school buildings with a small church as an appendage. That sight is also a visible reminder of a remarkable accomplishment. Without great resources the Catholic community in America developed the most complete nonstate system of schools in the world. Bishop Hughes could not have asked for anything more from his fellow aliens in Zion. In the hundred-year span from the 1850s to the 1950s, they remained true to that plain goal hammered out amidst the perilous struggles of the mid-nineteenth century—to keep Catholic Americans Catholic. Here, as perhaps nowhere else in the sweep of Christian *paideia* in America, we can discern the power of a vision of the future.[4]

An Uncertain Present

This swift glance at an earlier period reminds us of the enormous changes that have overtaken American religion in the last fifteen years. Consider, for a moment, the recent troubles of the Catholic parochial schools.

Their problems reach deeper than just a shortage of money and a decline in religious vocations. The old rationale—keeping Catholic Americans Catholics—is no longer persuasive ideology. The mainspring of this system, the power of alienation, has grown slack in recent years. With the election of John F. Kennedy in 1960 and the Vatican II reforms in ensuing years, the Roman Catholic Church has become more like another denomination, content to sell its wares in the religious marketplace alongside other groups. Meanwhile the secularization of the Catholic schools proceeds apace, and even their most zealous defenders will be hard pressed in the coming years to prove their uniqueness on the American scene. In short, Catholic education has reached the end of an era.

Can the same be said of Protestant education? There is no one answer to that question because of the varying pace of change in different quarters of American Protestantism. The traditional ecology of educational institutions is still intact in those communities of faith which have adhered to the spirit and forms of nineteenth-century evangelical Protestantism. For confirmation of that fact, one might look to the "right" of the denominational spectrum, well beyond such powerhouses as the Southern Baptist Convention, to the lesser-known movements like the Nazarenes or the "holiness" churches. In those so-called fringe groups (a label that is rapidly becoming misleading), the older pattern of Sunday school, church college, seminary, and other agencies is still very much in evidence.

As the observer scans leftward across the spectrum, some changes become noticeable. All kinds of distress signals emanate from the broad center where the established, "mainline" denominations hold sway. It is not only the seminaries and Sunday schools that are experiencing a case of misplaced identity; the other companion educational institutions—i.e., the colleges, the denominational boards of education—are likewise scrambling to stay afloat. The distress is *system wide,* a fact which could indicate that the larger pattern is gradually dissolving.

Yet this educational ecology represents only the visible portion of our inheritance from the nineteenth-century evangelicals. What happens to its invisible counterpart may be of more importance. I doubt that the old Protestant image of the future will play the same role that it did earlier in the century. The historian Henry F. May once commented that Americans in the early 1900s looked to the "unfolding American future" as the "main guarantee of universal morality."[5]

So it has been until the last ten years. From Woodrow Wilson's crusade to "make the world safe for democracy" to the inaugural address of John F. Kennedy, Americans have been entreated to bear the burdens of a secular missionary nation. Then came the Vietnam debacle, and after Vietnam, what? No one knows for sure. My own hunch is that it will be far harder for many Americans to revert to an earlier state of innocence. Our faith in America as Zion has been damaged, if not destroyed. It will probably never be quite the same again.

That makes the immediate future of liberal Protestant education all the more uncertain. Despite its appearance of modernity and relentless relevance, white Protestantism of the liberal hue is rooted in the ethos of Victorian America. Whenever that foundation is shaken, the reverberations rattle the present structures. Few "mainline" Protestants can escape the sounds of these deep rumblings. They are echoed, for instance, in the pervasive loss of a sense of mission and direction in history, in the growing difficulty of defining the purposes of church programs, in the diminished self-confidence of denominational and ecumenical leaders, and above all in the quiet erosion of old loyalties and enthusiasms. These subtle and shadowy changes of the ethos are of greater import than crisp statistics about Sunday-school attendance or church giving. If I read the signs of the times correctly, liberal Protestantism is undergoing a crisis of confidence far more severe than anything experienced even at the height of the controversy over biblical criticism in the early 1900s. That state of crisis will affect all aspects of "mainstream" Protestant education for some time to come. What lies ahead, in all likelihood, is an extended season of restiveness and experimentation.

In the retrospective judgment of future historians of American education, the 1960s will mark the beginning of an end. That transition continues through this decade. One chapter in the story of Christian *paideia* is concluding, while another has yet to be written. What will Christian education be like in the 1980s and 1990s? Here are one person's speculations about the next chapter.

Three Questions About the Future

Several years ago the Catholic educator, Gabriel Moran, confessed to "great skepticism" about venturing any "predictions for the year 2000." "I have difficulty with predicting next week," he commented. "The only place I look for the future is in the depths of the present."[6] But the art of plumbing the "depths of the present" is no less arcane or risky than writing scenarios about life in 2000. In exploring three guesses about what lies in those depths, I am aware of how murky the view usually is.

The first question concerns a ghost out of recent history. Will there be another resurgence of progressive education, and if so, what form will it take in the domain of religious education? That is a crucial query for Protestant and Catholic educators, since the cause of liberal Christian nurture is very much intertwined with the career and vitality of progressive education. At first glance the phrase *progressive education* may suggest more of the early twentieth century than of the 1980s and 1990s. When Lawrence A. Cremin published his fine history of progressive education, many of us (including this writer) read *The*

14

Transformation of the School (1961) as though it were the epitaph for a movement which belonged to an irretrievable past. Actually Cremin's work provided a very apt introduction to the creative educational impulses of the 1960s—for instance, to John Holt and his famous "how" books, to the thought of Paul Goodman, George Denison, and a host of others who sparked, sometimes unknowingly, a renaissance of progressive education. John and Evelyn Dewey's *Schools for Tomorrow,* an account of experimental schools, written shortly before World War I, made for fascinating reading in the late 1960s. It was almost as if the cycle of educational reform had come around to the exact place where it had been a half century before.

In church circles, too, the newest innovations seemed to resemble—at least in the estimate of veteran educators afflicted by a sense of déjà vu—the discoveries of the first generation of pioneers in the religious education movement. Once again the work of George A. Coe was deemed relevant while the criticisms of his neo-orthodox detractors of the forties and fifties were largely forgotten. The freshest expressions of the "new" educational thought came from Catholics whose predecessors had been often hostile to Dewey and his cohorts in the first decades of the twentieth century. In Gabriel Moran, for instance, the progressives of the sixties found their leading spokesman.

Perhaps it is premature to speak of the demise of progressivism à la Holt, Moran, John Westerhoff, and others. But clearly the educational enthusiasms of the last decade have lost some of their appeal. The bloom is off, and it may be some time yet before another generation strikes up the romance with progressive education. When that time comes (as I think it will during the next two decades), Christian educators should work to develop a version which is different from the previous incarnations in at least one respect.

The major exception will be to devise programs which are not necessarily dependent upon the presence and *imprimatur* of a professional educator. From the very beginning the founders of the religious education movement were intent upon developing educational leaders who were highly professional in training and outlook. American Protestantism could no longer rely, they believed, upon the amateurish efforts of Sunday school workers. This push toward professionalism has never been entirely successful. The director of religious education has lived in a twilight zone, caught between the clergy and the expectations of a volunteer staff. (The story of this ill-fated effort should be of more than casual interest to Catholic leaders who are now establishing similar posts in dioceses and congregations in an effort to find a substitute for the parochial school system.) For a while after

World War II this fledgling profession seemed to be gaining a toehold in Protestant church life. But as soon as the postwar period of religious prosperity slacked off and the pressure of inflation hit the congregations, the marginal character of this position became readily apparent. "The last to be hired, the first to be fired"—that was the fate of many a director of religious education.

One of the characteristic failures of the progressives (whether of the 1910 or 1960 vintage) was their political ineptitude in generating a movement that would sweep across the churches. A movement dominated by the professionals and their interests turns out to be no movement at all. In the future the progressive religious educators should reach beyond the easily gathered coterie of like-minded believers and appeal to a wide variety of Christians. Ironically enough, the most instructive model of that sort of movement in Christian education is the very organization which stirred the first generation of progressives into rebellion and action—the Sunday school system of the nineteenth century.

My second question points to another emerging challenge for Christian educators in the next two decades. Will the churches be able to come to terms with a media-oriented society? I suspect that the media, i.e., especially commercial television but also other forms of broadcasting and written communication, will take the place of the state as the central symbol of a whole range of educational policy matters.

In the last half century or so, religious leaders have lavished considerable attention upon certain church-state problems. The growing power of government and the public school system—its possibilities and spiritual pretensions—moved educators to argue fiercely over prayers and Bible readings in public school classrooms, the study of religion in public schools and public aid for parochial schools. These four issues pitted Protestant against Catholic, Christian against Jew, liberal against conservative.

Will these problems continue to be as divisive and inflammatory? Probably not. The Supreme Court decisions of 1962 and 1963 have been belatedly accepted, though there are still pockets of stout resistance. The dispute over public support of parochial schools will doubtless persist for some time to come. Yet even that matter is no longer the explosive, emotion-laden issue it was ten years ago.

It would therefore be a mistake for religious educators to continue reworking the old church-state issues as though this is the way to shape the future. For at least the next ten years the pervasive presence and influence of the media will remain a tangible reminder of a set of major educational problems and difficulties. Other forces in American society have long recognized and feared the potential educational power exercised by the major television networks. Indeed both the political left and right can agree on one thing: The network moguls are, in effect, the value-brokers of contemporary America. The essential correctness of that conclusion has been confirmed by a recent study conducted at the Annenberg School of Communications of the University of Pennsylvania. "Never before," declared one of the researchers, "have such large and heterogeneous publics—from the nursery to the nursing home, from ghetto to penthouse—shared so much of a system of messages and images, and the assumptions embedded in them." As a result, televised fare becomes the source of "a new religion that provides viewers with a complete world view. It offers them an acceptable view of society in which problems are solved and the inexplicable is explained." Along the same lines another researcher asserted, "If you don't watch television more than four hours a day, you're in the culture, but not of it."[7]

If it is true that television constitutes our society's cultural mainstream and embodies a potent form of religion, then here is a fact of substantial importance to Christian educators. Yet for the most part the current leaders in church education have not come to terms with that fact. Born in a pretelevision era and largely dependent upon theories of education that were developed before the advent of broadcasting, these educators are inclined to treat television as another means of communication. A "school" mentality inhibits full understanding of a different kind of educational space and time—that, for instance, the most important educational space in America may not be the classroom, but rather the area before the twenty-one-inch screen in the living room, or that the TV schedule and its sequences could be more significant than the rhythms of the school calendar.

Perhaps some John Dewey of the late twentieth century will illumine the problems and possibilities of education in a media society, much as Dewey himself helped several generations to make the schools of an industrial society slightly more humane and generous. In the meantime, however, religious educators will be thrust into an uncharted terrain, where they will be contending with a gamut of strange policy issues. To wit: Since there is no realistic way of withdrawing from the ever-present media, can there be any countercultural Christian witness within that society? Or how can the American people be assisted in criticizing and transcending the type of functional popular religion—a world view via commercials, etc.—as described in the University of Pennsylvania study? Such queries, I submit, will be as crucial in the eighties and nineties as the standard church-state arguments were in the mid-twentieth century.

My third major probe into the future anticipates the emergence of a strikingly different phase in the American experience. Will Christian educators be able to work in a post–youth culture? A post–youth culture in America? A decade ago that notion would have seemed the unlikeliest, the most implausible of all possible futures. Few modern countries have been so obsessed with the virtues of being young. Our national preoccupation with youthfulness dates back to the early days of the nineteenth century. If in agrarian America children were potentially valuable as "hands" to work the fields, the younger generation in the industrial period came to symbolize progress and a living reminder of hope for tomorrow. Of course that romantic spirit will linger in certain sectors of American society for years to come. Nothing so deep and so permanent a part of our history suddenly vanishes overnight.

But nowadays there are occasional signs of resistance to a child-centered way of life. In the early seventies a new work was introduced into the secular litanies of confession. *Ageism* took its place alongside racism and sexism as descriptive of American waywardness. *Ageism* refers to a wide variety of behavior and attitudes—an easy condescension toward the elderly and their capacity for continuing contributions to the common life, prejudice against another person based solely on age, the segregation of generations, the blatant use of youthfulness in advertising, and the fear of aging. So far these complaints about *ageism* have not made any great impact upon the thinking of the American public.

Yet, as the median age of the population slips upwards in the late seventies and eighties, the American value system may start to tilt in a slightly different direction. I would never predict a complete flip-flop so that someday American culture would celebrate oldness. In between these extremes lies the possibility of a post–youth culture, i.e., a society conscious of itself as living in an interim, beyond the attachments and values of an earlier period.

If and when this shift does occur, the Christian education establishment in this country will be hard pressed to shuck off the weight of a century-old tradition. The conventional wisdom of the past has proclaimed the imperative of reaching children and young people first and then using "adult work" as a supplementary means of appealing to the younger generation. And so adult education has remained the starved and neglected sector of church life. In each decade since World War I, its importance has been discovered, widely touted and praised, and then forgotten, only to be rediscovered several years later. A witless repetition of this forgetfulness in the coming eighties and nineties could be a costly mistake.

There, in brief, are three glimpses into the "depths of the present." Only time will tell. What is finally important about these speculations (or any ruminations about the future) is that they provide the occasion for rethinking our history and our responsibility in the present.

NOTES

1. Plumb, *The Death of the Past* (Boston: Houghton Mifflin, 1971), p. 17. In this essay I will not deal extensively with the history of religious education. If any reader is interested in learning more about this fascinating topic, consult the following introductory articles: Marvin J. Taylor, ed., *Religious Education: A Comprehensive Survey* (Nashville: Abingdon Press, 1960), pp. 11-23, and *An Introduction to Christian Education* (Nashville: Abingdon Press, 1966), pp. 21-31. For a closer look at the developments in American religious education during the nineteenth and twentieth centuries, the reader might investigate William Bean Kennedy's *The Shaping of Protestant Education* (New York: Association Press, 1966), or Robert W. Lynn's *Protestant Strategies in Education* (New York: Association Press, 1964). The story of the American Sunday school is told briefly in Robert W. Lynn and Elliott Wright's *The Big Little School* (New York: Harper & Row, 1971).
2. Vincent P. Lannie, *Public Money and Parochial Education* (Cleveland: Western Reserve Press, 1968), p. 253.
3. *Ibid.*, p. 255.
4. Most of the material in this section appeared in my article, "Sometimes on Sunday: Reflections on Images of the Future," *Andover Newton Quarterly*, 12 (1972), 130-39.
5. May, *The End of American Innocence* (Chicago: Quadrangle Books, 1964), p. 14.
6. Moran, "Religious Education: Past, Present and Future," *Religious Education*, 66 (September-October 1971), 337.
7. Malcomb G. Scully, "TV, Our Society's New Cultural Mainstream, Study Concludes," *The Chronicle of Higher Education* (January 21, 1974).

Chapter 2

THEORY IN
RELIGIOUS EDUCATION

Charles F. Melchert

Until the late nineteenth century there had been little theoretical interest in religious education. Through the centuries, religious education was conducted by means of straightforward transmissive, didactic, even catechetical methods with a heavy emphasis upon memorization of texts, especially the Bible and the catechism in recent centuries. It was assumed that the purpose of these activities was to enable the learner to "get right with God" or "be in a saved relation with God" by knowing the Word of God and right doctrine. Indeed, in America, most schools in the colonial period were founded with that avowed intent.

As schools were gradually secularized, religious education was left more and more to churches, synagogues, and the family, although it was widely assumed through the nineteenth century and into the twentieth that the public school was a firm support for Protestant religion.

In the course of the nineteenth century, with increasing state control of the schools and with rising professional standards for schools and teachers, there began to emerge increased awareness of the potential theoretical and scientific explorations that could be performed on processes of teaching and learning. This in turn led religious educators to reflect more systematically upon their own endeavors and to begin to write more theoretically and systematically about religious education and to perform some empirical investigations about religious education.

With the emergence of such leaders as George Albert Coe, Paul Vieth, William Clayton Bower, Luther Weigle, Adelaide Case, and the like, religious education came to have a sense of being a venture with some integrity and autonomy of its own. Until that time it was typically regarded as little more than a method whereby children and adults were made Christian. Religious education was simply one form of the salvific activities of the church. Indeed, this is probably still

Charles F. Melchert is Associate Professor in the Department of Curriculum and Instruction, Faculty of Education, Memorial University of Newfoundland, St. John's, Newfoundland, Canada.

the view of the majority of those directly involved in teaching and learning in the name of religious education.

What the leaders above tried to do was take seriously the educational nature of religious education. Prior to this time, and again in the forties under the influence of neo-orthodoxy, religious education was regarded as more religious than educational. As has repeatedly been observed, religious education originated because persons wanted to make others Christians, Jews, Catholics, Methodists, etc, as themselves, not primarily because they wanted them to become truly educated. In America there has long been a deep distrust of becoming too educated, especially in the sphere of religion, for fear that too much education will lead one away from a right or saving relation with God. As a result, most theorizing in religious education in the past has been little more than providing a theological rationale for the place of education in church activities. It has seldom been significantly based upon or linked with empirical research in education and in religion.

Do Religious Educators Need Theory?

To answer the question of religious educators needing theory, we might first ask, What is theory? Most familiarly, theory is contrasted both with common sense and with practice.

Theory differs from practice in that it typically entails the giving of reasons for various practices. Theory differs from common sense in that the reasons given are expected to be systematically coherent with one another, and they are expected to be grounded not solely in tradition or custom, unless such traditions and customs can be shown to have empirical validity. Common sense is also limited by the shortsightedness which results from its closeness to first-hand experience. This limit becomes most clear when there is a change of historical or social context, and suddenly it is discovered that what has been accepted as common sense is no longer common, nor does it seem to make sense in the new context.

On the other hand, theory is not simply something in abstraction from practice, for in its most fundamental sense all theory arises from practice, and every individual participates in theory-forming from birth onward. From the beginning of life, the infant forms hunches about the masses of information that flood the senses. To survive, one must begin to bring some order to that chaos of data, that is, to make some sense out of it or bring meaning to it. One way of ordering the chaos which is essential to survival and adaptation is to begin to be able to predict (though not yet in a form capable of verbal articulation) what behaviors will produce which responses in one's environment. In other words, theory-forming, in both its most rudimentary and its most sophisticated senses, is a form of mental economizing, or as Bruner aptly puts it, it is a "way of keeping in mind a vast amount while thinking about a very little."[1]

An adult, such as a teacher, behaves in a similar fashion (although the range and complexity of the data being considered has vastly increased) while at the same time the symbolizing processes and the experience which enter into the theory formation are both more sophisticated and more extensive. What is important to note here is that at root theory is not exclusively for specialists, but is a way of using the mind and the imagination, creatively and constructively. More scientifically speaking, it seems there are two kinds of theories, complementary yet distinct. One can construct theory to understand some process, or one can construct theory to predict the outcome of some process. These goals are separate and the structure of theories used to attain each is distinct.[2]

A theory can be constructed which accurately predicts the outcomes of a process, such as predicting election results from various known population samples and their previous behaviors, without having an understanding of how or why it works that way. This has been called the "black box" approach to theory since what is needed is knowledge of what goes into the box, knowledge of which inputs lead to which outputs, and then predictions can be made about what comes out of the box without needing to understand what interactions go on inside the box itself. This kind of theory could be useful in religious instruction. If I know that treating this group of children in M and N manner over B period of time under C conditions will produce D kinds of habitual religious behaviors among the children, that knowledge gives me considerable precision, even if I do not understand the why and how $(M+N)(B+C)=D$. No teacher will lightly scoff at results. This kind of theory enables one to say more precisely *what* will happen.

On the other hand, one may want to understand *why* these factors produce this result, and such an understanding may be attained even without a corresponding ability to predict exact outcomes. For example, Freud has given us a powerful explanation of human behavior without being able at the same time to predict what a person will do from minute to minute, day to day, month to month, or even year to year. At the same time, Freud's theory has had profound effects upon the day-to-day behavior of thousands of people, perhaps even helping reshape entire social and cultural patterns. This kind of theory is closer to common sense in some ways and has been most typical of the kind of theory found in religious education. Yet a teacher or a planner is often interested both in understanding and in being able to produce predictable results. Thus a theory for religious education would be a coherent system of statements that would help explain what happens when a person or a group helps another become educated in religion and which enables predictions to be made about which practices under what conditions will lead to what outcomes.

Now to answer more directly the question posed earlier. I would claim that not only do religious educators need theory, of both kinds, but also that they cannot do without it. As long as one is thinking about what one is doing, theories are being formed and used. The remaining question is whether such theories will be consciously and critically examined, related to empirical data, tested and evaluated against the ongoing practices and results that emerge as such theories are being tried out in the educational process. For both kinds of theories the critical test of adequacy is empirical, that is, Does the theory accurately and completely fit the process to which it refers?

What Does a Theory Do?

1. *Functions.* A theory tells us what to look for. Without it, we could not even know what to count as data. The theory also defines which data are relevant for this understanding or that result. It tells us what a datum could mean or signify or what it could lead to under certain circumstances.

For example, a theory tells us what kinds of activities would legitimately be included in religious education and which should be excluded. A theory may focus attention upon the activity of the one doing the educating and thus direct our attention to the teaching side of the process. Or it might suggest that religious education is more constituted by the act or process of being educated, thus directing our attention to the learner or the learning process. A theory might direct attention to the results of both the above, that is, to the abilities produced in or possessed by the one who is educated. Or, to cut it another way, some authors seem to presume that the cognitive is focal and that religious education is essentially complete when the learner has achieved mastery of a certain set of concepts. Other theorists would claim that religious education is not complete until a lifestyle is achieved which is marked by the presence of some behaviors and the absence of others. Still others, who might not deny the above, would focus attention rather upon the presence of certain feelings so that the depth, range, and intensity of certain feelings is the mark of educational success in religion. However, one of the things that distinguishes serious theory from popular journalism in religious education is that the theorist is under some obligation to justify his choice of what to focus attention upon.

Perhaps it would be more descriptively accurate to say that if a theory had only one of the above foci, it should be called a theory of instruction, not of education; or a theory of affective learning; or a theory of behavioral outcomes which could as well be produced by educational or noneducational means. In other words, a full-blown educational theory would entail not only a description of what to look for in teacher behavior but also in learner behavior, and, in the learner's resulting behaviors or abilities, the manners by which such transformations can be achieved, together with a justification of why these various things qualify as educational processes and outcomes as compared, for example, with maturational or chemical outcomes. Thus, not just any form of behavior by a teacher which might effectively lead the learner to the desired goal could be accepted as an educational style of behavior, since there are implicit yet necessary value dimensions to the educational endeavor. Thus, for example, a teacher may not legitimately deceive a student into believing certain things, nor can the teacher achieve the desired end by hypnosis and still be allowed to call it a fully educational process. The offering of justifications for one's theoretical choices is immensely difficult for religious education since the range of data and the forms of justification are inherently complex and often controversial. It is important for a theorist not to get seduced into offering theological justifications for religious outcomes while ignoring the need to justify them as viable educational outcomes.[3]

Thus a full-blown educational theory in religion will consist of many subtheories, each having its own more specific focus, such as a theory of learning and a theory of teaching. Each subtheory will specify which units to look for in its own domain. Formally speaking, the minimal structure of a theory of education could be represented by the formula "X is fostering or seeking to foster in Y some disposition D by method M." Differing theoretical views of education are shown by changing the variables in the formula.[4]

Whatever type of unit a theory directs attention to will shape the nature of that theory. For example, a theorist might use teacher (X), student (Y), and subject matter (D, M) as units, which might lead to explorations of what kinds of teachers are needed for what kinds of students and "subjects." If, instead, the theorists focused upon the skill functions, the memory functions, and the deliberative functions (D) which the teacher (X) and the learner (Y) use in their treatment of subject matter, the change of the units from substantive bodies to activities or relationships completely changes the nature of the theory.[5]

2. *Principles of interaction.* Once there has been identification of the units of the particular theory, then the theorist must state the laws or principles which govern the interactions of these units. For example, using the units in the above illustrations, a law might be that an open-minded teacher will create an open-minded learner more quickly and more completely than will a close-minded teacher. Or again, the ability to infer and hypothesize depends upon memory functions and certain specific skills and thus will be achieved later in time. Subsequent empirical exploration or research will be directed toward demonstrating or disproving these principles or defining them more precisely.

3. *Boundaries.* A theory must also include a specification of its boundaries—for example, that this is a theory of learning and not a theory of instruction or education. A fully educational theory will also specify how each subtheory relates to the others and then to the whole endeavor called education in religion. A theory might also include specification of the role or function of education within the domain of religion or religious life, which will also help determine the boundaries of this particular theory.

When all these factors have been explicated, statements can be made about what is true in this model and what results can be expected from the use of this model. Then empirical indicators can be formed which will give the researcher the ability to make judgments about the accuracy of those propositions and the validity or "fit" of the theory with the world it is intending to describe.

Of What Use Is Theory in Religious Education?

Once a theory has been formed, it can provide many useful services for those involved in religious education.

1. *Research.* Theory can provide the grounding and context for research, which in turn supports and tests theory. This process may, in turn, help make more effective practice possible by demonstrating what does and does not lead to certain desired ends.

2. *Policy decisions.* Theories help guide policy decisions of all sorts. If one has a theoretical position which has some demonstrable basis in fact, one can perhaps more confidently decide what kind of an

institutional structure is needed for particular educational styles and outcomes, what kinds of teachers and material resources would be most appropriate, what kinds of training experience would most suit the teachers for the tasks desired, and so on.

3. *Planning decisions.* Theories are used in the day-to-day planning decisions facing teachers and learners as well as administrators. A theory can help inform a teacher about a particular learning sequence which might be most useful to this particular child with this particular learning style and present condition. A theory can help planners in choosing curricular resources for particular groups, times, places, and abilities.

Theories are also valuable in a much less tangible way. Theories give a teacher a sense of being competent because one has a sense of what leads to what, a sense that one has a grasp of the whole, that one can significantly help direct activities into meaningful directions and not allow them simply to remain random attempts at learning.

Very often competing theories will stimulate not only reevaluation of one's own present position, but also will help stimulate "the envisioning" of the whole of education, which may enable reappreciation of education's role in forming the whole person.

How to Criticize Theories When Offered

It is increasingly important to be able to make judgments about the adequacy of theories being offered for part or all of the religious educational tasks. Here are a few bench marks by which a theory can be assessed.

1. What kind of theory is it? Does it intend to offer predictions for practice or understanding of the internal and external interactions of its components? For example, does the theory tell what specific behaviors will produce a specific piece of learning, or does it tell why people under certain conditions persistently tend to evidence a particular sequence of behavior? Is it a theory of religious education? Or of education alone or of religion alone? Is it a theory of learning or of teaching? How does each of these potential "parts" of a theory of religious education fit into a more wholistic theory?

2. Is the theory internally self-consistent? Are there logical non sequiturs? One clue to internal consistency is the stability and precision of the language being used. Does the meaning of terms shift in the course of the argument? Or are terms being used which are ambiguous or poetic and thus not operationally precise enough to prevent "slippage" in descriptions of events, patterns, or predicaments?

3. Is the description adequate to the data or the phenomena in question, or are there obvious omissions or distorted perceptions? (*Distorted* here does not mean twisted from some theological frame but incompatible with data in question.) This is a particularly important test in religious matters since many researchers and theorists about religion seem tempted to either reduce religious experience to terms that none of the participants would recognize as having anything to do with what they experienced, or else to so overdescribe an experience that it seems to almost carry inherent with it a particular theological position.

4. Are the assumptions adequate or taken into account? Every interpreter brings along some understanding of the world. Each must watch that such an understanding does not so color the formulation of theory that the bias gets unconsciously written into the theory uncritically. This is particularly true with relation to value questions and theological positions. It is not possible to operate without either in forming theories, but it is possible, even necessary, to try to be aware of one's own bias, and then master it rather than allow it to determine what is seen and thought.

Most debates about theories arise from debates about the assumptions which precede the theories themselves. If one theorist assumes that religion cannot be supernatural and another assumes that it cannot be other than supernatural, then it is quite possible their resultant theories will not be identical. If they are trying to predict the occurrence of some religious outcome, then their theories may have quite different forms and prescriptions. If they do not, then one should check to see if they are both internally consistent.

5. Are there overgeneralizations from the data? Overgeneralizing is one of the most common errors in theorizing, especially in theories intending to predict outcomes. For example, theories of instruction may explain with considerable power what one needs to do as a teacher to produce certain behaviors in the one being taught. Often it is then assumed that the one being taught has thereby been religiously educated. That assumes an identity between "being taught" and "religious education" which is nowhere justified, and which some would argue cannot be justified. When dealing with a phenomenon as complex as religious education, it is vitally important to be aware of the limitations imposed by the data one is using. Other data, or the same data handled differently, may provide alternative understandings which lead to new theoretical formulations.

Resources for Theories of Education in Religion

There was a time in the not too distant past when it was easier to decide what data were needed to form principles of education in religion. It was (is?) widely assumed that if one had personal religious experience and cared for children, one was prepared to teach. Gradually, as education became subject to more scrutiny in its own right and not simply as something to do with others, there was increased awareness of the complexity of the process. Suddenly a teacher needed not only experience and theology plus sincerity, but also methodologies, sociology, anthropology, epistemology, history, sociology of knowledge, and much, much more.

This expansion of the relevant data which bear upon understanding and predicting effective educational practice in religion has continued unabated in recent years. Indeed, there are signs now that the biological sciences, neurophysiology, and the psychology of consciousness will also be added to the data relevant to religious education.

As those fields enter the picture for the religious educator, they not only increase the complexity of one's understanding of the task but also often challenge many of the fundamental issues which have long been assumed to be so. They also entail more complex forms of investigation for the researcher, the theorist, and the practitioner. This is the more so with the creation of newer interdisciplinary fields, such as the sociology of knowledge, the psychology of consciousness, genetic epistemology, future studies, etc. Each of these fields holds promise for theory in religious education, yet they also call for almost full-time study in their own right.

One important implication of these observations for the future of religious education is the necessity of interdisciplinary cooperation among specialists. No longer can our field (or any other) rely solely upon the isolated practitioner or theorist who works more or less alone. Teams of specialists will increasingly have to work together— as has long been the case among those who have the responsibility for constructing programs of curriculum materials.

As the data feeding into theories become more complex, and as there is increasing need for teams of experts, there is also a new awareness of the personal attributes effective theorists must have. In order for a theoretician to be able to formulate adequate theory, he or she must be capable of precise analytical and synthetic thought, as well as having all the intuitive creative ability possible. In addition, the theoretician also must be: (1) fundamentally open-minded to new data, especially data which seem to contradict or call into question existing theories or principles; (2) open to critical responses to one's own formulations; (3) willing to learn from unexpected sources; (4) cognizant of one's own humanity or finitude and thus a relativistic understanding of one's own endeavors and a sense of community with other theoreticians, researchers, and practitioners. Clearly not all great theoreticians in the past have had these qualities, and the absence of some of these has not always hindered their forming significant theories. But the point at which their greatness was limited was also the point at which one or more of these qualities prevented them from moving beyond an established position to a more wholistic or more adequate conception of the reality with which they were dealing.

Bibliography

Belth, Marc. *Education as a Discipline*. Boston: Allyn and Bacon, 1965.

Brauner, Charles J. *American Educational Theory*. Englewood Cliffs, N. J.: Prentice-Hall, 1964.

Doyle, James F., ed. *Educational Judgments: Papers in the Philosophy of Education*. International Library of the Philosophy of Education. London: Routledge & Kegan Paul, 1973.

Dubin, Robert. *Theory Building*. New York: The Free Press, 1969.

Hardie, Charles D. *Truth and Fallacy in Educational Theory*. Cambridge: Cambridge University Press, 1942.

Langford, Glenn and D. J. O'Connor, eds. *New Essays in the Philosophy of Education*. International Library of the Philosophy of Education. London: Routledge & Kegan Paul, 1973. See especially the articles by P. H. Hirst and D. J. O'Connor entitled "The Nature and Scope of Educational Theory."

Wilson, John. *Philosophy and Educational Research*. National Foundation for Educational Research in England and Wales, 1972.

NOTES

1. Jerome Bruner, *The Relevance of Education* (New York: W. W. Norton & Co., 1971), p. 15.
2. Robert Dubin, *Theory Building* (New York: The Free Press, 1969), pp. 9ff.
3. Charles Melchert, "Does the Church Really Want Religious Education?" *Religious Education*, 69 (January-February, 1974), 15-16.
4. William K. Frankena, "The Concept of Education Today" in *Educational Judgments: Papers in the Philosophy of Education*, James F. Doyle, ed. (London: Routledge & Kegan Paul, 1973), pp. 21ff.
5. Marc Belth, *Education as a Discipline* (Boston: Allyn and Bacon, 1965), pp. 75-76.

Chapter 3

THEOLOGY AND
RELIGIOUS EDUCATION

Sara Little

The "Clue" to Christian Education:
A Historical Comment

In 1950 Randolph Crump Miller said that the "clue" to Christian education is theology. Timing for that statement was superb. Moving into the ferment characteristic of the forties, as educators struggled with neo-orthodoxy, Miller offered a slogan and a battle cry that could and did bring increasing consensus into the educational work of the church. By 1966 Howard Grimes, writing in *An Introduction to Christian Education,* predecessor to this volume, said, "The struggle for the recognition of the crucial nature of theology in relation to Christian teaching has probably been won." [1] Yet hardly a decade later the question arises as to the relation between theology and religious education, and the answer is that theology is no longer the clue. The victory—if it was a victory—was short-lived.

What happened?

As a part of the theological confrontation, educators were accused of being imperialistic and trying to "take over" the church, of viewing education as a kind of messiah, of giving inadequate attention to the explicit and implicit theology that was taught. Increasingly, theology became the dominant discipline that influenced religious education in the fifties and early sixties, as symbolized by Miller's comment. To be sure, the influence manifested itself in different ways. When Miller spoke of the "clue," he was not referring to a "correct" theology formulated as doctrine to be transmitted through education. For him, theology had to do with the "truth about God in relation to man." Truth lay in the experienced reality of the relationship—theology, in the interpretation of that reality, informed by the biblical witness.

In contrast, theoreticians, like James Smart, with more attention to the necessity for correct belief, showed great concern for the

Sara Little is Professor of Christian Education at Union Theological Seminary and the Presbyterian School of Christian Education, Richmond, Virginia.

educational task of developing a theologically literate generation. The Christian Faith and Life program of the United Presbyterian Church, giving form to his vision, embodied a new approach to Christian (rather than religious) education. Even with divergence in viewpoints, the writings of these and others, as well as curriculum developments in churches, evidenced the new détente between theology and education. Resultant motivation and the sense of clarity brought a new vitality into the work of educators. A brief period of stability emerged in the educational scene.

It lasted about a decade. If one were to use Barthian theological categories for analysis of the causes of changes that occurred in the sixties, she or he might anticipate that the great new programs and the trust in theology would engender false confidence. As Karl Barth said, people tend to substitute "some plan or programme or method . . . some new 'interpretation of the truth,'" for fearing and loving God above all things.[2] If one were to use historical or sociological tools for seeking out the causes, the conclusion would be that the "turbulent sixties," as Sidney Ahlstrom calls them, brought new "cosmic signs" and "a fundamental shift in American moral and religious attitudes." There were John Kennedy and Martin Luther King, the "death of God," and Vatican II, years that brought "excitement and liberation to some, bewilderment and pain to others."[3] The shift was far-reaching and complex.

Thus, forces from without, as well as self-criticism from within, shifted the world of religious education again. By the seventies, theology was no longer the clue. General educational philosophy and practice were again "respectable." What then is the relationship between theology and education? In that connection, consider two preliminary questions: What are the possible alternative relationships? What is the situation in theology?

The Relation Between Theology and Education: Possible Alternatives

Five possibilities present themselves. There may be others, but these five can be observed operating to some degree in the mid-seventies.

Theology as content to be taught. Theology, viewed by Webster as the "rational interpretation of religious faith, practice, and experience," offers to a religious community the basis for a common language and understanding. When theology is neglected, the community loses its identity and sense of mission. When theology is one item in the whole scope of human knowledge, it becomes diffuse, probably erodes, and Christian education has no distinctive function. Although conservative, evangelical branches of the church often hold to this view, other segments of more liberal churches do also. With them, indoctrination is not the goal. Rather, exploration of meaning becomes the instrument for appropriation.

Theology as norm. To some degree, when creeds or theological systems are predetermined by church officials as subject matter to be learned, theology can be said to function as a kind of norm. What is meant here, however, is more comprehensive. Contributions from the behavioral sciences, or from any discipline, are to be screened with reference to their appropriateness to theological presuppositions. Educators are to take the stance of a theologian, as it were, and engage in the critical work of analysis and evaluation of the practices of the church in its teaching work in the past and the present for the sake of the future. Because theology serves as a point of reference both for what is to be taught and for methodology, it functions in a normative way.

Theology as irrelevant. A third view, drastically opposed to the first two, holds that education itself is essentially religious. Its intention is personal growth and the search for truth. Wherever truth is found it functions as meaning, as religion for the seeker. One can only speak of education or religious education, then, never of Christian education.

There is another perspective for viewing theology as unrelated. Education is considered to be primarily the work of practitioners, operating pragmatically. It is means to an end. Practice is more important than reflection on the relationship between means and ends.

Here is where education becomes autonomous.

"Doing" theology as educating. When *theology* is converted into a verb and used thus—"theologizing about the meaning of experience" or "situational theologizing"—the assumption is that God is still active in human history and that the way to be "educated" is to inquire about the meaning in the events, with reference to God's presence and activity in the past and his purpose for the future. Obviously, this is not too unlike Miller's "clue," interpreted in the context of his theory. It means that one is educated as one theologizes. Daniel Day Williams, in fact, says that one way to define Christian education is to speak of it as theological inquiry. He says this:

> Since theology in the church is an interpretation of the Christian way of believing and living, all those who reflect crit-

32

ically upon Christian experience become theologians. Christian educators therefore not only draw upon theological insight provided by the tradition and thought of the church; but they help to create the body of materials and the reflective criticism which make a living theology possible.[4]

When this approach is operative, the educative process not only educates, but also develops a substantive contribution to the theological formulations of the church.

Education in dialogue with theology. One assumes here the independence of various disciplines, each with its recognizable functions. Theology, along with such disciplines as psychology, sociology, and anthropology, both influences and is responsive to these other disciplines. Decisions about the educational task emerge from the dialogue. They do not emerge from some "application" of theological or theoretical formulations. Decisions are constantly adapted and indeed remade as the dialogue continues. Theology may function in a somewhat normative fashion, but that is not necessarily the case. The significance of a discipline varies according to the situation and the nature of the decision to be made. What is called for is a collegial approach to education.

Is any one of these "the" way to relate education and theology? Probably not. Reflect on the alternatives as we consider the theological scene in the mid-seventies.

"Between" Theologies, or Theological Fragments

When theology was a clue to Christian education, it was dominated by great scholars producing ideas and systems that were stimulating to other theologians and to the church at large. It would have been unthinkable for education not to have responded. The situation is quite different now. After the "death of God" and the "secular theologians" of the sixties—but probably more because of the social ferment of those years—in many ways confusing or alienating theologians, we come to a period when it is risky to offer any generalizations at all about theology. Are we "between" theologies—that is, waiting for some new giants to appear and point us in new directions? Or are there numerous offerings to be viewed as theological fragments, the most appropriate response to the current situation? Whatever the designation, theology is in trouble. That is one clear reason for difficulty in stating the nature of its relationship with education.

On the one hand, we do seem to be "between" theologies. Martin Marty, church historian, speaks of the "unfound generation" in the seventies. "Where is everybody?" he says. "Ten years ago the under-30 people carved out a place for themselves. . . . The space seems never to have been filled." Hugh Kerr, editor of *Theology Today,* states in an editorial that "we live in the midst of moral and ethical chaos" and concludes, among other points, that "we desperately need in the area of theology a new chapter on the interlocking relation between religion and culture." William Hordern, theologian, says that systematic theology is "in the doldrums . . . a not surprising outcome of the theological history of the '60s." But men are "theological animals," he says, and the scene is very similar to that of 1919—"ripe for a theological renaissance." [5]

It would be inaccurate to suggest that no substantive theological work is being done. Wolfhart Pannenberg, of Germany, with his "circle," continues to explore the relation of revelation to universal history, via the Judaic-Christian tradition. Process theology, in the United States, with John Cobb, Schubert Ogden, Gregory Baum, and others, is probably the most significant theological enterprise here. Providing continuity to the Whiteheadian philosophical tradition, it appears peculiarly appropriate for a world self-conscious about change. Iris Cully, Christian educator, says, "Here is a theology for the space age." She sees in it a position compatible with educational presuppositions, one which brings a "cosmic dimension to the concerns of power, conflict, and self-determination." [6]

More conservative theologians continue to work steadfastly at the theological task; some are moving deliberately to place theology in its historical framework and to relate it to social concerns. Bernard Ramm, in *The Evangelical Heritage,* cites evidence to indicate that there are tens of millions of evangelicals, many of them in mainline denominations. Unless their needs are to be met, he says, they may be driven into sectarianism. His call to evangelical theologians is to do responsible theological work as a part of their Christian stewardship, a task in which he is engaged.

Other instances could be offered to suggest that we are not just "between" theologies, that steady systematic theological work is under way. On the other hand, much theological reflection that is being done seems to be related to problems, not systems of thought. Or it arises out of cultural situations. There is liberation theology and black theology and feminist theology. There is theology in art and the theology of group experience. Some of the most productive work being done, with pioneering flavor, is coming out of these efforts.

James Cone, for example, sees black theology as "exodus" theology and the black church as the instrument of liberation. Mary Daly sees feminist theology as moving people beyond the present into new dimensions of understanding, as suggested in her *Beyond God the Father.* Nathan Scott, commenting on the general instability of the numerous theological programs, says that "the literary imagination remains for me (most especially in its great classic modern expressions) a primary repository of insight—and the discipline of literary criticism, therefore, an important medium for theological work." [7] Whatever the "handle" the theologian uses, whether it is theology in the arts or theology in bioethics, the theological reflections that result are characteristic of the seventies. One wonders whether a new way of doing theology may emerge from the decade. And even in this quick sampling, possible relationships to education begin to be apparent.

Educational and Theological Pluralism

The relation between theology and religious education seems much clearer for the fifties than for the seventies. Perhaps that clarity was not so apparent in the midst of the arguments then, but in retrospect it seems that theology was a dominant, controlling force. It was fashionable then for educators to become amateur theologians or for theologians to function as educators, often without any recognition of need for investigation of history or theory of education. Today, the relationship between theology and education is somewhat more mystifying to representatives of both fields. No easy statement can be made. In fact, more often than not, the question of the relationship is ignored—and that is irresponsible.

But perhaps some observations can be made, growing out of the effort to relate the possible alternatives mentioned earlier to the scene in theology. That effort or investigation, undertaken from an educational perspective, must take seriously the cultural situation, characterized by both theological and educational pluralism. Such an investigation is a "doing" of educational theory. What results is the conclusion that only one alternative relationship is unacceptable. The other four can be affirmed as options appropriate to certain current theological processes and as potentially useful in carrying out constructive education. The variety of possibilities takes seriously what is going on, indicates unwillingness to make a "final" pronouncement, and calls for active evaluative reflection in educational decision-making.

First, the alternative that is unacceptable. When theology is viewed as irrelevant, what happens may be education, but it is not likely to be religious education and certainly not Christian education. It is more likely to be conditioning or training than education. Guidelines are to be found in fads—franchised or packaged "programs," words like *creative* or *relevant* or *innovative,* techniques like value clarification or the latest planning process in one of the organizational development schemes. Educators become consultants or specialists in some activity. Many of these specialties or techniques are quite valuable, but not when utilized indiscriminately and constantly without adequate reference to purpose, context, rationale, and insights from appropriate disciplines. Theology is likely to be one such discipline. Even when education is viewed as a never-ending search for truth, theology is one area that should be explored.

Then, as to the investigation of the other alternatives in relationship to the present situation, four propositions are offered here that may suggest some guidelines for the educator in knowing how to choose or deal with theology today. Obviously, more than one approach or pattern will emerge as "good" if these propositions are affirmed and become functional. Consider the four.

1. *There is a gospel message which is independent of the various processes by which it is communicated—a message which becomes available in different ways, depending on the particular process operative at any given time.* One implication of this proposition is that theology, in relation to education, may become content to be taught. Whether the apostle Paul, Martin Luther, or Martin Luther King is interpreting the gospel, one benefits by the varying views and comes to perceive some central reality underlying the differences, a reality which is not restricted by the words, which exists independently of them and yet is made partially available through them. Indeed, according to Gerhard Ebeling and Ernst Fuchs, theologians of the new hermeneutic, reality becomes available or comes into existence only when it is spoken of. Moreover, just because the person is a rational creature, in distinction from an animal, she or he never approaches maturity unless there is deepening understanding and the satisfaction —even delight—in seeing meaning, patterns, relationships. Thus the value of the exploration of the work of scholars like Wolfhart Pannenberg, with his new interpretation of the resurrection; Jürgen Moltmann, with his eschatological concerns; or Gordon Kaufman, with his models of transcendence.

Theology is offered through preaching, through drama, through visual arts, and through other forms. Implicit in what has been said here is the assumption that *teaching* is the avenue under consideration. A certain view of teaching is doubtless evident "between the lines" or in the phrasing of ideas. Indoctrination, though it has a function in teaching, is not what is intended here. That approach which encourages a person to explore, to ask questions, to find what is reasonable to believe, is at the heart of the activity called teaching, according to Thomas Green.[8] It is with that kind of teaching that theology may become a "content to be taught."

2. *The message, or content, to some extent at least, should help shape the process by which it is communicated. It offers a point of reference for interpretation and evaluation of practices, systems, and structures set up as instruments for communication.* In a way, then, theology may be said to serve as a norm. What is not acceptable is for the theologian to stand outside the educative process and prescribe doctrinal formulations to be learned by young children irrespective of their level of cognitive development or to direct educators to function solely as technicians, where methodology is viewed as extrinsic to the content. On the other hand, the theologian does serve the church as interpreter, making available knowledge about the tradition and the community out of which the tradition emerged. Particularly in a creedal church, the theologian has the task of helping make clear the position of the church, in order that persons may make informed decisions about their response.

There is another way in which theology may appropriately function as a kind of norm, preferably when the educator takes the stance of a theologian and raises questions about practices. This is especially true in these days of almost unprecedented use in religious education of techniques from every conceivable source. Thomas Oden, reflecting theologically on that fast-growing social phenomenon, the encounter group, offers both criticism and potentialities of deep religious significance. Phoniness and anti-intellectualism he condemns. Focus on feeling, experiencing, confession in a trusting community—these he sees as a "new pietism" paralleling historic Jewish and Protestant emphases.[9] A Christian encounter group, although similar to, is also distinct from a secular encounter group. Whether or not theology is serving as "norm" here, it *is* serving as an important factor for evaluation and planning. Any educator could list dozens of areas in which theological reflection is called for. Consider the widespread use of behavioral objectives, obviously useful in many ways, but in need of theological reflection.

Perhaps the term *norm* is overstated. If so, the intention is to propose a possible corrective to certain excesses by appropriate reference to theological insights.

3. *Knowledge is comprehended, synthesized, internalized, changed, and enlarged when it is integrally related to issues in human existence.* In other words, "doing" theology is a way of being educated, and at the same time, of contributing to theological reformulations. The

times call for just such a view of the relation between theology and education. If it is true, as Nathan Scott proposes, that reflection on the arts is one way to do theological work, it is also true that the educator today is making widespread use of such reflections. In addition, as persons are encouraged to express meaning through artistic channels, they, too, are doing theology in a process which is educative.

Martin Marty and Dean Peerman, focusing in their 1973 *New Theology No. 10* on "Bios and Theology," comment on the cluster of issues dealing with common, secular life—the genetic alteration of humans, cloning, ecological issues about people's place in nature and their control of nature. They say that the Jewish and Christian traditions provide some help for dealing with these subjects, but "to say . . . that there are resources is not to say that there will not have to be reconceptions." As they say, "the Christian tradition . . . has newness built into its program and character. 'Behold, I make all things new!' " The "biotic theology" represented in the essays presents a process that is educational. To the degree that the process enables the actual making of ethical decision, the hope of both educator and theologian will be realized.[10]

Reference has been made to cultural involvement in theology, to liberation theologies. Donald Dawe says that "the disenfranchised peoples of the world are no longer willing to accept the theology of white, Western man as the norm. . . ." In fact, "the indigenization of Christ to non-Western cultures is becoming a fact that may re-shape Christology far more radically than any alternative now at work in academic circles." [11] Such a theological process is compatible with the theory of such educators as Paulo Freire. What happens is not only a contribution to theology, but a reshaping of the very self.

Much of what is going on in theology, then, is most appropriately related to education in this alternative. The relationship is organic and is possible only when theology and education are both viewed as dynamic, not static, processes.

4. *The theoretical work of the educator necessitates consideration not only of situations and cultural conditions, but also of contributions and insights from appropriate disciplines—theology, for example, as one of the more important disciplines for religious education.* When education is in dialogue with theology, a situation is set up in which independence of the disciplines is maintained, with possibilities of mutual benefit. In the work of Daniel Day Williams, for example, one may see a kind of dialogue between process theology and education. This particular alternative seems most appropriate to the work

of the theoretician. Philosophical statements about education, or designing of educational systems, emerge from the interaction of numerous relevant disciplines. Such statements are informed by and understood in the context of historical analysis. Theology, crucial as it is, must be related to psychology and social sciences as educational decisions are made. Social science is not the "clue" any more than theology. No one thing is. The intention is to do education and to think about education in a constantly changing situation, in a way that takes into account the "gifts" of the members of any given religious community, viewed increasingly in its universal setting.

The Future as Venture

Education, like theology, is dependent on the vitality of the life out of which it emerges and which it seeks to perpetuate and reshape. In spite of signs of vitality and "rumors of angels," according to Martin Marty and Dean Peerman, there is a kind of *anomie,* emptiness, and directionlessness today.[12] Such a statement raises questions about the future, about the value or validity of propositions and alternatives. Or better, the question is how *both* theology and education, separately and in relationship to each other, can actually make a difference in the lives of people and in the world.

A second, more practical question can be raised. In the wealth of curriculum resources presently available, what is the place of theology? A cursory look suggests that all five alternative relationships may be found, including the one in which theology is held to be irrelevant. Both educational and theological pluralism is evident, and affirmed, with help in utilizing this pluralism constructively. There is obviously a need at least to raise the question of theological content and function as one evaluates these resources and considers the systems within which they are to be used.

There is another question. Most of what has been proposed here is directed to organized teaching or schooling, although not exclusively so. Significant educational leaders like John Westerhoff are proposing a socialization model, taking seriously the total life of the religious community, with attention to ritual, experience, and action. What is the relationship of theology to that approach to education? If that approach is one of the next ventures into the future, certainly "education in dialogue with theology" is a viable option, even a necessary one. It should produce constructive results.[13]

In the final analysis, then, whatever the shape of the future, the "health" of religious education is intertwined with that in theology.

Bibliography

Cully, Iris V. *Change, Conflict, and Self-Determination.* Philadelphia: The Westminster Press, 1972.

Greeley, Andrew M. *The New Agenda.* Garden City, N.Y.: Doubleday & Co., 1973.

Marty, Martin E., and Peerman, Dean, eds. *New Theology Nos. 7-10.* New York: The Macmillan Co., 1970–73.

Ramm, Bernard L. *The Evangelical Heritage.* Waco, Tex.: Word Books, 1973.

Robinson, James M., and Cobb, John B., Jr., eds. *Theology as History,* vol. 3 of *New Frontiers in Theology.* New York: Harper & Row, 1967.

Shinn, Roger L. *Man: The New Humanism,* vol. 6 of *New Directions in Theology Today.* Philadelphia: The Westminster Press, 1968.

Sontag, Frederick, and Roth, John K. *The American Religious Experience: The Roots, Trends, and Future of American Theology.* New York: Harper & Row, 1972.

NOTES

1. Marvin J. Taylor, ed. (Nashville: Abingdon Press, 1966), p. 39.
2. Edwyn Hoskyns, trans., *Epistle to the Romans,* 6th ed. (London: Oxford University Press, 1933), p. 373.
3. *A Religious History of the American People.* (New Haven: Yale University Press, 1972), pp. 1080, 1082.
4. Williams, "Current Theological Developments and Religious Education" in *Religious Education: A Comprehensive Survey,* Marvin J. Taylor, ed. (Nashville: Abingdon Press, 1960), p. 52.
5. Marty, "The Unfound Generation in Religious Thought," *Christian Century,* 91 (February 27, 1974), 225; Kerr, *Theology Today,* 31 (April, 1974), 2; *Ibid.,* p. 4; Hordern, "What's in Store for '74?" *Christian Century,* 91 (January 2-9, 1974), 15; *Ibid.,* p. 16.
6. Cully, *Change, Conflict, and Self-Determination,* (Philadelphia: The Westminster Press, 1972), pp. 81, 83.
7. Scott, "What's the Big Idea?" *Theology Today,* 30 (January, 1974), 333.
8. See Green, *The Activities of Teaching* (New York: McGraw-Hill Book Co., 1971).
9. See Oden, *The Intensive Group Experience,* (Philadelphia: The Westminster Press, 1972).
10. Marty and Peerman, *New Theology No. 10* (New York: The Macmillan Co., 1973), pp. xviii, x.
11. Dawe, "Christology in Contemporary Systematic Theology," *Interpretation,* 26 (July, 1972), 275.
12. Marty and Peerman, *New Theology No. 10,* pp. xi-xii.
13. Westerhoff, "A Socialization Model," in his *A Colloquy on Christian Education* (Philadelphia: Pilgrim Press, 1972), pp. 80-90.

Chapter 4

A HERMENEUTICAL APPROACH TO EDUCATIONAL THEORY

H. Edward Everding, Jr.

It has been appropriate for teachers to formulate educational theory on the bases of philosophy and psychology.[1] Infrequently has hermeneutics informed the theory, even though teaching is interpretation. My thesis is that hermeneutics provides the proper frame of reference within which to develop educational theory.

A hermeneutical approach to educational theory emphasizes the nature of interpretation and understanding, the study of which is hermeneutics. These words, *hermeneutics* and *hermeneutical,* derive from the Greek verb *hermēneuein* and noun *hermēneia* which are translated respectively "to interpret" and "interpretation." In ancient times these words were associated with the messenger-god Hermes whose function was to bring to human understanding the otherwise unintelligible messages of the gods. Today hermeneutics refers to a broad field of study including philosophical concerns of the nature of reality, human existence, language, epistemology, and psychological concerns of the interpreter's makeup.[2] Yet, the aim of hermeneutics is to unpack what is involved in the interpretive process, and this is its distinctive contribution to educational theory.

This essay focuses on the interrelationship of biblical interpretation and teaching. This is appropriate for two reasons. First, contemporary hermeneutics has for the most part grown out of biblical studies, even though it has now reached wider proportions within theology and may be said to constitute its own discipline.[3] Second, teachers regularly and dramatically confront the "hermeneutical problem" every time they teach the Bible. Each student, as well as the teacher, has his own understanding of a text. This often results in multiple and sometimes conflicting interpretations. This phenomenon frequently leaves the teacher with many unanswered questions such as: How do I account for these different interpretations? Are they all correct, or is there one normative meaning of the text? What then should be my goals in teaching the Bible? What can I do to achieve these goals? Hermeneu-

H. Edward Everding, Jr., is Associate Professor of New Testament at the Iliff School of Theology, Denver, Colorado.

tics does not provide simplistic answers to these questions but does provide a frame of reference within which each teacher can develop his own responses. Moreover, this essay seeks only to introduce what is involved in the process of interpretation while highlighting some of the central issues characterizing recent hermeneutical discussion. More thorough treatments of the subject are found in the literature mentioned in footnotes. In conclusion, I shall explore some implications of hermeneutics for educational theory geared to teaching the Bible.

A Profile of the Interpretive Process

The technical and theoretical aspects of hermeneutics become concrete and meaningful the more we realize that all life is interpretation. When looking at a movie, playing tennis, talking with a friend, reading a newspaper, or checking the time, we are grasping meanings which help us know who we are and what we are to do. From birth to death we engage in the ongoing and complex process of assimilating and accommodating external stimuli. Hermeneutics in all its refinements is linked to this common human experience. To be sure, different subjects such as science and the humanities will require hermeneutics to be formulated in specific directions. But these are extensions of the general interpretive experience which characterizes human existence. In this broad view, interpretation is "perhaps the most basic act of human thinking; indeed, existing itself may be said to be a constant process of interpretation."[4]

The interpretive act is comprised of three ingredients—the interpreter, what is interpreted, and the relationship between the two. This relationship is the locus of the hermeneutical problem, the transfer of meaning from the one to another. Persons experience this problem in conversations as they seek to translate and appropriate what the other says. In interpreting ancient texts, such as the Bible, the hermeneutical problem is intensified because of the distance in time, space, language, and thought between the text and the interpreter. Moreover, the text cannot respond orally to the interpreter's questions. The problem then is how to interpret or translate meaning from one historical and cultural context to another. Hermeneutics is the resolving of this problem. It is the understanding of the interpretive act, concerned especially with the principle by which the interpreter and text are meaningfully related. Before delineating representative views of the *scope* of this relationship, we shall identify current issues pertaining to the interpreter and the text.

A HERMENEUTICAL APPROACH TO EDUCATIONAL THEORY

The Stance of the Interpreter

It is a truism today that interpretation without presuppositions is not possible. Each interpreter stands within a horizon of understanding determined by his cognitive and ego development, theology, communities of understanding, culture, and central interests. He presupposes an understanding of reality, the world, human existence, and the nature of understanding. Even the method of approach, including the so-called objective historical-critical method, delimits what the interpreter sees.[5] His stance shapes the way he views and questions the text. This accounts for the plurality of interpretations the educator hears when teaching the Bible. An individual's presuppositions cannot be eliminated, although they can be realigned through dialogue with others and the text. The interpreter can, however, bring to consciousness and acknowledge his stance for what it is.[6]

Acknowledgement of one's presuppositions, moreover, is necessary for interpretation. As a participant in life, the interpreter already presupposes a relation to the text which is an expression of life. This pre-understanding between interpreter and text makes interpretation possible. By determining the way he questions the text, the interpreter's pre-understanding shapes the meaning he will discover. The grasping of meaning, however, is a dialogical process. To understand a text, the interpreter must already pre-understand its subject; but only by getting into the text is he led to its more complete meaning. This complex dialectical process which we experience in everyday conversations is the "hermeneutical circle." A partial understanding draws the interpreter into the text which alone gives the context for its own further understanding.

Since pre-understanding determines the questions the interpreter puts to the text, it is crucial for him to ask if his pre-understanding is appropriate to the text's subject matter. Does a rational understanding of reality let one fully understand the world of miracles? Does a doctrinal understanding of Christian faith let one fully understand the world of New Testament theologies? Can a person who thinks in concrete operations comprehend Paul's argument about the Law in Galatians 3? As the interpreter engages his source through the dialectical process, he may discover that he needs to restructure his presuppositions as he seeks to understand the subject matter expressed in the text.

The Source to Be Interpreted

While the interpreter approaches his task within the general framework of the interpretive process, the source itself may occasion a particular set of problems. A text may require him to ask different questions because of its distinctive content and form. For example, the interpreter may need to develop varying skills appropriate to the form and content of a novel, a poem, a painting, or a sculpture. The interpreter of biblical literature will also adjust his viewing and questioning procedure according to the source's particular literary form and content (e.g., law, history, myth, prophecy, apocalypse, gospel, or letter). The source to be interpreted, therefore, exerts an influence on the interpreter.

A source's distinct problems of interpretation are determined by the horizon of meaning in which it stands. The text is located in various contexts of understanding. The *linguistic* context is determined by rules of grammar and the range of meaning of the text's vocabulary. The *literary* context includes the text's sources, individualized style and form, as well as its place in a document or collection. The *historical* context is comprised of the specific occasion of the text within its own historical epoch. The *traditional* context refers to the history of tradition behind the text and the history of interpretation the text sets in motion. The necessary involvement of the *author* in the text he has created is also a significant part of this horizon. The interpreter, then, is confronted with the task of entering the text's multifaceted and moving horizon of meaning.[7]

The interpreter enters the text's horizon through its language. Although the nature and function of language is the central topic of current hermeneutical debate, we shall here only try to indicate some of the reasons why this is so crucial. First, the interpreter's primary access to the text's meaning is through what it says. Since the Bible was originally composed in Hebrew, Aramaic, and Greek, the interpreter is faced with a major problem of interpretation. If language is culturally conditioned, then not only the translation, but also the initial speaking is an act of interpreting one's experience. Moreover, biblical literature is frequently the writing *about* events which once happened or were spoken, so the writing is itself further interpretation. The text's language, therefore, may present an interpretation of an interpretation of an interpretation. So whether the interpreter reads the text in the original or reads a translation, he is dealing with multiple interpretations within which the text's meaning is lodged. What principle, then, helps him to reach that meaning? Second, the form and function of the text's language determines the direction interpretation takes. For example, some biblical language is figurative, not descriptive or objective. It is mythopoetic, the language of metaphor and symbol whose function is to refer and not designate. This kind of language does not always mean what it says or say what it means. The interpreter is drawn to discover the world of the symbol, the intention of which is partially hidden in the mythopoetic expression. Again the interpreter needs a principle which will help him reach the meaning to which this language refers.[8]

The intention of a text, which is the goal of interpretation, is thus disclosed or hidden in the language of the text. On the text's surface, the intention is discovered in the point being scored about the subject matter. This is discerned by analyzing the structure or pattern of words and measuring their range of meaning in their literary and historical settings. Moreover, what is not said may be as important as what is said. This procedure, however, may miss the depth of intentions in a text composed from sources or layers of traditions. The interpreter may find multiple intentions in a given text. If he seeks to identify a continuity or unity to these intentions, then he will again need to select a principle to uncover this "true" meaning. In any event, the intention of a text may not be found solely by analyzing what the text says on its surface level.[9]

In light of the preceding issues about the interpreter's stance and source, contemporary hermeneutics is concerned with establishing a systematic basis for interpretation. By this is meant an approach which recognizes and safeguards the integrity of both interpreter and text. The text must be heard and the interpreter must ask his own questions. The distance as well as the points of contact between the two must be maintained. The subjectivity or horizons of understanding of both must be allowed to merge in dialogue. This is a concern not for scientific "objectivity," but for a controlled relationship between text and interpreter and a principle of interpretation which allows meaning to emerge. Given this concern, the scope of interpretation in contemporary views differs considerably.

The Scope of Interpretation

The broad scope of interpretation in the ancient period provides a convenient backdrop against which the distinctive emphases of recent theories can be viewed. Interpretation included the activities of speaking, translating, and explaining. *Speech* referred to clear proclamation of the obscure, language itself being the interpretation. *Translation* is transferring meaning from a foreign language into one's own language. *Explanation* or commentary is clarifying something formerly unexplained. Interpretation, therefore, was not just theory, but the practice of the art. All three dimensions of this practice characterized the history of biblical interpretation to the Enlightenment.[10]

With new understandings of man and reality occasioned by the Enlightenment's discovery of reason, science, and history, the scope of interpretation narrowed. Texts were viewed as "objects" to be analyzed and explained by the "objective" rational interpreter. The aim of his historical exegesis (from the Greek *exēgēsis* meaning "showing" or "explanation") was to describe what the text originally meant. Exegetical practice was distinguished from hermeneutical theory which was limited to philological, historical, and literary aspects of texts. In short, the scope of interpretation was equated with the historical-critical method which itself provided the control for interpretation. This theory is "traditional" for biblical interpretation in the sense that it has provided the foundation for contemporary biblical studies. Its value has been to free the Bible from forced doctrinal interpretations and for a reading in its own historical context of meaning. Exegesis firmly recognizes the text's distance from the interpreter whose historical imagination and method allow him to bridge the gap. Although not concerned with translating the Bible's contemporary meaning, exegesis has pinpointed and intensified the problem of translation by its recognition of the Bible's pastness. The task of applying the text (labeled hermeneutics by some), however, is delegated to the theologian or preacher, but not the exegete.[11]

Traditional historical interpretation has set in motion the variety of contemporary styles of interpretation. Out of discontent with a preoccupation with the past and a tendency to dissolve the Bible into unrelated bits of antiquated facts, they seek to broaden interpretation to include appropriation of meaning for the present.[12] For example, biblicism asserts that the text says what it means and means what it says. However, it naïvely ignores the distance between text and interpreter and the force of the interpreter's theological and cultural presuppositions. More sophisticated approaches start with historical interpretation but further seek to identify and abstract noble ideals, the author's personality, spiritual truths, rational doctrines, or religious experience. Although claiming objectivity, such approaches endanger the text's independence by projecting their categories upon the text. Nevertheless, the general concern to broaden the scope of interpretation created the need for a system which took into account the text's pastness and underlying meaning and the interpreter's subjectivity and involvement with the text.

Existentialist interpretation is today the most influential hermeneutical theory in respect to its number of opponents, as well as proponents. Through its inception by Rudolf Bultmann to its refinement in the new hermeneutic, it is the only systematic theory of the interpreter's involvement with the historical text. Moreover, it broadens the scope of interpretation to include explaining, translating, and speaking.[13] Traditional exegesis is absorbed into a larger process in which the goal of interpretation is to disclose, translate, and proclaim the "event" which originally occasioned the text.[14]

The need for interpretation in this broader sense is caused by the language of the text. For Bultmann, the Bible's mythological language distorts its subject matter. Myth is a way of talking about God, who cannot be objectified, in seemingly objective terms (e.g., God descends or fights). The interpreter, therefore, needs to grasp the inner intention of this language. He cannot eliminate it but can "demythologize" or interpret its meaning. For the new hermeneutic, language itself is regarded positively as an interpretative proclamation of the text's meaning. Language is the interpretive tool in and through which the interpreter gains access to the event or intention which brought language to expression. The intention, therefore, is not to be equated with the text's linguistic expressions. Likewise, translation is not finding equivalent words but respeaking the text's intention even if the contemporary words contradict the original.

The original intention of the text is retrieved through a dialogic process guided by the interpreter's own questions. The dialogue is made possible by the common participation in human existence of interpreter and text. The interpreter's "pre-understanding" of human existence provides the principle (i.e., the hermeneutic) which enables him to understand the subject matter of the text. Questions about existence—his estrangement from his true self—lead the interpreter to what the text says about the meaning of existence. The text's subject matter, however, is not an object to be mastered but a subject or word which addresses the interpreter and calls for his decision about its view of existence. The new hermeneutic particularly stresses the active and performing function of language. In this encounter the traditional idea of subject-object is reversed so that the interpreter is interpreted by the text he seeks to interpret. This dynamic interaction of text and interpreter is the heart of the interpretive process. But the process is not completed until the interpreter speaks or proclaims the text's meaning so it again can become an "event" to his hearers. For Bultmann this is the proclamation of the *kerygma* ("message") of how God works a believing self-understanding through the salvation event in Jesus Christ. For the new hermeneutic this is the proclamation of the word-event, the revelatory Word-event, in which God is brought to expression in such a way that the hearer is led to certainty or faith.

Existentialist interpretation, particularly in the form of the new hermeneutic, presents a holistic approach to interpretation akin to the ancient period. This broad scope is shaped and controlled by the view that language is the medium in which man exists. Hermeneutic is then not just a theory but the practice of an art in which language becomes an event of meaning. And insofar as Christian theology seeks to translate the Bible so that God's Word-event can address the world today, hermeneutic is equivalent to theology.[15]

New directions in hermeneutics are, in large part, responses to existentialist interpretation. In this sense, the new hermeneutic is a language-event which sets in motion trajectories of meaning. One trend broadens the scope of interpretation by reconsidering the nature of history. For example, Wolfhart Pannenberg criticizes the individualism of the new hermeneutic and introduces the category of universal history. He distinguishes between the two as follows:

> Both have to do with texts. Both arrive at the interpreter's present on the basis of the text and draw the interpreter into the interpretation of the text. However, the hermeneutical outlook apparently moves solely between the past text and the present interpreter, whereas the universal-historical outlook first goes back behind the text, and considers the essential content (*Sache*), i.e., the event being inquired into behind the text, in its universal-historical context of meaning, including also the interpreter's own present era.[16]

His historical understanding includes verifying the "objective historicity" of certain past events which have normative meaning for faith and need no translation (e.g., Jesus' resurrection). Process metaphysics broadens the hermeneutical scope by seeing history in cosmological perspective and stressing the past's conditionedness but relatedness to the present. In this context, the Bible is interpreted as the unrepeatable primal form of the historical emergent, Christian existence, as well as the occasion for trajectories of meaning into the present, Christian tradition.[17]

A second trend seeks to narrow the scope of interpretation by reconsidering the nature of language. For example, in distinguishing between the meaning of what a text says from the significance which the reader finds in it, E. D. Hirsch, Jr., defines hermeneutics as "the philological discipline which sets forth the rules by which valid determinations of the verbal meanings of a passage may be achieved." [18]

A third trend broadens the scope by stressing social contexts of meaning in contrast to the existentialists' focus on one's own existence. For example, in conjunction with his understanding of the impact of the future on the present, Jürgen Moltmann proposes a "political hermeneutics" in which interpretation eventuates in changes of the present social and political order.[19]

A fourth trend broadens the scope by taking an interdisciplinary approach to the interpretive process. For example, current ethical issues provide a context for a communal approach to interpretation which probes the text for the images of faith which shape human behavior.[20] In these and other developments of the scope of interpretation, it becomes even clearer that life is interpretation.

Implications for Educational Theory

The issues stressed in the preceding interpretation of the interpretive process have direct bearing on teaching. Nevertheless, there is need for caution about making too neat correlations between hermeneutics and educational theory. Here I propose only to sketch programmatically some of the implications for the teacher's views of the student, educational goals, and teaching style.

The Student as Interpreter

In teaching the Bible it is important to recognize that the student is an interpreter. He comes at the text from a particular horizon, and only he can interpret it for himself. Although the teacher also interprets the text, his main purpose is to help the student develop his interpretive abilities and not to force an interpretation on the student. The heart of this facilitating process is the teacher's awareness of the presence and function of his own presuppositions and those of his student. The knowledge that each student will have his own interpretation can at least minimize frustration occasioned by unexpected diverse student interpretations. The teacher can be free to encourage individual and perhaps contradictory interpretations because each is determined by how persons see the text for themselves. In this connection, theories of how persons develop can help the teacher appreciate more fully what kinds of distance and points of contact exist between student and text. Educational goals, therefore, can be designed to help the student interpret according to his cognitive and affective level of development.[21]

Educational Goals

If the main purpose of teaching the Bible is to help the student interpret, then one goal for the student is to learn how to read what the text says. Teaching frequently informs the student *of* the Bible, but does not enable him to work *with* the text and hear it for himself. Access to the text's meaning is gained only through careful and disciplined reading which lets the text speak. The selection of texts and reading expectations, to be sure, are determined by the student's reading ability. Whether at an elementary or advanced level, however, the student can develop listening techniques which safeguard the text's integrity and open up its meaning for him.

Second, to discover the meanings of the text is certainly the ultimate goal of biblical interpretation and teaching. But meaning is determined as much by the interpreter's presuppositions as by what the text says. The history of biblical interpretation, therefore, would support a contextual or relative view of meaning. Each generation or person interprets the Bible's meaning in light of a particular setting and stance. There is, then, no absolute and unchanging interpretation, for each person's interpretation is correct since it is his own. There are, of course, continuities of meaning which have surfaced throughout the history of interpretation. Yet, even these have been variously understood in terms of facts, ideals, doctrines, symbols, self-understandings, etc. This does not mean that the search for meaning is without controls. The control of meaning is located first of all in the reality of what the text says, given contingencies related to the text's language, transmission, or translation. It is also controlled by the interpreting community, whether a small study group or the church seen in its totality. The interpreting community provides a system of checks and balances, challenges and supports in which pluralism of interpretation can be both tolerated and encouraged.

A third goal is to help the student understand himself in relation to the text's meaning. When the scope of interpretation is broadly defined to include the active involvement of the interpreter, the Bible becomes an interpretive tool which interprets the interpreter. The Bible can have this effect whether it is viewed as the literal Word of God, a source of revelation, the primal form of Christian tradition, or just good literature. In any case, confrontation with the text enables the student to learn about himself, to restructure his way of thinking, and therefore to shape his life values.

Teaching Style

The activity of interpretation suggests a participatory style of education. The student learns to interpret by interpreting. Furthermore, the hermeneutical circle of interaction between text and interpreter suggests that this style be confluent, a "flowing together" of input (text) and response (interpreter). This flow can be structured through strategies which allow the student freedom to work with the text. The learning which takes place through this process warrants relativizing the importance of a lecture style designed to "cover all the material." That is, there is a clear distinction between the student who "learns" how to interpret a text by doing and the student who "learns about" a text by hearing. The latter stocks his memory. The former shapes his thinking.[22]

The interpreter's appropriation of meaning in the interpretive process suggests a confessional style of teaching. This does not mean that the teacher should proclaim his idea of what the Bible means. Rather, it refers to a climate of challenge and support, conflict and trust which allows the student to apply the text for himself. This includes the interplay of thinking and feeling in which the student opens himself to the meaning of the text so that it becomes part of his personal structure of symbolic meanings. This is a teaching style which lets the student make an appropriation of the text *his own.*

How one interprets the processes of interpretation and teaching is determined by his horizon. Significantly contributing to one's stance toward biblical interpretation and teaching is how he views the issues of biblical inspiration, revelation, and authority.[23] As Holy Writ, the Bible is supposed to be relevant and regulative for contemporary faith. As ancient literature, the Bible is conditioned by its own language and historical setting. The juxtaposition of these views has occasioned the contemporary crisis of how to interpret and teach the Bible faithfully and legitimately in the modern era.

This essay has sought to introduce the broad scope of this crisis by exploring the dynamic structure of the interpretative process. This crisis, however, is not restricted to *biblical* interpretation and teaching. It affects the *total context of Christian education.* Similarly a hermeneutical approach to teaching the Bible undoubtedly has ramifications for the entire process of Christian education as it pertains, for example, to Christian history, doctrine, or social views. For as a hermeneutical approach to the teaching of the Bible allows the student to claim the text as his own, in the broader context of Christian faith a hermeneutical process may allow the student to claim this *faith* as his own.

NOTES

1. For example, Van Cleve Morris, *Philosophy and the American School: An Introduction to the Philosophy of Education* (Boston: Houghton Mifflin, 1961); Wayne R. Rood, *Understanding Christian Education* (Nashville:

Abingdon Press, 1970); Hans G. Furth, *Piaget for Teachers* (Englewood Cliffs, N. J.: Prentice-Hall, 1970).

2. The cross-disciplinary nature of hermeneutics is thoroughly discussed in Roger Lapointe, O. M. I. "Hermeneutics Today," trans. L. Sabourin, *Biblical Theology Bulletin*, 2 (June, 1972), 107-54. The best comprehensive treatment in English of current hermeneutical theories is Richard E. Palmer, *Hermeneutics: Interpretation Theory in Schleiermacher, Dilthey, Heidegger, and Gadamer* (Evanston, Ill.: Northwestern University Press, 1969).

3. Accounts of this development are found in Gerhard Ebeling, "Hermeneutik" in Kurt Galling, ed., *Die Religion in Geschichte und Gegenwart*, 3rd ed., vol. 3 (Tübingen: J. C. B. Mohr, 1959), pp. 242-64; James M. Robinson, "Hermeneutic Since Barth," in James M. Robinson and John B. Cobb, Jr., eds., *The New Hermeneutic: New Frontiers in Theology*, vol. 2 (New York: Harper & Row, 1964), pp. 1-77; René Marlé, S. J., *Introduction to Hermeneutics* (New York: Herder and Herder, 1967); and William G. Doty, *Contemporary New Testament Interpretation* (Englewood Cliffs, N. J.: Prentice-Hall, 1972), pp. 1-51.

4. On the distinction between general and specific hermeneutics see Palmer, *Hermeneutics: Interpretation Theory*, pp. 36-38 and *passim*. Biblical interpretation does not require a special hermeneutics as argued by Rudolf Bultmann, "The Problem of Hermeneutics," in idem, *Essays: Philosophical and Theological*, trans. James C. G. Grieg (New York: The Macmillan Co., 1955), pp. 257ff; Palmer, *Hermeneutics: Interpretation Theory*, p. 8.

5. Rudolf Bultmann, "Is Exegesis Without Presuppositions Possible?" in Schubert M. Ogden, ed. and trans., *Existence and Faith: Shorter Writings of Rudolf Bultmann* (New York: Meridian Books, 1960), pp. 289-96.

6. This critique of method has been made most forcefully by the philosophers Martin Heidegger and Hans-Georg Gadamer whose theories are described by Palmer, *Hermeneutics: Interpretation Theory*. From the perspective of the Bible as canon, a holistic hermeneutic which includes serious use of the history of biblical interpretation is proposed by Brevard S. Childs, *Biblical Theology in Crisis* (Philadelphia: The Westminster Press, 1970).

7. The practical dimensions of this task are described by Victor Paul Furnish, "Some Practical Guidelines for New Testament Exegesis," *Perkins Journal*, 28 (Winter, 1975), 1-16.

8. A comprehensive analysis of current understandings of language is given by Robert W. Funk, *Language, Hermeneutic, and Word of God* (New York: Harper & Row, 1966). Doty, *New Testament Interpretation*, works out the practice of these views for New Testament interpretation.

9. For example, see the penetrating analysis of Genesis 32 by Gerhard von Rad, *Genesis: A Commentary*, trans. John H. Marks, The Old Testament Library (Philadelphia: The Westminster Press, 1961), pp. 311-21.

10. Each word is a possible translation of *hermēneuein* and *hermēneia*. Palmer analyzes their modern significance in *Hermeneutics: Interpretation Theory*, pp. 12-36; Robert M. Grant, *A Short History of the Interpretation of the Bible*, rev. ed. (New York: The Macmillan Co., 1963).

11. Underlying this division of responsibility is the traditional distinction between what the text *meant* and what it *means*. For example, the descriptive task of the exegete sets the stage for the hermeneutical task of the theologian, according to Krister Stendahl, "Biblical Theology, Contemporary," in George A. Buttrick, ed., *The Interpreter's Dictionary of the Bible*, vol. A-E (Nashville: Abingdon Press, 1962), pp. 418-32.

12. Robinson, *New Hermeneutic*, provides a survey of the moves away from traditional hermeneutics. See also Amos N. Wilder, "New Testament Hermeneutics Today," in William Klassen and Graydon F. Snyder, eds.

Current Issues in New Testament Interpretation: Essays in Honor of Otto A. Piper (New York: Harper & Row, 1962), pp. 38-52. Representative of Roman Catholic biblical interpretation which today does not differ considerably from Protestant is Raymond E. Brown, S. S., "Hermeneutics," in Brown et al., eds., *The Jerome Biblical Commentary* (Englewood Cliffs, N. J.: Prentice-Hall, 1968), pp. 605-23. See also Marlé, *Introduction to Hermeneutics,* pp. 94-123.

13. Robinson, *New Hermeneutic;* Doty, *New Testament Interpretation;* and Marlé, *Introduction to Hermeneutics,* present good introductions to Bultmann and the new hermeneutic of which Gerhard Ebeling and Ernst Fuchs are the chief representatives. More extensive and readable is Paul J. Achtemeier, *An Introduction to the New Hermeneutic* (Philadelphia: The Westminster Press, 1969).

14. The new hermeneutic is closely associated with the new quest for the historical Jesus in whom God's Word became event. For example, see Ernst Fuchs, "The New Testament and the Hermeneutical Problem," in Robinson and Cobb, *New Hermeneutic,* pp. 111-45, and Norman Perrin, "The Modern Interpretation of the Parables of Jesus and the Problem of Hermeneutics," *Interpretation,* 25 (April, 1971), 131-48.

15. Gerhard Ebeling, "Word of God and Hermeneutic," in Robinson and Cobb, *New Hermeneutic,* pp. 78-110.

16. Wolfhart Pannenberg, "Hermeneutic and Universal History," in idem, *Basic Questions in Theology: Collected Essays,* vol. 1, trans. George H. Kehm (Philadelphia: Fortress Press, 1970), p. 99.

17. The contours of a process hermeneutic are currently being drawn as, for example, William A. Beardslee, "Notes Toward a Whiteheadian Hermeneutic," (paper presented at the annual meeting of the Society of Biblical Literature, Washington, D.C., October 24, 1974).

18. Palmer, *Hermeneutics: Interpretation Theory,* p. 61.

19. Moltmann, "Toward a Political Hermeneutics of the Gospel," *Union Seminary Quarterly Review,* 23 (1968), 303-23.

20. Important examples are the phenomenological approach of Paul Ricoeur, *The Symbolism of Evil,* trans. Emerson Buchanan (New York: Harper & Row, 1967), and the psychoanalytic perspective of Walter Wink, *The Bible in Human Transformation: Toward a New Paradigm for Biblical Study* (Philadelphia: Fortress Press, 1973); H. Edward Everding, Jr., and Dana W. Wilbanks, *Decision-Making and the Bible* (Valley Forge, Pa.: Judson Press, 1975).

21. See James E. Loder, "Developmental Foundations for Christian Education," chapter 5 in this volume.

22. For example, George Isaac Brown, *Human Teaching for Human Learning: An Introduction to Confluent Education* (New York: Viking Press for the Esalen Institute, 1971).

23. Sara Little, "Revelation, the Bible, and Christian Education," in Marvin J. Taylor, ed., *An Introduction to Christian Education* (Nashville: Abingdon Press, 1966), pp. 42-49. Although Little suggests that Christian educators investigate "the idea of *hermeneutic* in relationship to their approach to the Bible," I am not aware that this has been done. Furthermore, as noted below, I suggest that hermeneutics has significant implications for Christian education as a whole.

Chapter 5

DEVELOPMENTAL FOUNDATIONS
FOR CHRISTIAN EDUCATION

James E. Loder

In order to provide a general definition of *development* and a principle for discriminating among developmental theorists, we can begin with a basic premise. That is, normal human development is an emergent reality, a resultant of the interaction between a personality and its environment whereby the potential structures of the personality are given particular and varied shapes over the course of a lifetime.

For example, language, a uniquely human endowment in its fullest form, is in its general structure a potential of the personality that is given particular and varied shape depending upon the interaction between the person—his/her age and the personal qualities by which he/she embellishes that structure—and the cultural environment in which he/she develops.

By locating development "between" the personality and its environment and by asserting that it is an emergent gestalt, synthesizing environmental influences and personality potentials, we have already discounted certain views that have been—and to some extent still are —prominent in developmental studies.

For instance, we have discounted *preformationism,* a naïve seventeenth-century notion held by Anton van Leewenhoek. Studying sperm in his microscope, van Leewenhoek believed he saw miniature animals which he thought simply expanded into maturity. By this view, development takes place in a balloon fashion; it is simply the expansion of a preformed miniature. Naïve as this seems, it is nevertheless quite common to revert to essentially this same view as when we fall into thinking of the child as just a little adult.

A second view which we have discounted is *predeterminism* in which it was assumed by persons such as G. S. Hall that preset biological mechanisms exercise exclusive determination over development. Hall, founder of child psychology in America in the late nineteenth century, propounded a developmental Darwinism summed up in the phrase "ontogeny recapitulates phylogeny." This view fails to take

James E. Loder is Associate Professor of Christian Education, Princeton Theological Seminary, Princeton, New Jersey.

sufficient account of the uniqueness of human development, assuming, as it did, that children's minds develop in the same fashion as, say, a mature frog develops from a tadpole.

A third view which is discredited by our basic premise is *environmentalism*. This view of the early behaviorists, notably John Watson, assumed that by controlled training any newborn child could be molded into any type of adult. Contemporary behaviorists such as B. F. Skinner take more account of genetic factors and neurological findings than did Watson, but they make similar claims regarding the power of the environment to determine the shape of adult personality. Environmentalism makes the same mistake as predeterminism, but from the outside in rather than from the inside out. It fails to take account of human uniqueness, assuming that persons can be shaped in all registers of behavior by the same techniques that shape laboratory rats and pigeons.

Each of these discredited positions has made some contribution to more adequate understandings of human development, but what follows here will depart from these views. We will discuss those theories of development which are based upon primary research and treat development as a complex emergent resultant of the interaction between the person and his/her environment.[1]

Psychodynamic Views

The most widely used notions of development in mental health are Freudian or neo-Freudian. Freud's assumption, based primarily upon clinical experience with regressed patients, was that generalized sexual energy focused upon erogenous zones of the body of the developing person. Such eroticized zones are the physical—and basically the psychological—means that the developing person has for giving and taking in relation to the objects of his affection. The earliest zone upon which the child's libidinal energy is focused is the mouth. In this *oral phase,* characteristics of receptivity, dependency, as well as oral gratification are fostered, so that, even though this period is usually past by eighteen months or two years, a person may be fixated at this stage and manifest the characteristics of orality long after he has properly outgrown it.

The next phase is the *anal.* During the period of eighteen months to two and one-half years, the libidinal energy of the child is transferred to the anus and just prior to or during this period, toilet training is undergone. In this presumably crucial time for the child, he is taught for the first time to introduce between the cue and the response a socially determined choice which either affects delay or prompts release. Here, some clinicians believe, is the ground of the adult capacity to choose for or against socially structured restrictions and demands. Confusion or excessive frustration at this period may also cause fixation and subsequent personality characteristics such as tightness, messiness, a fondness for collecting, stubbornness, aggressiveness, and/or shamefulness can result.

At two and one-half or three, the child enters the so-called *phallic period* in which libidinal energy shifts from the anus to the phallus. In little girls the much-debated presupposition is that they have penis envy, sensing their physical differential they envy the male phallus. Little girls come to desire the father, and little boys develop a sexual desire for the mother. But, since incest is taboo, a new frustration sets in. This is the Oedipal conflict (Electra for girls) which is biphasic; that is, the conflict at this period of development is resolved temporarily by identification with the parent of the same sex, but it will return in adolescence, at which time it receives its final resolution. The period of temporary resolution is called *latency,* and the final resolution is called the *genital phase* in which it is presumed that the ego has achieved sufficient stability so as to "love and work" as Freud phrased it.

There have been many elaborations on various aspects of this basic scheme and not the least of the elaborators was Anna Freud, whose work emphasized psychological development in childhood. The most significant basic shift in emphasis has been from the dynamics of the libido to the developing formation of the ego.

Ego psychology stresses the view that the ego has a developmental plan of its own, not exclusive of all libidinal instincts or reality considerations, but sufficiently autonomous to negotiate for a place of its own on the psychic terrain. Most significant early figures in this movement were Henry A. Murray, David Rapaport, Heinz Hartman, Ernst Kris, and H. S. Sullivan. However, the most influential and widely read ego psychologist, whose work has stressed the developmental perspective, is Erik Erikson.

Erikson was analyzed by Anna Freud, but his background is not medical and his writing is less technical than other ego psychologists. However, his books have wide-ranging intuitive—even artistic—and academic import. His work is almost as significant for literature, history, and social psychology as it is for clinical psychology and human development. For the purposes of this chapter, three central notions can be used to characterize Erikson's theoretical distinctiveness. The first is his multidisciplinary approach to ego development. The second is his elaboration of the principle of epigenesis from birth through death stressing the identity crisis and generativity as much or more than the early years of development. The third is his constructive application of psychoanalytic concepts to value formation and religious belief.

Erikson's approach is not multidisciplinary in any strict sense, since he seems to disregard the methodologies of the disciplines which are influenced by his thought; yet he makes it clear that the formation of the ego is a biologically based, psychologically located, socially shaped, and culturally controlled and articulated phenomenon. Any less complex treatment will not be sufficiently comprehensive to account for certain essential aspects of the ego's development. In his earliest volume, *Childhood and Society,* he built upon the Freudian foundations, elaborating the psychological dimensions of physiological relations with important objects of affection. But he went much further to show through clinical observations, anthropological studies, and experimental play situations that human interactions (e.g., mother-child relations; male and female identity; the older person's relation to his family) are culture bound even as they yield to a presumably cross-culturally valid psychodynamic interpretation.

At each stage of its development, the ego comes up with a new sense of itself. The term *sense* is used with discretion because the patterns of ego formation which Erikson describes are not able to be objectified by the subject himself; he rather senses that they are there and tests this sense of himself in his behavior (via the social and cultural context) to discover whether his intuitions about himself prove valid. Each ego state is a kind of multidimensional equilibrium which, for all of its interrelatedness to physical, psychic, social, and cultural factors, has a relatively stable autonomy of its own. The dynamics of development follow from stage to stage: as one ego state finds itself too heavily and persistently conflicted from such factors as physical growth, emerging competences, and environmental demands, so the ego either expands in complexity toward a new state of stable autonomy, or else it is overcome by the disintegration imposed by growth factors and reaches a state dominated by negative affective relations toward the several dimensions of its context.

Development in Erikson's scheme follows a conflict-resolution process throughout life. It is probably not sufficiently stressed just how Hegelian Erikson's scheme is; it is always the case that a positive ego state, a successful resolution, represents a synthesis of affirmative and negative aspects, but the negative aspects have been converted into assets in the struggle for adaptation rather than liabilities. For instance, the newborn child is, according to Erikson, in an eighteen-month existential struggle to determine whether or not he can trust the new extrauterine environment into which his growth has thrust him. It is the mother's task to construct with her body, by stroking and nurturing of the child, an environment which simulates the comfort, support, and assurance to which the child has become accustomed for nine months or so. But the child makes the transition from uterus to trust, not simply by replicating the earlier situation, but also by learning what can be reached and not reached, what hurts to bite, and how it feels to fall and be left alone. He learns trust not simply by trusting everything, but also by learning to mistrust certain things, situations, persons, and impulses and yet continuing to reach out, exploring his world and himself. Thus trust incorporates limits and grows all the more trusting because of learning what must be mistrusted.

So much for ego development in a multidisciplinary context. For Erikson, the pattern of development through the life span is called *epigenesis*. This notion has its basis in the step-by-step physiological development of fetal organs. Each organ has its appointed time for emergence. If it does not arise at that time, it will never be able to express itself fully because the appointed time for some other part will have arrived, and this will tend to dominate the less active organ. Moreover, failure of one organ to develop fully tends to impair the whole developmental schedule and the hierarchy of organs. By analogy and extension of this physiological model, Erikson has proposed that lifetime ego development follows an epigenetic schedule through eight major stages. Each phase is characterized by a critical opposition in one's sense of himself, and, according to the schedule, the phase passes, resolving the opposition with a dominance of one side over the other. The model taken rigidly would seem to say that each resolution is destiny for that person, but Erikson does not hold strictly to this view. Such a view would seriously undermine psychotherapy and analysis. On the contrary, the whole conceptual scheme is to be used as a model of ego structures for reflection upon both therapy and development.

Erikson's acceptance in religious circles has been built on the basis of his studies, *Young Man Luther* and *Ghandi's Truth,* and his developmental view of virtue. In the first two studies Erikson shifts the conventional psychoanalytic view of religious behavior from an exhaustive explanation (cf. Freud's *Future of an Illusion* and *Moses and Monotheism*) to one perspective among others. This has the effect of accounting not only for the psychodynamic aspects of general religious behavior, but accounting in developmental terms for some of the personality formations in a prophetic religious genius. Erikson does not completely overcome the reductionistic tendencies of his perspective, but there are new far-reaching insights. For instance, his description of the homo-*religiosus* as one who has effectively leaped from identity to integrity—the fifth to the eighth stage—is a valuable but, as yet, not a fully developed insight.

In *Insight and Responsibility,* Erikson set up a schedule for the development of virtues—pervading strengths—which follows the epigenetic sequence but describes how the ego comes to manifest its structures of biosocial adjustment at any particular stage in relation to macrostructures of the social order and even the cosmos. Such manifestations are reciprocal interactions between the ego and its environment, which have been stabilized as strengths upon which the ego can rely. They build into the personality qualities of actual life which combine over the course of development to integrate the whole person in relation to his world.

Below, a typical chart listing the eight stages of development and their corresponding contexts in personal, social, and cultural order.[2]

Psychosocial Crises	Radius of Significant Relations	Related Elements of the Social Order	Rudiments of Ego Strength
Basic trust vs. Basic mistrust	Maternal person	Religion and the cosmic order	Hope
Autonomy vs. Shame, doubt	Paternal person	Law and social order	Will
Initiative vs. Guilt	Basic family	Theater and ideal prototypes	Purpose
Industry vs. Inferiority	Neighborhood school	Technological elements	Competence
Identity vs. Role confusion	Peer groups, models of leadership	Ideological perspectives	Fidelity
Intimacy vs. Isolation	Partners in friendship, sex, competition, cooperation	Patterns of cooperation and competition	Love
Generative vs. Stagnation	Divided labor and shared household	Currents of education and Tradition	Care
Ego integrity vs. Despair	"Mankind" "My kind"	Collective wisdom	Wisdom

Structuralism

Structuralism, taken generally, says that the human mind has innate formal properties which determine the limits within which all types of behavior occur—psychic, social, and cultural. These formal properties, here called "structures," are perhaps best described briefly by analogy. For instance, a common spider will suspend its web on three up to twelve points of attachment, but the radial threads will always intersect the lateral ones at equal angles. This takes place because of a fixed code of rules or "structure" built into the spider's nervous system. In a person, the structure is a deep, innate capacity which emerges to structure surface behavior as a result of the interaction between the organism and its environment.

Developmentally, structuralism argues that transformation of cognitive structures takes place in stages.[3] In response to growth in the organism and increased environmental demands, stage transformations occur normally in the direction of increasing complexity and flexibility so as to increase the reciprocity between the developing person and his environment.

The major representative of structuralism in human development is Jean Piaget. Piaget was originally a biologist who wrote his first scientific paper at the age of ten and had published twenty such papers by the time he was twenty-one years old. Studies in philosophy brought his biological background into a concern for the wider notion of epistemology. After a period with Freud in Vienna and Simon in Paris, Piaget began to study cognition in children and to develop an interdisciplinary structuralism. His position in its current form states in essence that the cognitive structures applicable to all realms of knowledge develop through discernible stages from birth through adolescence. Thus, Piaget is not in the strict sense a psychologist, but a genetic epistemologist.[4] His methods of "clinical interview" with children have been criticized as being too subjective, but in recent years his major results have been confirmed by independent investigators.

Four major notions can be used to characterize Piaget's theoretical position. First is his organic model of intelligence. In this model there are two basic invariants: the organization of the organism and the process of adaptation by which the organism adapts to its environment. Adaptation has two subdivisions—assimilation and accommodation. *Assimilation* refers to the organism's capacity to change elements of its environment in order to incorporate them; *accommodation* refers to the changes the organism itself undergoes in order to incorporate environmental elements. The balance between assimilation and accommodation constitutes the mode of adaptation in any given instance.

In the adaptational process of eating, a child will simultaneously accommodate his mouth to the contours of the object and break down its tissues in assimilating it to his own organic system. At a more complex level of behavior, "play" in children represents a dominance of assimilation over accommodation, and "imitation" (not play) represents a predominance of accommodation over imitation. However, both are modes of adaptation less symmetrical than intelligent adaptation which is the balanced relation between assimilation and accommodation that amounts to a dynamic equilibrium between the organism and its environment.

The basic structural units of intelligence are patterns of adaptational action called "schemas." Sucking, in an infant, is a schema which both accommodates itself to the nipple and assimilates the nipple in a process of *intelligent adaptation* at the most rudimentary level. Schemata combine to form ever more complex modes of adaptation. An example of a supraordinate schema would be thumb-in-mouth-curl-up-and-go-to-sleep. Such sensori-motor schemata are all action-based structures which constitute the rudimentary ground of mature conceptual intelligence. Mature intelligence is the result of a series of complex transformations of supraordinate schemata.

In this interpretation of intelligence, it is important to notice that Piaget is pointing out the formal aspects or structures of adaptation inherent to the nature of the human mind. This has nothing directly to do with the content of knowledge, so Piaget claims cross-cultural validity for his model in its power to discriminate between levels of intelligence in developing persons.

A second major concept in Piaget's system is *egocentrism*. His studies show that young children are egocentric not in the sense of choosing to be selfish, but in that they unreflectively construct and live in a world which is always composed around their own ego as the center. Such a child simply cannot put himself in another's position and look at the world from that person's point of view. The development of intelligence can then be described generally as the child's movement from an egocentric to a sociocentric basis for the composition of and reflection upon his world. As the child learns to put himself in another's position, he is also learning to take up and reconcile several different perspectives upon the same object. This allows him to gain the capacity for conceptual continuity of quantity in an object while it undergoes several changes in appearance or shape. This sort of continuity requires mental reversibility, the ability to restore an object mentally to an original state. This is central to the formation of objectivity which in turn is central to the development of mature intelligence.

The third major notion is the *stage sequence* itself. Piaget has discriminated between four major levels of intelligence each of which has internal gradations. The first is sensori-motor intelligence, the second is preoperational intelligence, the third is concrete operations, and the fourth is formal operational intelligence. The term *operation* suggests first the fact that all levels of intelligence are action-based; but more than that an operation is a tightly knit, consistent pattern of mental activity which is repeatable at will.

The distinction between the levels is manifold, but a few major characteristics will help to discriminate between the processes of behavior involved. Sensori-motor intelligence is dominated by physical action exerted upon the environment. Even the minimal amount of language used before eighteen months is given its meaning on the basis of sensori-motor schemas. For example, holophrastic utterances such as *ball* are sounds assimilated to a sensori-motor schema as its basis for meaning. If the child could put it into propositional form, it would be some schematized form of action such as "roll me the ball." Up to two years of age, then, the development of intelligence depends heavily upon hierarchically ordered, sensori-motor schemas.

Between eighteen months and two years, a new aspect emerges, namely, the *semiotic function*. By use of this new capacity the child can transpose schemes of action from a given external scene to a mental scene, preserve them, and reproduce them spontaneously at a different time in a new setting. This is indicative of the child's new power to differentiate a signifier from the thing signified, to internalize the signifier and use it as a provocation for his own experience. This capacity begins to move his intelligence out of its egocentrism toward the place where the child can symbolically construct with accuracy the viewpoints of other persons as distinct from his own. The child matures immensely in intelligence from age two to seven, but this is the general period in which spontaneous, partially organized constructs or intuitions hold sway.

The transition to concrete operations (the period from seven to eleven) is a transition to the use of coherent and integrated cognitive systems by which he can organize and manipulate the world around him. He can consistently structure things of the present in terms of past categories. He is not easily reduced to perplexity like the child of the earlier period because he has an established set of categories involving reversibility, class-inclusion, and the basic logical operations (as in formal logic) at his command.

However, the starting point for concrete operational thinking is always the present and the real rather than the future and the potential. His categories are designed to organize what is before him, but he does not seek to delineate all possible eventualities in confronting a problem. He does not have sufficient formality in his system of categories to extract an essence from an appearance, to attain a content-free concept. Finally, he does not have sufficient overlap in his categorical systems to interrelate patterns of organization with any facility.

When the child moves into formal operational intelligence (about age eleven), he has attained the peak of intellectual maturity in the structural sense. There are obstructions (such as a characteristic omnipotence of intelligence during adolescence) to his using this new capacity, but this is the period when one makes the final great stride in the growth of his intelligence. In this stage his thinking is characteristically propositional and hypothetico-deductive in the textbook sense of scientific. In fact, this stage of thinking bears a remarkable resemblance to John Dewey's description of 'how we think' in his book by that title. Problems are propositionalized (*intellectualized* is Dewey's term), and all possible hypothetical solutions are explored and then examined for their anticipated consequences. The most satisfactory hypothesis is selected and finally put to an empirical test.

These phases in the development of intelligence presume to say that logical structures are present in the conscious human mind as its internal structure. By a process similar to what Erikson described, one phase of equilibrium in intelligence breaks down when the complexity of growth and environmental demand become too great to manage with the present level of organization. This process continues through formal operational intelligence which Piaget sees as the optimal structure of the human mind.

The final major notion to be mentioned here is Piaget's concern for the development of a wide variety of dimensions of human experience other than logic-based intelligence. However, all such dimensions, he believes, are consistent in their development with his view of intelligence. He has studied the development of the child's view of the world, concept of reality, judgment, imagination, affect, and morality to mention a few especially relevant to Christian education.

Following Piaget's structuralist hypotheses are three investigators whose findings are especially pertinent here. The first is Lawrence Kohlberg, whose work is an elaboration of Piaget's work on moral judgment. Kohlberg, following Piaget's method, asked children to judge the morality of conduct described in a series of stories which pose moral dilemmas. By analysis of responses, he set up six stages by which moral judgment moved out of its egocentrism to a final stage which Kohlberg called "conscience." In the order of their appearance in development, a person's moral judgments are: (1) heteronomous, in which there is egocentric deference to a superior power in order to avoid punishment; (2) need-satisfying by means of exchange and self-interested reciprocity; (3) stereotypical, conformed to "good boy" or "nice girl" images in order to please others; (4) oriented to doing one's duty, as in law and order; (5) socially contractual in that right behavior may be determined by corporate agreement when established rules are not sufficiently complex to deal with the situation; (6) a matter of conscience in that judgments are made according to universal principles.[5]

Apparently, at this point in Kohlberg's research, children up to the age of ten tend to make most of their judgments in a serial order of frequency. Most judgments are at level one, and fewest are made at level six. By the time children are seventeen, the order is reversed from whatever level of moral judgment the person had attained. Most Americans do not get beyond level four or five in a lifetime, though apparently potentialities for all the higher levels appear before age seventeen. It should also be noted that the developmental progression is one stage at a time; each stage has its own kind of integrity which is necessary to the optimal development of subsequent stages. Finally it is important to note that a person can comprehend only one stage above his own. So, frequently, more complex moral judgments at, say, stage six are misunderstood by persons at stage four, and the stage-six person may then be erroneously condemned as seeming to be only at stage two or so.

Kohlberg's research is still in progress with most recent changes being made at levels five and six and a seventh under construction. The first four stages seem to be relatively well established as distinct levels of moral development. The age-level correlations for these as well as stages five and six are still somewhat in flux.

Although Piaget has written one article on religion, his views in this area have not been significant. To interpret religious concerns in structuralist perspective one must look to persons such as Ronald Goldman and, more recently, James Fowler.

Goldman has taken some of Piaget's assumptions into research on the development of religious thinking from childhood through adolescence. This study assumes that religious thinking is the same as ordinary thinking except that it concerns itself with religious subject matter. Goldman's research essentially confirms Piaget's findings regarding the levels of thinking about religious matters, but he introduces two notable differences.

First, he suggests two intermediate stages: one intervening between intuitive thinking and concrete operations, the other, between concrete and formal operations. Second, Goldman advances the theory that the age periods in which the various levels of religious intelligence emerge come significantly later than the age periods designated by Piaget for each level of general intelligence. For Goldman, intuitive, or pre-operational, thought pertains up to about seven or eight years; concrete operational thought, from seven/eight to thirteen/fourteen; formal operational thought from thirteen/fourteen years onward.

Goldman has said that religious thinking occurs in a context containing a wide variety of complex factors, all of which contribute to the personal meaningfulness of religious conceptualization. In his application of his research in *Readiness for Religion* he has stressed the use of life situations as the optimal context within which religious thinking can mature. However, this aspect of his work beyond the development of religious thinking has relatively little basis in research.

James Fowler's work must be treated briefly because it is still in its earliest stages. The starting point here is faith as an active form of knowing which has a discernible structure. The structure matures in a fashion which is roughly analogous to the Piaget-Kohlberg viewpoint. That is, it is a movement out of egocentrism toward greater complexity and differentiation in all the major aspects of faith. In theological terms, Fowler says faith is a tripolar form of knowing by which persons apprehend themselves as related to the transcendent and to other persons. His research centers upon the inner structure of a person's faith, i.e., that structure by which one knows himself as related to what he considers to be transcendent. Because Fowler is concentrating upon the formal aspects of faith-knowing, his research may be expected to have cross-cultural significance but limited usefulness in interpreting distinctively Christian aspects of theology.[6]

Several other approaches to human development might be examined, but the foregoing are basic research and models which have or probably will have considerable influence upon education in a Christian context.

Integrative studies are much needed, but not as yet available in complete or systematic form. Peter Wolff has done one such study integrating psychoanalytic and structuralist views for the very early years of development.[7] Jerome Bruner's writings, stressing a structuralist perspective, interrelate psychology and culture for the developmental foundations of education.[8] Broader integration can be seen in Talcott Parsons' comprehensive studies which extend from biological functions through psychoanalytic interpretations of the person to the structures and dynamics underlying social and cultural systems.[9]

Religious development is addressed from a variety of standpoints, including theoretical and empirical studies focused on Christian education in a major collection of papers entitled *Research on Religious Development.*[10]

Longitudinal studies are not available in sufficient quantity and quality to have had a significant impact on theoretical thinking about Christian education. Even the classic study of this type by B. S. Bloom by no means settles the question of educational readiness, and similar studies of religious development would be much more complex and probably even more debatable in terms of their applications for readiness in religious education.[11]

Finally, it should be pointed out that theology and the psychology of human development tend to move in separate orbits, and it is past time for the two disciplines to engage each other formally. It would be most desirable both for giving direction to continuing research and for the construction of Christian education theory and programs if theology would address itself to persons at various age levels in the life span. Currently there is no theology for which children, youth, and aged are the principle audience. Moreover, it is still the fundamentally rationalistic tendency of behavioral science which governs research even in religious development. Theological views of human nature should begin to play an active part in guiding research as well as in evaluating its significance. When theology and the study of human development engage formally and systematically, then we can begin to build an integrated foundation for Christian education that is both developmentally sound and theologically informed.

NOTES

1. Some such discussion may be found in Harry Munsinger, *Fundamentals of Child Development* (New York: Holt, Rinehart and Winston, 1971).
2. Adapted from Erikson, *Insight and Responsibility* (New York: W. W. Norton & Co., 1964); idem, *Psychological Issues,* vol. 1 (New York: International Universities Press, 1959); idem, *Childhood and Society* (New York: W. W. Norton & Co., 1963).
3. This is not uniformly maintained. For instance, Noam Chomskey and his followers do not agree with Piaget on the stage development of language.
4. *Genetic* here refers less to genes than to the genesis and generation of the structures of knowledge. See J. H. Flavell, *The Developmental Psychology of Jean Piaget* (Princeton, N. J.: D. Van Nostrand Co., Inc., 1963).
5. For a firsthand view of Kohlberg's work, especially in relation to structuralism, see *Handbook of Socialization Theory and Research,* ed. David A. Goslin (Chicago: Rand McNally & Co., 1968).
6. For introduction to James Fowler's work, see *Religious Education,* 69 (March-April, 1974), 207f.
7. Wolff uses orthogenesis as interpreted by Heinz Werner (see *Comparative Psychology of Mental Development,* rev. ed. [Chicago: Follett, 1948])

among other such principles to develop his integration in *Psychological Issues* (monograph 5, vol. 2, 1960), which is entitled "The Developmental Psychologies of Jean Piaget and Psychoanalysis."

8. For a view of Bruner's general research in development, see *Studies in Cognitive Growth* (New York: John Wiley & Sons, 1966). For his approach to education, see *The Process of Education* (New York: Random House, 1960), *The Relevance of Education* (New York: W. W. Norton & Co., 1971). For Bruner's sensitivity to the creative side of learning and development, see *On Knowing: Essays for the Left Hand* (New York: Atheneum, 1965), and *Beyond the Information Given* (New York: W. W. Norton & Co., 1973).

9. Talcott Parsons, *Family: Socialization and Interaction Process* (Glencoe, Ill.: The Free Press, 1955), and *Toward a General Theory of Action* (New York: Harper & Brothers, 1961).

10. Merton Strommen, ed., *Research on Religious Development* (New York: Hawthorn Books, 1971).

11. Bloom, *Stability and Change in Human Characteristics* (New York: John Wiley & Sons, 1964); David Elkind, *Children and Adolescents, Interpretative Essays on Jean Piaget* (New York: Oxford University Press, 1970), p. 128.

Chapter 6

CONSCIENCE, VALUES, AND RELIGIOUS EDUCATION

C. Ellis Nelson

Conscience and values are both vague concepts. However, in ordinary life they determine almost by habit the hundreds of judgments we make every day; and they form the basis on which our most important decisions are made. Although the power and ubiquitousness of both are present in the earliest biblical writings and have been analyzed by theologians throughout the history of the church, they did not become the objects of systematic study until the twentieth century. With the development of psychology and sociology as separate fields of inquiry, the general terms *conscience* and *values* have been broken up and examined under more specific rubrics such as ego ideal, superego, attitudes, behavior modification, internalized control, class values, cultural values, sentiment, socialization, internal moral standards, guilt feelings, moral judgments, internalization, motivation, resistance to temptation, denial of blame, identification, and many other terms of powers and processes that attempt to understand a person's moral choices. The purpose of this essay is to describe in general terms the way conscience and values as agents of morality develop and function and to suggest to religious educators how they can relate to these natural processes.

How Conscience Develops

Conscience is a complex phenomenon which develops slowly from a variety of sources. It starts almost from the first day of life so that some of its components are in operation before a person begins to become self-conscious. The baby is at first aware only that there is authority in the surroundings which orders life and that this authority has power to enforce its will. Parental authority may be kindly, but it controls the baby's life and the baby must adjust to it. As the baby becomes self-conscious and more adventuresome in her/his running about, she/he is physically restrained or punished for transgressing whatever boundaries have been set. At this early stage, it is not possible

C. Ellis Nelson is President and Professor of Christian Education at Louisville Presbyterian Theological Seminary, Louisville, Kentucky.

to reason with the baby because it cannot talk or think. What the child learns is obedience based on the rewards or punishments that are administered hundreds of times each day. The punishments, especially spanking or threats to withhold affection, sink deep within the child's receptive mind because it has no ability to defend itself or to escape.

Thus, the first part of conscience is developed out of feelings associated with what a person must do. As the child grows older, parents, baby-sitters, neighbors, school teachers, and policemen all direct the child's behavior with a certain amount of authority. The growing child unconsciously accepts a good deal of required conduct. In Freudian terms, this is the superego—the generalized power of parents and community functioning inside a person about a fairly specific code of conduct.

This part of conscience is sometimes called negative because it is primarily about what one should not do, although it does also include what one must do. The must-do part was called "fierce goodness" by Karen Horney because its motivation was an obedience to authority rather than a freely chosen desire to be helpful. The internal authority that powers the negative conscience is nonrational. It was created out of the feelings engendered when the small child was struggling with parents and others who made a social being out of her/him.

Two types of reaction are laid down in one's personality by this process. One is inhibitory. We learn that certain things are wrong, and we develop a strong nonrational desire not to do them. Recognizing that some object or property belongs to someone else and successfully resisting the temptation to steal it is an illustration of an inhibition. The other reaction is guilt. Often we do or say something we know we should not do or say—and we feel guilty. This feeling is extremely disturbing. It must be placated in some way. The healthy and constructive way is to admit the wrong and make restitution. Most often we allow an immature reaction such as denying we were wrong, trying to justify our action by saying we were really trying to help the other person rather than hurt him, or we scapegoat the guilt by projecting it onto a person or group as illustrated by racial or ethnic prejudice.

Exactly what causes these two reactions of the negative conscience is not known. One theory is that the way the rewards and punishments are administered makes the difference. If they are administered before a prohibited act, then the child learns to inhibit the action; if the punishment is carried out afterwards, the child learns to feel guilty. Others speculate that the child is such a weak person before the power and knowledge of the parent that the child "introjects," i.e., incorporates the parents' commands within her/himself. Whatever the cause, we know that the child reacts to what the parents' real attitudes are, not what the parents say they are. This also means that the reactions are emotionally conditioned. There is great variety from person to person and, within a person, she/he will have different reactions to different situations. The child, for example, may learn to feel little guilt about lying because his/her parents do it frequently; but this child may have a very strict prohibition against stealing because she/he was punished for that type of behavior.[1]

Conscience also has a positive component. As children grow, they realize that they are loved and enjoyed as persons in their own right. Parents do good things for and with them which cause the children to want to be the kind of persons these significant adults desire. By this process of identification, children incorporate within themselves the ideal image of what they should be and what the values of the family should be. There are several unique factors in this part of conscience that need to be noted. The children voluntarily accept the ideals of the parents so that these become a part of what they really want; thus, the children's well-being or good feeling about themselves is involved. The thing toward which the children are motivated is an ideal or mental picture and may never be obtained. But the ideal can be described enough for children to understand approximately what it is and how they should shape life's events to move toward the ideal. Because this positive side of conscience is formed later than the negative, it is not as strong a force for motivating behavior as the negative conscience.

When one does something that violates the positive conscience, one feels shame. Shame is a general feeling that one has not lived up to what others expect and what one wants to be. Because shame is more in the conscious mind than guilt, one is aware of shortcomings and has a yearning to correct them. In short, guilt is the breaking of a code that was enforced by authority, and the self only wants to regain equilibrium. Shame is the breaking of the expectations that were formed by loving human relationships, and the self wants to correct its behavior in order to get back into the good graces of the loved ones.[2]

Taking conscience apart this way helps us understand its complexity; yet we should not assume that any matter of conscience follows a simple or predictable course. Shame and guilt are intermingled in almost any infraction of a person's conscience. Moreover, much of conscience functions in the unconscious mind formed by relationships with persons rather than by the logical working of the mind. Thus, a person will have a conviction that certain things are right or wrong even though there is little evidence to support such a belief. Or, a person may hold to the conviction that it is wrong to steal, not because she/he has thought it out, but because she/he was "trained" that way as a child. Because conscience is formed early in a child's life, it is a powerful determinant of conduct; and it remains remarkably consistent and active throughout a person's life with modifications most likely occurring during adolescence and the early years of adulthood.[3]

Social Values

So far we have been looking at moral development from the standpoint of the person and the way she/he reacts to parents and the surrounding community. To help complete the picture, let us now look at the other side of the coin—society—and see how it shapes the moral life of the individual.

Society means the organized or formalized understanding by which people live. Although individuals in our Western nation have considerable freedom to live as they please, society is a reality which constantly shapes individual lives and through its laws can command the individual to go to war or to pay taxes. This money may be distributed in ways the individual does not approve of. The substance of a society can be identified by describing its laws and customs, but the underlying reality is values.

Clyde Kluckhohn's definition of values is instructive: "A value is a conception, explicit or implicit, distinctive of an individual or characteristic of a group, of the desirable which influences the selection from available modes, means, and ends of actions."[4] Note three main ideas. First, values are conceptions, that is, they exist in the minds of people. They are broad generalizations that a person believes accurately describe society and to which she/he has strong loyalty. Values may not be formulated in precise language, but they work incessantly within the mind to shape the thought and action of individuals. Second, values are what a person thinks desirable for all people as distinct from what she/he knows to be his/her personal tastes and preferences. It is this sense of oughtness that makes value the basis of moral judgments. When a person says an action or opinion is right, wrong, better, or worse, she/he is expressing an opinion based on what she/he thinks is proper and appropriate for good social living. Since social life is an absolute necessity for our well-being, these opinions are stated with considerable conviction in a variety of ways. Third, values influence action. A person always has a variety of actions she/he can take in any human situation. In our ordinary life, we select specific actions in the way we use our money, the clothes we wear, or the vocation we select. Underlying each action is a value such as: money should be saved (or enjoyed), clothes should be serviceable (or stylish), or work should be pleasant (or useful to society).

We acquire our values from the group of human beings with whom we grow up or to whom we attach ourselves. The family is the primary agent for inculcating values, these values being reinforced by the neighbors, schools, and church. Since the United States is made up of different racial, ethnic, and class groups, it may be helpful to identify different types of values. We might describe national values as those represented in the Constitution and Bill of Rights. Abraham Lincoln's Gettysburg Address is famous because it sums up in simple language some of the major values of our nation. Social classes and ethnic groups develop their own special values and their own interpretation of the national values. For example, one of the most important values of the middle class is the importance of deferred gratification. Unless a child learns early in his/her life to wait to eat until mealtime, to save some money for later spending, to study for later rewards, and so on, one cannot be a professional or hold a job that brings middle-class benefits. Perhaps the best-known summary of middle-class values is the twelve Boy Scout laws.

Emile Durkheim connects conscience with values by saying the content of conscience is social—that is, what specific moral thoughts and actions a person has come to him from society and are expressed in society.[5] Although this view is too restricted, it suggests that there is a close interaction between self and society in the moral realm. This can be illustrated in three areas. The first, suggested by Durkheim, is that society gives a person his or her values. For the vast majority of people there is little doubt that this is so. Very few people ever go against commonly held values of their group or even resist an unjust law such as restrictive covenants sometimes written into real estate contracts. The second area is the perceptive system one develops out of his/her values. Our values cause us to see certain events and close our eyes to other events. If a white person has the assumption that black men should do hard manual labor, his or her eyes, seeing such activity, confirm his or her belief so quickly she/he hardly notices the event. She/he would, however, be startled to see young white girls digging up a city street with an air hammer. Some people have the assumption that young white women should be secretaries, clerks, or airline hostesses. The third area is companionship. Since values are formed, refurbished, and kept alive by groups, an individual will seek out friends who incorporate his/her values. This often is a controlling factor in the selection of a congregation, a neighborhood to live in, or a social club to join. Values are so much a part of one's inner life that a person feels restless unless his self-image is supported by people with similar beliefs. By this same token if a person wants to change his or her position in life, she/he will search out the group which personifies those values. People who want to overthrow the government form revolutionary cadres; others, seeking to bring about a new life-style form communes.[6]

Struggle of the Self

So far the description of moral development leaves little room for a person to shape his/her own life. Given the high degree of conformity in the moral realm, we must not underrate the power of parents and society to shape personhood. How much of our morality is thrust upon or into us will vary considerably from person to person, but we must not forget that the individual is involved in a struggle with morality from the time she/he becomes self-conscious until she/he loses it.

When one becomes conscious of him/herself as a living reality, she/he cannot avoid managing the self in relation to society. The "I" of the self (ego) knows itself through memory; it has the ability to see, feel, and hear the world and the mental capacity to understand what is happening. Moreover, as the "I" gains experience, it develops habits and responses to the outside world, which give it confidence or fear in the face of new circumstances. Self-consciousness is by definition the "I" of the self, managing the incessant struggle of inner forces. As one grows, one becomes more aware of the necessity to master instincts, yearnings, dreams, fears, urges for retaliation, and logical thoughts that exist in a dizzy and dazzling array within the self.

Theorists who have studied the development of morality have different ideas of how the self masters this inner realm. However, they all seem to agree that the child starts from an amoral position and, if she/he matures properly, will move through several stages and emerge with the ability to make moral decisions based on rational principles permeated with altruism. Few people ever achieve the highest level, and even fewer are able to maintain that level in all areas of their lives; but the rational-altruistic goal is a possibility. They also agree that moral behavior is made up of a number of closely related factors and forces within the person. However, the theorists disagree on exactly what these factors and forces are and on the number and sequence of stages through which a normal person goes.

Jean Piaget gave special attention to how a child learns rules for playing marbles and then how the child thinks about certain moral situations. From these investigations he outlined four stages of moral judgment-making: (1) premoral, (2) heteronomous, obedient to adult authority, (3) autonomous, reciprocity, and equality oriented, (4) autonomous, ideal reciprocity, and equality.[7]

Robert F. Peck and Robert J. Havighurst, after administering a wide assortment of tests to school children, defined five moral character types. (1) Amoral—the infant is egocentric. (2) Expedient—in early childhood, the person acts in accordance with what is expected. (3a) Conforming—the older child conforms to what is done in his/her social group. (3b) Irrational-conscientious—the older child behaves according to his/her own standards but in a rigid, nonrational way. Both forms of the third type are stable, and some people will not go beyond this stage. (4) Rational-altruistic—stage reached in adolescence and is based on a stable set of moral principles. A person is able to apply them in a flexible manner with a concern for the welfare of others.[8]

Lawrence Kohlberg, building on the works of Piaget and testing people up to the age of adulthood in several different cultures, has devised a six-stage theory. He believes a person must proceed sequentially through these stages and that culture and religion are relatively unimportant as the mind develops the capacity to make moral judgments. (1) Punishment and obedience—a person judges the goodness or badness of an act on the basis of the physical consequences. (2) Instrumental relativism—a person judges the rightness of an action on the basis of how well it satisfies his/her needs. (3) Impersonal concordance or good-boy/good-girl—"Good behavior is that which pleases or helps others and is approved by them." (4) Law and order—"right behavior consists of doing one's duty, showing respect for authority and maintaining the given social order for its own sake." (5) Social-contract legalistic—"right action tends to be defined in terms of general individual rights and in terms of standards that have been critically examined and agreed upon by the whole society." (6) Universal ethical-principle—"right is defined by the decision of conscience in accord with self-chosen ethical principles appealing to logical comprehensiveness, universality, and consistency." [9]

There are other theories. Erik Erikson, relating psychoanalysis to culture, has proposed an eight-stage model of human behavior. Each stage has strong implications for morality.[10] Some efforts have been made to show the correspondence between some of the theories.[11] However, there is no grand, overall theory of the development of morality that social scientists and moralists agree takes account of all the factors that go into moral living. Given this lack of agreement, perhaps all we can do at this time is note some of the problems with which the self must struggle.

First, the self must learn a moral code, then doubt it, and finally transcend it. This is exceedingly difficult psychological work at each point. All theories say this must be done, although they differ widely on how and when it happens. If it does not happen, then a person becomes locked into a conventional code of conduct and his/her personality is restricted, defensive, or inadequate to changing circumstances. If it does happen, a certain amount of personal anguish and social delinquency occurs. The typical situation is in adolescence when a person goes through what Erikson calls "ego-identity" crisis. At that time the moral code of childhood is often tested by petty stealing. Defiance of authority is also a common form of testing anew the limits of acceptable conduct. In young adulthood when one starts one's career, another sphere of reality opens up, having to do with the way labor unions operate, businesses function, or professionals relate to the public. In all of these periods, the "I" of the self must adjust moral codes learned at an earlier period with an ever-widening sense of responsibility.

Second, the self must manage feelings—as well as reason—even though they do not mature at the same pace or in the same way. The negative and positive conscience with their reaction patterns are laid down and function smoothly by the age of six and have become sturdy parts of the personality by the age of twelve when ordinarily the mind is just becoming capable of logical thought and historical reasoning. This imbalance is not easy to correct: most people are never able to bring the affective side of their personality under the control of their reason.

Third, although the mind may develop through sequences which can be described, other parts of the self may be arrested or accelerated because of unusual circumstances. A person may be fairly mature in social philosophy—working and voting for political reform which would extend human rights to a larger number of people—while in personal relationships be highly competitive and even vindictive toward people who disagree with him/her. Thus, the self is always trying to manage the claims made by affective and cognitive elements while at the same time it is struggling with immature elements of the self and may at times be dominated by a surge of fear, anger, or jealousy.

The Role of Religious Education

The role of religious education in the proper development of conscience and good social values is to help individuals develop what E. Mannsell Pattison calls "ego morality." The notion assumes that the struggle of the self is the principal thing in morality. According to Pattison, "reviews of child rearing practices reveal that parental attempts at specific training and 'good' habits fail to produce consistent moral behavior; whereas effective nurturance of a child as a significant, lovable individual with the use of firm, kind, consistent discipline does produce moral capacity." [12] For the moral self to develop, the "I" must be able not only to control and manage the forces within it, but it also must learn to help form and adjust to the values of the human group to which she/he gives allegiance. In practical terms this is the congregation. At this point psychology and theology agree; a person in the Judeo-Christian tradition is never an isolate. She/he is a person answerable to God as an individual, but in terms of his/her relation to the community of believers. It is important to keep this individual-congregation dialetic in mind because that is the source of the great things in religion: faith, hope, love. These sentiments come from human relations where persons have commitments to one another and to God.

In practical terms there are three major areas that can be used to foster "ego morality." First, as already indicated, is the congregation. If the congregation in its work and common worship is a living example of what it professes in its theology, then it is a powerful force for forming and reforming moral standards. Educators in the church have generally overlooked the dynamism of the congregation as an educational agency. Church-night suppers, picnics, and small groups of six to eight families in some kind of regular association for study and play all provide the environment where persons can learn to know and appreciate one another as individuals. Such personal knowledge leads to sharing of problems and mutual emotional support in times of disappointment and tragedy. It also makes possible a probing of moral matters on an informal basis so that a person is challenged to both state and restate his/her position in a lively and realistic dialogue with others who share his/her common life purposes.

Second, adults are responsible for the moral tone of the congregation. What adults do (the kind of situations they define as moral and how they think about them and the administrative decisions that are made about church programs and policies) represent the hard-core moral values which make a difference. This is the laboratory where values are defined, redefined, and adjusted to particular cases. Such a laboratory is essential because valuing is a mental act, a blend of facts, circumstances, and reason, and there is no other way to blend these things except in serious conversation. Moreover, the moral life as we have seen from the earlier discussion of conscience is a continual struggle and must be properly nurtured or it becomes hardened in the codes of law without the possibility of mercy.

This means that some of the finest religious education of conscience can go on in official boards and committees of the church about routine business. Many important ethical issues involved—such as the salary paid to the janitor, items in the budget for institutional luxuries, the investment of endowment funds, the position of being a tax-free institution in a community—are often avoided by looking upon them as administrative matters that have to be decided quickly. Serious, well-prepared discussion of issues such as these would probably do more to help adults think ethically than sermons on the topic. Also, regular adult classes on ethical issues in our society are essential for helping adults keep their conscience in tune with the times. Such discussions have an important by-product—they help adults who have children to become better parents. We need to remember that one of the ways children develop their conscience is by identifying with their parents. If they see their parents involved in a lively struggle to know what is right, the child may incorporate that characteristic into his/her own selfhood.

Some efforts have been made to use the family as an agency for religious education. Margaret Sawin, for example, has developed what she calls "family clusters." Four or five family units meet in the church for common activities that include a deliberate effort to deal with interpersonal relationships. Because feelings as well as religious ideas are a point of the discussion, such clusters hold out the possibility of developing the whole person better than the traditional Sunday school.[13]

Third, schools of the church can engage in moral education. Church schools, whether parochial or part time like the Sunday school or Confraternity of Christian Doctrine program, can do a great deal in direct education for moral living. The content of the Judeo-Christian religion through its stories, history, and teaching refers mostly to morals; yet our school leaders are not often acquainted with the stages of moral development nor with teaching techniques that are helpful at different age levels. Just telling children about the morals of religion is inadequate and ineffective. Perhaps the first thing the church leaders should do in this regard is to realize that the school is a social institution and has many opportunities for direct teaching of and influence for morals. Barry Sugarman's *The School and Moral Development* gives a careful examination of the various elements in school life which relate to morals, as well as teaching strategies that may be employed.[14] How classroom teaching can be used to help pupils clarify their values has been well-developed. Although these methods are religiously neutral, they are practical and useful for starting discussions which can lead to profound questioning of conventional moral standards. Also, value clarification techniques have a "fun" quality that makes them adaptable to informal church groups.[15]

Public and parochial schools are increasingly aware of the breakdown of traditional values and the changes in our society that have weakened the home and community as places where moral values are inculcated. Schools will increasingly need to become aware of their role in forming values and become better prepared to do explicit teaching in this area, including ways to help parents coach their children who come of age under social conditions vastly different from those that the parents experienced in their childhood.[16]

Bibliography

Bull, Norman J. *Moral Education.* London: Routledge & Kegan Paul, 1969.

Chazan, Barry I., and Soltis, Jonas F., eds. *Moral Education.* New York: Teachers College Press, 1973.

May, Philip R. *Moral Education in School.* London: Methuen Educational Ltd., 1971.

Medtcalf, Lawrence E. *Values Education.* Washington: National Council for the Social Studies, 1971.

Mount, Eric. *Conscience and Responsibility.* Richmond: John Knox Press, 1969.

Williams, Norman and Sheila. *The Moral Development of Children.* London: Macmillan & Co., 1970.

Wilson, John, Williams, Norman, and Sugarman, Barry. *Introduction to Moral Education.* Baltimore: Penguin Books, 1967.

Wright, Derek. *The Psychology of Moral Behavior.* Baltimore: Penguin Books, 1971.

NOTES

1. Justin Aronfreed, *Conduct and Conscience* (New York: Academic Press, 1968), pp. 2-6.

2. Helen Lynn, *On Shame and the Search for Identity* (New York: Harcourt, Brace Jovanovich Publishers, 1958).

3. This overview has followed the general psychoanalytic model. For a description of how conscience is formed from the standpoint of developmental psychology, see Dorothea McCarthy, "The Development of the Normal Conscience," in C. Ellis Nelson, ed., *Conscience: Theological and Psychological Perspectives* (New York: Newman Press, 1973), pp. 263-91.

4. Talcott Parsons and Edward A. Shils, eds., *Toward a General Theory of Action* (Cambridge: Harvard University Press, 1954), p. 395.

5. For the purpose of this essay see Durkheim, *Moral Education* (New York: The Free Press, 1973).

6. A fuller discussion of how social values influence personality can be found in my book *Where Faith Begins* (Richmond: John Knox Press, 1967), pp. 35-67. Another book that explores how anthropology can be helpful to religious educators is by John Westerhoff and Gwen Neville, *Generation to Generation* (Philadelphia: Pilgrim Press, 1974).

7. Piaget and Barbel Inhelder, *The Psychology of the Child* (New York: Basic Books, 1969), pp. 122-28.

8. Peck and Havighurst, *The Psychology of Character Development* (New York: John Wiley & Sons, 1960), pp. 3-11.

9. Kohlberg, "Stages of Moral Development as a Basis for Moral Education," in C. M. Beck, B. S. Crittenden, E. V. Sullivan, eds., *Moral Education* (Toronto: University of Toronto Press, 1971), pp. 86-88.

10. The eight stages are described by Erik H. Erikson in "Identity and the Life Cycle," *Psychological Issues*, vol. 1, 1959, (New York: International Universities Press, Inc.), pp. 50-101. See also chapter 5 in this volume.

11. A. William Kay, *Moral Development* (New York: Schocken Books, 1968), p. 218.

12. Pattison, "The Development of Moral Values in Children," in C. Ellis Nelson, ed., *Conscience: Theological and Psychological Perspectives* (New York: Newman Press, 1973), pp. 238-62.

13. A brief account of Margaret Sawin's idea of "family clusters" was written by Edna Stumpf in John Westerhoff, ed., *A Colloquy on Christian Education* (Philadelphia: Pilgrim Press, 1972), pp. 152-57.

14. Sugarman, *The School and Moral Development* (New York: Barnes & Noble, 1973).

15. Louis E. Raths, Merrill Harmin, Sidney B. Simon, *Values and Teaching* (Columbus, Ohio: Charles E. Merrill Publishing Co., 1966).

16. One illustration of this trend was the formation of Dendron Publishing, Inc., in 1973 dedicated to the creation and publication of educational materials for public and church schools in the realm of "valuing and meaning making." Richard J. Payne, the managing editor, expects to publish materials for use in grade 1 through the adult level. The junior-elementary unit, grades 1-3, was published in January, 1975. Editorial offices: 1865 Broadway, New York, New York 10023.

Chapter 7

LIBERATION THEOLOGY, BLACK THEOLOGY, AND RELIGIOUS EDUCATION

Grant S. Shockley

"Of the Dawn of Freedom" entitles chapter 2 of *The Souls of Black Folk* by the brilliant black American scholar, W. E. B. DuBois. In the opening sentences of that chapter are his words, "The problem of the twentieth century is the problem of the color line,—the relation of the darker to the lighter races of men in Asia and Africa, in America and the islands of the sea." Fifty years later (1953), DuBois republished this book. When asked if he still affirmed his position he responded:

> I still think today as yesterday that the color line is a great problem of this century. But today I see more clearly than yesterday that back of the problem of race and color lies a greater problem which both obscures and implements it: and that is the fact that so many civilized persons are willing to live in comfort even if the price of this is poverty, ignorance and disease of the majority of their fellowmen.[1]

This addendum brings into sharp focus three issues that will be discussed in this chapter: human oppression in its various dehumanizing forms; liberation programs and their signs of hope; and religious education, potentially an enabling means toward the end of realizing "love, power, and justice" for all persons. These issues, which constitute a challenge to the churches, are restated by Lerone Bennett, Jr., historian of the black revolution in America, and Paulo Freire, liberationist educator of Latin America. Bennett said:

> We can see that challenge in its clearest form in the educational field. . . . For blackness raises total questions about the meaning of education in a situation of oppression . . . an educator in a situation of oppression is either an oppressor or a liberator.

Brazilian educator Freire at the Bergen World Consultation on Education held in Holland said: "There is no such thing as neutral education.

Grant S. Shockley was Professor of Christian Education at the Candler School of Theology, Emory University, Atlanta, Georgia, and is now President of the Interdenominational Theological Center, also in Atlanta.

Education is either for liberation or against liberation and therefore in favor of domination." [2]

The challenge to the educational programs of churches in these statements is clear, and it raises several insistent questions for the religious educator. Rosemary R. Ruether articulates some of these from the life of a local congregation:

> What kind of Christian education is possible in America in the third quarter of the twentieth century . . . where our cultural forms and institutions taken for granted have become quaint cultural artifacts and where the name "Christian" seems a more and more parochial image. What kind of Christian Education is possible in a world of youth and revolution, black revolution, and world challenge to imperialism?

In attempting to resolve these questions, Euro-American theology has not been too helpful and has often been reluctant, if not reactionary. Some of the reasons for this necessitate the brief historical background that follows.[3]

During the nineteenth century, Calvinism and revivalism united to form a "New England" system of theology, emphasizing repentance, conversion, and personal piety. With the passing of the western frontier, the advent of Darwinism, the historical-critical method of biblical study, urbanization, and strong criticisms of Calvinism, New England orthodoxy gave way to "Evangelical Liberalism," putting stress on freedom, growth, choice, and progress. Its most notable achievement was the initiation of the Social Gospel movement (1876–1917). Between 1919 and 1939, Karl Barth's influence and insistence upon "desecularizing" the gospel by getting rid of all "entangling alliances" with science and philosophy dominated the theological scene. Important for this chapter is the fact that Barth's anti-empirical posture militated against movements which could have enriched American religion's understanding of the then future phenomenon of the Third World and the already desperate racial issue in America. Actually, theological investigation during this period (1900–40), excepting the critiques of H. Richard Niebuhr (1929) and Reinhold Niebuhr (1932), almost totally neglected the black experience.[4] Similarly, Euro-American theology neglected contact with the rapidly growing fields of the social sciences, especially education. In religious education theory development, curriculum construction and teaching systems were moving in the direction of social concerns and criticism. Excepting the work of George A. Coe, however, even religious educators paid scant attention to racism. The Sunday school movement found the black population a source of continual embarrassment to the churches, despite their aim to carry it to "every destitute place."[5] Horace Bushnell, considered the founder of modern Protestant religious education in America, was a firm believer in the racist doctrine of Manifest Destiny and its corollary, white (specifically Anglo-Saxon) superiority. To Bushnell, Indians were "among the feebler, wilder races" and, together with black people, were only salvable through assimilation. Bushnell, however, did desire slaveholders to acknowledge "the immortal mind and manhood of your slave," but he also believed "that the African race in this country, would soon begin to dwindle towards extinction . . . if emancipated."[6]

Not until the publication of Coe's *What Is Religion Doing to Our Consciences?* (1943) did religious educators in America begin to examine, even generally, this critical dimension of responsibility. In 1965 Randolph C. Miller (Bushnell Professor at Yale) wrote in relation to the involvement of religious education in the social sphere that it was "one of the untravelled roads in contemporary Christian thinking." In the same paper, he also felt obliged to say, "slowly the churches have become aware of the Christian interpretation of race relations . . . . To some extent, the recognition of this problem is finding its way into Christian education."[7]

In the theological arena in America, parties in the church-society dichotomy began to show signs of desiring unification and serious dialogue after World War II. As a result of the landmark meeting of Euro-American theologians at the Cambridge (England) Conference on International Affairs (1947), theological trends began to move "toward constructive rather than polemical thinking." During the fifties and the sixties the center of gravity in Euro-American theological thought moved rather boldly from a past-oriented traditional stance to a present-oriented, if not an existentialist, posture. Included in this reorientation were the emergence of such movements as: the "new hermeneutic," attempting to interpret more authentically, the biblical past in the present; "secular theology" and its effort to draw theology "increasingly into a new worldliness" and freedom to fashion the future; and "theologies of hope," engaging the world and Christians in future-oriented history-making in the "now" of the present.

A question is posed by this historical survey of the response (or rather the lack of it) of theology and religious education to the insistent cry of "the wretched of the earth" for liberation and development.[8] Why, except for its racism (and elitism) has religious education in America failed to see its responsibility for applying its recent research and insights about change and humanization to the poor and the minorities? This inability or unwillingness or both posed the dilemma that both "liberation theology" and "black theology" sought to resolve.

Black Power and Black Theology

In America, racism—the unwarranted assumption that persons of nonwhite ethnic backgrounds are inherently inferior—has been the vortex into whose center our entire national history has been drawn. Racism under the guise of Manifest Destiny condoned and allowed white settlers in America to confiscate from the Indians most of the land which now comprises the United States.[9] Racism contributed to the corruption of the social, economic, and political structure of the nation—North and South—through the system of chattel slave labor, "the vilest that ever saw the sun." [10] Spanish American lands were taken in illegal wars of "territorial expansion," and Asian Americans, whose poorly paid labor developed much of the West and its farmlands, were "rewarded" with racist-inspired exclusion acts and relocation (detention camps) centers.[11]

The classic and most dramatic example of racism in America remains her black population who, since the early seventeenth century, has endured in both the churches and the general society every conceivable form of abuse. They were considered only three-fifths human in the Constitution of "the most enlightened democracy on earth." [12] In 1854 the Supreme Court maintained that black people "had no rights that whites were bound to respect." In 1896 the Supreme Court legalized the segregation of its "free" citizens on the basis of skin color. The United Nations was not three years old (1947) when it received from the black constituency of the United States, a charter member, a document entitled "A Statement on the Denial of Human Rights to Minorities in the Case of Citizens of Negro Descent in the United States of America and an Appeal for Redress." It was 1954 before the Supreme Court recognized that the 1896 decision was a travesty upon justice and that *separate* in an open society is by definition "unequal." In 1964 and 1965 Congress legislated its first comprehensive civil rights bills in a century, including the right of franchise for millions of disfranchised black people in the South.

The years 1964-66 were years of disenchantment. The Civil Rights movement crested with Martin Luther King's eloquent "I Have a Dream" address (Washington, D. C., 1963). In 1964-65 deep frustration developed as unenforceable laws were substituted for justice, and tokenism in employment for comprehensive fair-employment practices.

The extremity of black patience, with gradualism, legalism, tinkering reform, and conciliation was reached. Then it came—the black revolution for power—Black Power! This movement galvanized the white (and some sectors of the black) community. It was a totally new, "audacious" way for black people to act. It meant a new assessment of power—not to achieve equality of opportunity, but to achieve equality of advantage and results. With this new concept of power other insights were born. Black power came to signify a new understanding of one's blackness, worth, dignity, and heritage. It meant affirmation rather than negation, activity rather than passivity, self-pride instead of self-hate. In this new light, black survival meant black control. Educational, economic, social, political, and religious institutions must become imbued with black self-determination.

Generally, what had been the witness of the churches in the long struggle for black civil rights and liberation from white racism? At best it had been paternalistic. But in terms of the mandate of the gospel, it had been (and still is) apostate. It had acquiesced in segregation—failed to identify, define, or articulate critically or challenge effectively a single aspect of the problem of racism faced by 10 percent of its national population, 80 percent of whom were fellow Christians.

While the churches did produce, periodically, sincere dissenting voices who exerted a positive though not a crucial influence, it is only honest to say that this was the limit of their participation. As the black revolution escalated in the direction of challenging the root systems of power that enabled racism and called to accountability the centers of power that supported it, most, though not all, of the white "liberal" voices receded into the background. At this point, two things became clear. The black struggle for justice and liberation must become independent. There could be no sure reliance on "reformers." The struggle would have to seek a base of support within the black community and most likely in the black churches. Second, the black churches themselves would have to be committed to the black masses and their liberation. A new generation of black youth began to question the credentials of an institution that could not or would not act courageously on issues it claimed were aborting its mission, violating its fellowship, and mocking its witness. It was this situation in the general society and in the church which gave birth to a liberation movement of its own—one that would combine the yet remaining faith of black people in the black church and their new determination to obtain corrective justice.

Black theology became the name of the movement that "religiocified" black power in the black church. A unique and indigenous development on the American theological scene, black theology, like its counterpart black power, was more than a new, "blackenized" version of Euro-American theology. It was a new way of doing theology. It saw as its mission raising questions, developing concepts, and patterning motifs about the basic nature of the Christian faith, forcing a reconsideration, "if not a redefinition of, every major theological category." Cone states it clearly:

> What is Black Theology? Black Theology is that theology which arises out of the need to articulate the significance of Black presence in a hostile white world. It is Black people reflecting religiously on the Black experience, attempting to redefine the relevance of the Christian Gospel for their lives.[13]

Black theology in America had its inception with the publication of the "Black Power: Statement" by the National Committee of Negro Churchmen in 1966. This statement had come as a result of a decision of a sizeable group of black clergy to endorse the then nascent Black Power movement. The thesis of the statement was a deep concern on the part of the black churchmen that the "important human realities in the controversy about 'black power' not be ignored because of its militant rhetoric. The fundamental distortion facing us on the controversy about 'black power,'" they said, "is rooted in a gross imbalance of power and conscience between Negro and white Americans." The black clergy made it clear that they would no longer abide by the assumption

> that white people are justified in getting what they want through the use of power, but that Negro Americans must, either by nature or by circumstances, make their appeal only through conscience. As a result . . . the power of white men is corrupted because it meets little resistance. . . . The conscience of black men is corrupted because, having no power to implement the demands of conscience, the concern for justice is transmuted into a distorted form of love, which in the absence of justice, becomes chaotic self-surrender. Powerlessness creates a race of beggars. We are faced now with a situation where conscience-less power meets powerless conscience, threatening the very foundations of our nation.[14]

Since the publication of this statement, black theologians and other scholars in black religion have emerged and continued to build on this conceptual base. Their efforts have been varied in focus, method, and approach. James H. Cone introduced the term with his first title,

Black Theology and Black Power. After probing contemporary Euro-American theologians, Cone delineated a theological position in which the black experience became the hermeneutical principle for the interpretation of the Bible, theology, church life, ministry, and mission whose task is to "analyze the black man's condition in the light of God's revelation in Jesus Christ with the purpose of creating a new understanding of black dignity among black people, and providing the necessary soul in that people to destroy white racism.[15]

Black Theology and Religious Education

Black theology confronts religious education in both black and white churches in America with the critical challenge of effective participation in the liberation of oppressed black people and all oppressed minorities. This mission has historic significance. It is the first time in the history of American religious thought that a major racial minority has aggressively challenged the theological assumptions of the Christian faith on the basis of its racial ethic. Also, it is the first time that a major theological movement of protest and revolt against the violation of that ethic has been articulated in an alternative system and church style. In this section, primary attention will be given to some of the implications of the new black theology movement for religious education in black churches, leaving to the concluding section some comments concerning the relevance of black theology for white congregations.

At least three questions must be asked of black religious educators who are attempting to develop an educational program to complement black theology: What is the rationale for a program of Protestant religious education with a black perspective? What are its foundations? What is its design?

The rationale for a church education program developed from a black perspective is sixfold. First, black theology "suggests a felt need to reconstruct a world view as it concerns an entire people."[16] That world view is the new recognition by black people that "we are some-bodies"—free, black, beautiful, and proud. Second, the agenda of the American black community is being reshaped to define what this "somebodiness" means—individually, collectively, educationally, economically, socially, culturally, and politically. Essentially, it implied the humanization of the dehumanized, the liberation of the oppressed, and the empowerment of the powerless. Third, the black church has affirmed this agenda in its historic black power statement: "We commit ourselves as churchmen to make more meaningful in the life of our institutions our conviction that Jesus Christ reigns in the 'here' and 'now' as well as in the future he brings in upon us." Fourth, black liberation begins with black people's liberating themselves. It is not something that can be done externally. In solidarity with blacks and other minorities, in church education programs, the consciousness of historical, ethnic, cultural, and political identity must be negotiated. This may have to be done in a posture of temporary "dis-engagement" or withdrawal from the Euro-American value system. Fifth, implicit in any educational effort is the objective of change. Religious education fulfills a normative function when it creates "an understanding of the process of social change for justice and new humanity, and the necessary struggle, sacrifice, and conflict involved in such change." [17] Sixth, black Protestant educational programs, limited almost exclusively to Sunday schools and youth groups, reach only a minority of black people. An educational program with an effective liberation component would increase the black church's outreach and mission. Finally, the process of developing liberation components would reinforce the need of black churches, preconditioned by white models in Christian education, to rethink their position and become aware of the current black liberation agenda.

Toward a Black Liberation Educational Design

It may be helpful to use a conceptual frame of reference to consider, somewhat more practically, the implications of black theology for religious education. The model that is being suggested is simple. Its components are: (1) foundations, (2) guidelines, and (3) design.

The biblical-theological foundations for religious education that reflect the new black theology movement are both varied and tentative. Their variety comprises a wide spectrum of positions from black separatistic nationalism to humanistic universalism. Nor do these positions pretend to be final, closed systems. The entire movement is highly dynamic or, as William R. Jones describes it, "neoteric."

There is wide agreement among black theologians (and educators) that the basic and guiding purpose of religious education ought to be liberation or "that theology which arises out of the need to articulate the significance of Black presence in a hostile white world." This is also referred to as "committed" or "engaged" theology, for it makes a prior commitment to an ultimate goal.[18]

As black theologians evaluate one another, a spectrum develops which includes several views. Five of these will be mentioned here, briefly. Cleage (1968) offers a "religion of Black Power" in the form of a "Christian Black Nationalism," or "a black nation within a nation" based on the normative authority of the black experience. Cone chooses to develop a "theology of black power" for black liberation making it the only "medium of encountering the contemporary revelatory event of God in this society." Major J. Jones theologizes from the current "theology-of-hope" position, relating it to revolution creatively, and moving it toward the new community and beyond racism. Roberts, concerned that black theology move beyond a "religion of Black Power" and develop a redemptive component, suggests that liberation must include reconciliation. William R. Jones would enlarge the search beyond traditional Christian categories and raise some fundamental questions about the nature of the Christian and biblical faith "and . . . [urge] a reconsideration, if not redefinition of every major theological category." There is less wide agreement regarding the context and comprehensiveness of the task of liberation. For Cleage it is the recreation of a "black Messiah" under whose leadership a black church will lead black people from slavery to freedom within a separate, Christian, black nationalist state. Cone's theology of liberation focuses on radical change and a black "salvation history." In the Old Testament the Exodus God is the God of the oppressed, and in the New Testament Jesus "takes upon himself the oppressed condition so that all men may be what God created them to be." [19] Cone's only suggestion for reconciliation with whites is for them to identify with blacks. J. Deotis Roberts interprets the task of black theology as that of awakening the latent sense of justice for and between all men. For him, theology from a Christian perspective implies a doctrine of reconciliation and is incomplete without it. Major J. Jones advances the thesis that liberation theology must be accountable to the Christian ethic of love. In its role of protest and advocacy it cannot divorce ethics from theology.

Guidelines for developing the implications of black theology for religious education in black churches must include the following: (1) Education in the black church should be based on a theoretical and operational model that is capable of implementing the new black agenda of liberation. Historically, this agenda has been subverted and rendered powerless by white and some black churches. (2) The biblical witness to liberation is a fundamental and unequaled source of concepts, images, and models of black liberation climaxing in the supreme revelation of God in Jesus Christ the Liberator. Personal experiencing that "Jesus is freedom" imbues liberation theology with authenticity—and church education for liberation with integrity. (3) The philosophy of religious education that is most likely to correlate the insights of black theology and liberation-learning may be described as holistic, i.e., a philosophy that does not emphasize particular aspects of liberation, e.g., "nationalism" to the exclusion of others, e.g., reconciliation, but rather emphasizes the organic and functional relation between "parts and wholes" in the system. (4) The centrality of such concepts as "personhood," "identity," and "self-awareness" in black theology necessitates a careful study of personality theories and theorists to determine which can most adequately account for the exigencies of the black experience. (5) Enabling black people to envision new futures other than those that at present seem possible in their oppressed state and empowering them to believe in the possibility of such a future and to achieve it to the fullest extent possible is a major learning goal in religious education as it encounters the black experience. Basically the religious educator will find help from both black and white learning theorists at this point.

Liberation-oriented education in the local congregation will require a unique enabling style of leadership, committed to the concept of the black church as a potential agency for basic social change and to the belief that persons must and can come to a realization of the need for change. Black parents, teachers, group leaders, officials, and clergy in black churches will need immersion in and exposure to a variety of learning theories and leadership styles from which to glean and construct a personally meaningful style of leadership and learning method. Particular attention should be given to Rogerian learning theory stressing self-discovery learning and Cantor's dynamic learning theory, emphasizing integrative versus adjustive learning. In the area of leadership the "maieutic . . . or developmental leadership . . . or a process facilitator" portends help as black leaders and teachers strive to develop "fully-functioning persons capable of impacting society."

Black local congregational support is crucial in the implementation of a liberation-oriented program of religious education. The local black church is the most feasible setting in which to "do" liberation education, provided it is autonomous and not frustrated or financially sabotaged by nonsupport, as some black units of predominantly white denominations have been. Such a setting provides an opportunity for black people of the church and the community to come to a new awareness of their "situations of oppression"; to find reassurance in biblical reflection, fellowship, and worship; to specify church-community needs; to exercise self-determination in the choice and use of funds, grants, resources, etc.; to plan in a self-determining way; to respond to varied needs in the community; to be in mission as the church, liberating the oppressed. In the words of Preston N. Williams, "the black church and Black Theology enables black people to be both black and Christian."

The foundations and guidelines that have been outlined imply several things for a liberation-oriented church-education design. These will be considered under curriculum-teaching leadership development and support systems. The objective in curriculum and teaching the Christian faith in relation to the black experience is the facilitation of the development of black persons that they become aware of God as the God of the oppressed and of his self-disclosure in the redemptive and empowering love of Jesus Christ the Liberator; that they come to know who they are and what their human situation—the black experience—means and how they can best respond in love and faith through their black Christian experiences, personally and socially. All curriculum components—scope, context-learning task, organizing principles—are brought into focus by these objectives.

Religious Education and Liberation

The massive thrusts toward liberation in the Third World and in the American black community have brought into sharp focus the fact that peoples and nations now live in what Marshall McLuhan has called a "Global Village." A major consequence of this new awareness is the realization that this global village is also the orbit of a single moral universe. People everywhere must be dealt with on the basis of a single moral standard. The Universal Declaration of Human Rights has made this clear.

> Human rights are based on mankind's increasing demand for a decent, civilized life in which the inherent dignity of each human being will receive respect and protection. This . . . reaches beyond . . . comforts and conveniences . . . [to] those conditions of life which allow us to fully develop and use our human qualities of intelligence and conscience and to satisfy our spiritual needs . . . without them we cannot be human.[20]

This new situation requires a critical theological and educational analysis, radicalizing the issues of developmentism and racism and its concomitant value and power system. In terms of theology, Robert McAfee Brown suggests that "we are called upon to develop a theology of the world, more than a theology of the church; or if it is to be a theology for the church, it must be a theology for the church—that—exists—not—for—itself—but—for—the—sake—of—the—world." Further, Brown's suggestion of a complementary theological method for this is an ethical one. He reminds us that, historically, "ethics has been seen as an outgrowth of theology"; he now feels that "today it may be the case that theology becomes possible only as we grapple with ethics." [21] The contributions of black theology and other theologies of liberation are precisely at this point. They have articulated views of ultimate reality for the human situations and the social conditions presented by the existences of the oppressed. In highlighting this consciousness of oppression occasioned by developmentism and racism, they have given new and necessary directions for a world in revolution.

In religious education a similar challenge is presented. The new era of the human person calls into question past models, concepts, theories, programs, practices, and resources at all age levels and in all settings, demanding that they be evaluated in terms of their performance and potential in achieving the goal of humanization. Methodologically, religious education must become praxis oriented. It must liberate itself to be a free agent in dealing with the theologizing process as it grows out of the historical situation of learners. In Freire's words, "there is a unity between practice and theory in which both are constructed, shaped and reshaped in constant movement from practice to theory, then back to a new practice." [22]

Liberation theology and black theology confront Euro-American theology with the necessity of recollecting the radically historical character of the Bible. At every point in its development, it relates God's action to human response in the context of particular situations. Its language is anthropomorphized. Its abstractions are concretized. Its universals are particularized, and its absolutes are relativized to the extent that it is necessary for God to speak his liberating word to persons. The Bible is also the record of the acts of a God who was concerned with the oppressed and acted for their deliverance.

The only future that the church has as Christ's church is to be a community of liberation under the aegis of a God who is sovereign but who also suffers and who through and by his suffering, death, and resurrection has the power to free. Educational theory and practice will be affected by the new direction of liberation theology, especially its "engagement" character.[23] This particular aspect of liberation and black theology was enunciated more than a decade ago, though in a different connection, in David R. Hunter's concept of "Christian education as engagement." Under such a concept religious education must lead persons beyond the "encounter" of the notion of black theology—i.e., meeting its rhetoric and theory—to a real "engagement" or "involvement" in what black theology is doing. Such engagement leads to both communication and response. In Miller's words, "Our engagement with other human beings becomes in some way unknown and yet known, an encounter with God." [24]

Both liberation theology and black theology raise new questions for religious education about the "development" issue in minority communities in the U.S.A. and in nations of the Third World. Development must be defined more comprehensively. Its new central concept is the fullest human growth of the whole person in a creative and nourishing community for every man, woman, and child. *Development*, the newer term for "missions" and "missionary education," also implies that the mission of the church in development is to ensure that in every country, including our own, material necessities, equality of advantage, corporate justice, national integrity, and ethnocultural values are observed and encouraged. These human goals also imply a basic shift in policy from service to self-help and from charity to justice. A parallel responsibility is, candidly, the political task of involving persons in the kind of action, as Christians and citizens, that will ensure the implementation of these new directions. The implications for religious education at the parish level are several: (1) through praxis-oriented learning, all age levels should be brought to clearer awareness of their responsibility as Christians; (2) through direct political action Christians can be motivated to promote those programs of development that are consistent with self-help, justice, self-determination, and ethnic integrity and oppose those that are not; (3) as members of church denominations, Christians and others can be urged to support those church structures that aid this kind of development or seek to replace them.

The issue of pluralism, an emerging life-style for black churches in predominantly white denominations, is focused sharply by black theologian Gayraud S. Wilmore. "Black churchmen know well that the real question is not whether these churches can become truly integrated on Sunday morning, but whether in the next twenty-five to fifty years, these churches will have any meaningful contact with black people at all!" The even deeper issue that Gilmore raises is the issue of the equality of any possible future relationship. Will it "contribute to the dignity and humanity of both black and white people in a time of revolutionary change"? [25]

The total bankruptcy of the integration-assimilation approach to congregational church life in America for black and white pragmatically demands a search for a "new black church style." That style for many is developing into a transitional black ethnocultural pluralism empowered with a black theology for the purpose of recovering identity, integrity, and perspective for whatever future there might be with the white Christian church.

Reconciliation, a continuing goal in ethnocultural relations and religious education, is also a major issue in the emergent constructs of black theology and other theologies of liberation in the Third World. Under the impact of recent theological discussion it needs radical redefinition. Restoration to a condition of "wholeness" is a basic theological necessity for Christian faith. But the World Council of Churches Symposium on Liberation Theology (1973) felt that it could not be "subrepted" or misrepresented and made a form of "cheap grace" for the purpose of perpetuating dominance or regaining it.

> Black Theology, it was said, finds it impossible to communicate as long as people live in a world of oppressed and oppressors. And though the acts of the spirit can intercede and foster reconciliation, it would be unwise to write a theology on that possibility at this time. The Latin Americans concurred.

This situation suggests two things to religious educators. There exists, and will continue to exist for a time, a communication gap between liberation theology, black theology, and Euro-American theology. A "cycle of incommunication" may be necessary "until and unless there are concrete signs that oppression [is] being eliminated." [26]

The communication gap suggests to the religious educator a renewed emphasis on realistic dialogical teaching-learning. Albert Camus' observation on this point is apropos:

> I shall not try to change anything that I think or anything that you think . . . in order to reach a reconciliation that would be agreeable to all . . . the world needs real dialogue . . . falsehood is just as much the opposite of dialogue as is silence . . . the only possible dialogue is the kind between people who remain what they are and speak their minds . . . the world of today needs Christians who remain Christian. [27]

The radical issue that is posed by the current "incommunication," namely, the elimination of oppression, will not be resolved until and unless a "praxiological theology" can be educationally designed "to bridge the behavioral gap between proclamation and practice . . . and (work) for planned social change." [28]

NOTES

1. DuBois, *The Souls of Black Folk* (Chicago: A. C. McClurg and Company, 1903), p. 13; Martin Weinberg, ed., *W. E. B. DuBois: Reader* (New York: Harper & Row, 1970), p. 15.

2. Bennett, *The Challenge of Blackness,* Black Paper, no. 1, (Atlanta: Institute of the Black World, April, 1970); Freire, "Witness of Liberation," *Seeing Education Whole* (Geneva: World Council of Churches, 1970), p. 72.

3. Rosemary R. Ruether, "Education in the Sociological Situation, U.S.A. (Part A)," in Kendig B. Cully, ed., *Does the Church Know How to Teach? An Ecumenical Inquiry* (New York: The Macmillan Co., 1970), p. 79; cf. Arnold S. Nash, *Protestant Thought in the Twentieth Century: Whence and Whither* (New York: The Macmillan Co., 1951); John Dillenberger and Claude Welch, *Protestant Christianity* (New York: Charles Scribner's Sons, 1954).

4. Cf. H. Richard Niebuhr, *The Social Sources of Denominationalism* (New York: Henry Holt, 1929), chap. 9; cf. Reinhold Niebuhr, *Moral Man and Immoral Society* (New York: Charles Scribner's Sons, 1932), pp. 119, 208, 251-55, 268, 272.

5. See Coe, *What Is Religion Doing to Our Consciences?* (New York: Charles Scribner's Sons, 1943), pp. 8 (especially), 31, 48, 78, 82-83, 91-92, 98-99; cf. Robert W. Lynn and Elliott Wright, *The Big Little School: Sunday Child of American Protestantism* (New York: Harper & Row, 1971), chap. 2.

6. Quoted from Louis Weeks, "Horace Bushnell on Black America," *Religious Education,* 68 (January-February, 1973), 28-41.

7. Miller, "From Where I Sit: Some Issues in Christian Education," *Religious Education,* 60 (March-April, 1965), 102; *ibid.,* p. 103.

8. The title of the book, *The Wretched of the Earth,* by the black North African intellectual and revolutionist Frantz Fanon.

9. Dee Brown, *Bury My Heart at Wounded Knee* (New York: Holt, Rinehart and Winston, 1971), chaps. 1-2.

10. Lerone Bennett, Jr., *Before the Mayflower* (Baltimore: Penguin Books, 1966), chap. 4; Stanley M. Elkins, *Slavery* (New York: Grosset & Dunlap, 1959), chap. 2, App. B; Kenneth M. Stampp, *The Peculiar Institution* (New York: Random House, 1956), chap. 9; *The Works of John Wesley,* vol. 13 (Grand Rapids, Mich.: Zondervan Publishing House, n.d.), p. 153.

11. Milton L. Barron, ed., *Minorities in a Changing World* (New York: Alfred A. Knopf, 1967), chaps. 3, 4; George E. Simpson and J. Milton Yinger, *Racial and Cultural Minorities* (New York: Harper & Brothers, 1953), chaps. 11-15; Philip Hayasaka, "The Asian Experience in White America," *Journal of Intergroup Relations,* 2 (Spring, 1973), 67-73.

12. U.S., *Constitution,* Art. 1, Sec. 2c.

13. James H. Cone, "Black Consciousness and the Black Church: A Historical-Theological Interpretation," *Annals of the American Academy of Political and Social Science,* 387 (January, 1970), 53.

14. "Black Power: Statement by National Committee of Negro Churchmen," *New York Times* (July 31, 1966), p. E-5.

15. Cone, *Black Theology and Black Power* (New York: The Seabury Press, 1969), p. 117.

16. Leon E. Wright, "Black Theology or Black Experience?" *Journal of Religious Thought* (Summer, 1969), p. 46.

17. "Black Power: Statement," *New York Times;* Vincent Harding, "Seven Goals on Education" (Education Workshop, Institute of the Black World, Atlanta, May 13, 1973).

18. Cone, *Black Theology and Black Power,* p. 53; Jones, "Toward an Interim Assessment of Black Theology," *Reflection,* 69 (January, 1972), 1.

19. Cf. Albert B. Cleage, Jr., *The Black Messiah* (New York: Sheed & Ward,

1968); cf. James H. Cone, *A Black Theology of Liberation* (New York: J. B. Lippincott Co., 1970), pp. 32-33, 117-19, and chap. 3; cf. Major J. Jones, *Black Awareness: A Theology of Hope* (Nashville: Abingdon Press, 1971), chap. 1; cf. J. Deotis Roberts, *Liberation and Reconciliation: A Black Theology* (Philadelphia: The Westminster Press, 1971), chap. 2; William R. Jones, "Assessment of Black Theology," p. 3; Cone, *Theology of Liberation,* chap. 3.

20. *The United Nations and the Human Person: Questions and Answers on Human Rights* (New York: United Nations Office of Public Information, November, 1967), p. 2.

21. Brown, "Doing Theology Today: Some Footnotes on Theological Method," *Action-Reaction* (Summer, 1969), p. 3; *ibid.,* p. 4.

22. Paulo Freire, "Education, Liberation and the Church," *Risk,* 9 (1973), 36.

23. William R. Jones, "Assessment of Black Theology," p. 1.

24. Hunter, *Christian Education as Engagement* (New York: The Seabury Press, 1963), chap. 2; Randolph C. Miller, "Some Issues in Christian Education," p. 59.

25. Wilmore, "The Case for a New Black Church Style," *The Black Church in America,* H. M. Nelsen, R. L. Yokley, A. K. Nelsen, eds. (New York: Basic Books, 1971), p. 325; *ibid.*

26. Archie Le Mone, "Report on a Symposium: When Traditional Theology Meets Black and Liberation Theology," *Christianity and Crisis* (September 17, 1973), p. 178; *ibid.,* p. 178.

27. Camus, *Resistance, Rebellion and Death* (New York: Modern Library, 1960), p. 52.

28. Olivia P. Stokes, "The Educational Role of the Black Churches," report of Kresheim I Consultation, July 28-August 1, 1969, Kresheim Study Center, Philadelphia, Penn., p. 1.

Chapter 8

WOMEN, MINISTRY, AND EDUCATION

Emily C. Hewitt

Does Christianity affirm the common humanity of women and men? Let us assume, in faith, that the answer is yes. Let us assume that behind the story of the fall lies an ancient vision of partnership and equality between the sexes. Let us assume that the apostle Paul spoke for all time when he affirmed in Galatians 3:28, "You are all one in Christ Jesus." Let us be unafraid to reject Paul's advice to the Corinthians that women "should be subordinate." Let us not blink the misogyny in Christian tradition, but let us assume that the gospel calls us out of the straightjackets of stereotypes and roles.[1]

How does Christianity affirm the common humanity of women and men? This is the question for those committed to the task of religious education in the churches.[2] We cannot answer with confidence. All too often, women learn their inferiority to men as an integral part of their training in Christianity. Those of us who find in Christianity an affirmation of our full personhood realize that this has happened *in spite of* as well as *because of* our training. Many women never hear the message of affirmation at all. Some women have accepted the view that they are subordinate to men and may be excluded from a whole range of religious and secular functions. Other women, who hear no affirmation from the churches, do hear good news in the contemporary women's movement. Faced with an apparent choice between church and their own personhood, they choose personhood.

We should be involved in changing our training—not for the reason that we will attract more women to the churches, nor because we should be trying to conform the Christian message to the movements and fashions of contemporary society, but for the fundamental reason that we should try to conform the practices of our churches to the gospel, in this way as in other ways.

Emily C. Hewitt was Assistant Professor of Religion and Education at Andover Newton Theological School, Newton Centre, Massachusetts. She is currently a student at the Harvard Law School.

Church Education:
A Curriculum Within a Curriculum

Church educators, like American educators generally since John Dewey, have proceeded with cheerful optimism on the assumption that the way to deal with any problem is to set up a course on the subject or alter the style and content of an existing course. Recently, the attention of both secular and religious educators has been drawn to the practices which form the context of courses of direct instruction. We can now recognize that there are two types of formative processes going on concurrently in our churches: first, those programs set up with the expressed aim of educating the participants—church school classes, adult education courses, youth programs, and the like; and second, those activities which are not self-consciously designed to be educational experiences, but which teach nonetheless.[3] This "hidden curriculum" teaches attitudes toward women and men in the ways we worship, structure decision-making, assign tasks of leadership and responsibility. The day-to-day life of a community of believers is, in fact, the primary means of communicating our values, attitudes, and beliefs.

> The human interaction is the most powerful process we know for creating and sustaining values, affections, commitments. . . . . The process communicates whatever is lived. . . . The self-conscious human group worshiping, living, and working together is a learning community.[4]

Our first task as educators is precisely to become "self-conscious." We need to back off and look at what we do; we need to hear what we say; we need to make an effort to understand how our practices affect girls and boys, women and men. We need to take this disciplined look not just at the special province of church life traditionally assigned to the religious education committee, but at the whole life of the church as a "learning community."

We can only undertake this task in a spirit of openness to the future. To try to deal with what we teach about women and men—either explicitly in formal classes or implicitly in such areas as worship and decision-making—is to start on a journey that has no predictable conclusion. There is no one thing that we can change—either in our textbooks or in our common life—that will solve the problem of how the churches are to affirm the common humanity of women and men. We simply do not know what a solution would look like. What is before us in the seventies is the possibility of taking provisional steps toward reform that will, we can be sure, raise new questions and lead us toward new reforms.

The Hidden Curriculum

We are just beginning to search out the "hidden curriculum" of church practices for its messages about women and men. The composition of church leadership, the roles assigned to women and men on church boards and committees, and the ways we carry out worship and mission all communicate powerful, if often unnoticed, messages.

Church leadership is an obvious problem. While the majority of membership and attendance at most churches is female, the overwhelming majority of ministers and church executives is male. Whatever we may say about the equal capacity of men and women to assume responsibility and leadership in the life of the church, the fact of inequality undercuts our claims.

The situation for women in church leadership *is* changing. Since the fifties most of the major Protestant denominations have removed formal barriers to the ordination of women. In 1956, Methodist women became eligible for full annual conference membership. Also in 1956, the United Presbyterian Church opened full ordination to women. In 1964, the Presbyterian Church in the U.S. (Southern) followed. Two national Lutheran denominations—the American Lutheran Church and the Lutheran Church in America—admitted women to their ordained ministries in 1970. The Reformed Church in America began ordaining women in 1973. Barriers remain in the Episcopal and Missouri Synod Lutheran churches, as well as in the Orthodox and Roman Catholic communions.[5]

Not only have women been admitted, in principle, to the ordained ministries of their denominations, but they have sought to enter professional church work in increasing numbers since the late sixties. A number of seminaries report large increases in women's enrollments. These women come from denominations that still have bars to women in their ordained ministries, as well as from those denominations which have long permitted women in their pastorates. Women seminarians of the United Church of Christ increased from 87 to 136 between 1971 and 1973; women's enrollment in Episcopal seminaries jumped from about 40 to 155 in the same period. Between 1970 and 1973 the number of women studying in the 8 seminaries which make up the Boston Theological Institute went up from 128 to well over 300.[6]

It still needs to be said that our churches are far from showing forth equality in leadership. In some important areas women have lost positions of authority and responsibility that they held in earlier periods. As R. Pierce Beaver has shown in his study of Protestant women in foreign missions, the consolidation of women's boards of foreign missions with male-run denominational boards resulted in the gradual exclusion of women from leadership positions in the mission field. Other efforts to consolidate church bureaucratic machinery have had the same effect. In the American Baptist churches, the number of women serving on regional, state, or city staffs declined by 50 percent during restructuring in the late sixties. Women who do have professional training and ordination find it difficult to locate suitable positions. They are likely to be paid less than male counterparts for the same work, and they receive fewer fringe benefits. The traditional professional church position for women—directing Christian education—is a low-paying job by comparison with the pastorate.[7]

If the present slow trend toward acceptance of women in church leadership continues, we will teach something new about the possibilities for partnership between women and men. We will very likely also find that our conception of the nature of leadership in the church changes with the composition of leadership. This potential for change can be illustrated by one difficulty those in the Catholic traditions have when they contemplate women ordained to the priesthood. Even those who have no theological objections to women in the priesthood are puzzled by the question What shall we call them? Some would object to the suggestion of "Mother." *Mother* fails to connote the same authority as *Father*. Perhaps we could ask whether we wish to have clerical leadership that is appropriately designated by either *Father* or *Mother*. There is the possibility of seeing an ordained leader more as colleague in ministry than as capstone of a system of either patriarchy or matriarchy.

Women have often been excluded from ordained and other professional ministries for the reason that they have not been thought of as embodying the characteristics of leadership and authority necessary to the ministerial role. What has often been ignored is the fact that many ministerial tasks—counseling, comforting, and other acts of pastoral care, as well as the sacramental function of presiding at the Lord's supper (preparing and serving a meal)—are usually associated with femininity. In terms of qualities associated in our society with masculinity and femininity, most ministerial positions call for a truly androgynous combination of attributes. Our traditional image of the minister as a male has, in the first place, allowed us to ignore the feminine qualities of ministry. Where these have been recognized, the dominance of men in ministry encourages us to think that only men can embody both types of qualities.

With both men and women working in partnership in the ministry, perhaps we can learn to value contributions associated with both masculinity and femininity, whether they are brought to the ministry by women or men. Our traditional conceptions of minister as patriarch neither adequately represent the reality of ministerial roles nor allow space for women. While it is impossible to predict where the process of reconceptualization will take us, we can be fairly sure that there will be change.

An enormous amount of the work of the church is done not by the clergy but by the laity. Who does what and who gets credit for doing it tells quite a bit about what we think of women and men. There is no question that women have contributed quantities of time, energy, and resources to carrying on the day-to-day life of most congregations. But there has been an unfortunate division of labor between men and women. When women perform services on behalf of the church, they are likely to do important but invisible tasks. If there is a church supper, the chances are that women will organize it and prepare the food, while the most visible action—saying the grace before the meal—will be done by a man. If there is lay participation in a worship service, it is likely that women will do the behind-the-scenes tasks of preparing the altar, the vestments, the flowers, and the refreshments for the postservice coffee hour, but the visible roles—serving as ushers, lay readers of lessons, acolytes, and servers—will be performed by men and boys. When there are committees to be appointed, it is likely that women will be assigned to the altar guild and the children's education committee, but men will be appointed or elected to the decision-making boards—the session, consistory, vestry, the trustees, the finance and property committees.

The area of lay life and leadership is particularly important in the effort to cut through stereotyped expectations based on sex roles because it is an area that churches can change immediately. We do not have to wait for more women to be educated to fill professional ministerial roles, something that will take generations. We can look at the composition of our committees and the assignment of tasks and find the ways in which we are creating different expectations for men and women by the way we use their talents in parish life.[8]

As a two-minute cartoon filmstrip, *Included Out,* eloquently demonstrates, the worship practices of the community of believers can be a powerful vehicle for teaching our views of women and men. In the film, an Oriental woman visits morning worship at an American

Protestant church. She is assured by the other participants in whispered asides during the service that the words *men* and *brother* are meant to include her and all women. Confident that she has comprehended the "strange language" of the American church, she ventures after the service into a room marked Men. And out again. In hymns, prayers, and liturgies, we need to begin the process of revision.[9]

No one pretends that liturgical revision is easy. We may change Sunday school texts from year to year, but we sing the same hymns and say the same prayers decade after decade, even generation after generation. At present, innovations on these traditional forms are usually done as special "women's liturgies," prepared and attended mostly by women. What is necessary now is to move to make the regular service of worship inclusive. The present forms teach that woman is invisible, her identity subsumable under so-called generic terms for man.

It is easier to deal with language which refers to the people of God than language which refers to the Deity. We can drop *men* in favor of *persons* much more easily than we can begin referring to God the Creator or even God the Holy Spirit as "she." But revisions in language to refer to the people of God do lead to questions about revisions in the language we use to speak of God. The question is How far? What are we to do with "Our *Father*, who art in heaven, hallowed be thy name. Thy *king*dom come"? Difficulties are compounded when the language of worship is also the language of scripture. The best that we can do with liturgical revision, as with changing the composition of our leadership, is to begin, but with the acknowledgment that we are embarking on a venture that does not have a predictable conclusion. A hundred years ago, an artist's conception of a black Messiah would have appeared blasphemous to most white Americans. But our words and images can and do change.

Within the context of the liturgy, there are possibilities for immediate change in sermons and homilies. Preachers, with their task of lifting up our faith and its implications for our lives, need not wait for some special women's service or long-term revisions in liturgy to proclaim a gospel that can be good news for women as well as men. This is not just a matter of preaching sermons on women's liberation or of seeing to it that women occasionally have access to the pulpit. What is more important is that preachers make a serious effort to grapple with the problems of language, that they think through sermon illustrations, and that they cease their reliance on misogynist jokes, no matter what topic they address.

Even ministers who would like to assist the church in changing its views of women will dodge opportunities to deal with a theological interpretation of the status of women and men in Christian thought. To avoid the issue is to leave people with the suspicion that the Bible and the tradition lack the resources to support our claims for the universality of the gospel. The point is not to gloss over misogyny in the tradition, but to lift up interpretive principles that will help people sift through the mixed record of the past.

The renewal of preaching toward communicating a view of the cohumanity of women and men depends in large part on the development and dissemination of scholarly work in biblical and theological studies. While this work is expanding rapidly, it is still largely the property of the seminaries and women's groups. This situation can change if the implications of a Christian view of women become topics of exploration and study by clergy in the course of their continuing education. An example of what can be done in this direction is the symposium held in the spring of 1974 at the Virginia Theological Seminary. Conferences organized by women's groups are quite common. What was unique about the Virginia symposium was that the impetus for the conference came from (male) administrators of the school and officials of the alumni group. Other seminaries, judicatories, and clergy associations could all include the study of women's role in their regular offerings in continuing education.[10]

Direct Instruction

Direct instruction is easier to deal with than the often unintentional teaching with which it is surrounded. We can pick up the texts for a Sunday school class, study them, and decide whether or not they say what we think should be said. We can look at the offerings for adult education classes; we can examine the scope of planned activities for a junior high school youth group; we can read through the syllabus for a confirmation class. The material is there to be inspected. What we have to do is ask questions that help us see how the material may shape the student's perceptions.[11]

In 1970, Christ and Norberg published a bench-mark study, "Sex Role Stereotyping in the United Methodist Nursery Curriculum":

> The method was a simple one. Each story, song, or picture was examined for evidence of attitudinal bias in the following areas:
> 1. sex-typing of play activities, behavior, and feelings of boys and girls;
> 2. the role of mother and father;
> 3. evidence of girls helping mothers and boys helping fathers;
> 4. occupational sex-typing of men and women.

> The study revealed blatant sexual stereotyping of behavior, emo-
> tions, abilities, occupations, and life-style on almost every page.
> Men and boys were generally shown as active, brave, useful, shaping
> their environment, and happy in their world. Women and girls
> were portrayed as passive, powerless, waiting, needing help, watch-
> the action, and often unhappy.[12]

This kind of content analysis, which has many parallels in work
done by secular educators, has the power to bring us up short in the
middle of glib assertions about equality.[13] Similar investigations can
be carried out by any concerned committee or board. The problems
with curriculum materials, as with liturgy, are not just in our por-
trayals of boys and girls, men and women. Much more difficult issues
are raised when we examine the biblical and theological content.
Another study of curriculum materials observes:

> This study has discovered sex role stereotyping to be pervasive
> in every aspect of these curriculum materials, but there is a primary
> underlying concern which may be seen as one basis for our whole
> society's concept of female inferiority, and which must be mentioned
> at the outset. This is the masculine, patriarchal image of God. . . .
> The problem is compounded by the image presented by the
> women who are included in this curriculum material and by the
> way in which they are used. The most frequently mentioned are
> Gomer, Jezebel, Delilah, Bathsheba, the woman taken in adultery,
> the wicked woman who anointed Jesus' feet, and Mary Magdalene—
> all women explicitly connected by these authors with sexual
> wickedness. . . .
> The few women who are mentioned who play neutral or positive
> roles are portrayed as passive, obedient, humble, waiting, acted
> upon—virtues which women certainly do not need to have
> reinforced.[14]

The tradition itself has resources for overcoming patriarchy, but not
if the materials from the tradition are used in the way this study
describes. We always exercise selectivity in choosing what to teach,
and there is every reason to exercise that selectivity to communicate
a more expansive view of the people of God. As with liturgy, we still
have the problem of how we express our understanding of the Deity.
What of the fact that the incarnation took place in male form? We
respond quickly that it doesn't matter, the message is still universal.
One Sunday school teacher agreed that the message might be universal, but the ways we communicated it certainly weren't. She considered the effects of pictorial accounts of the Gospels on her class of
elementary school boys and girls. She concluded that the pictures,
rather than the text, communicated a message that excluded the girls.

She abandoned the pictures and used only the text, inviting the children to visualize the scenes by acting them out.

Attempts to deal with intractable "generic" pronouns are still clumsy, in both secular and religious texts. When we use pronouns to refer to God, what shall we do? A teacher of Bible classes for adult education switches back and forth between *he* and *she* for God at intervals during the class period. This may be unsatisfactory, but no less so than insisting that a God who transcends our categories of sexuality must therefore and always be "he." [15] We can expect explorations in liturgical change and scholarly studies to interact with and inform what we are able to do in the classroom. We are in a situation where we can expect to be involved in changing our curriculum again and again.

Religious Educators and Reform

I have argued that if we are concerned with what we teach about the roles of women and men in the church, we are not going to be able to set down our task at the door of the Sunday school or adult education classroom. The most effective lessons we teach about the personhood of men and women in the light of the gospel remain to be taught after textbooks are closed—in the way we worship, in the way we structure participation in the day-to-day work of the congregation, in the people we choose to serve as leaders and pastors. It is simply not enough for church educators to do an innovative, sensitive job in classroom instruction and expect that the lesson they wish to teach will actually get across.

Educators have the responsibility to interpret to congregations the educational impact of committee structures, hiring policies, pay scales, and liturgical practices on our views of women and men. Educators need not claim to have all the answers before pointing out that churches have a problem in what they are communicating. The point is to lift up the problem and engage people in joint efforts toward change. "Change" rather than a "solution" because we do not have a solution. At present we do not know all the implications of trying to live out the gospel affirmation of the common humanity and co-equality of women and men.

The spirit with which reform is undertaken is as important as the reform itself. If we undertake to change what we teach about women and men, we do so because of the gospel. No matter how much the churches have been pressed to reconsider their teaching by the contemporary women's movement, the only reason that they should respond is faithfulness to the good news that they wish to communicate. Because we are talking about an effort to preach, teach, and live the gospel, we are talking about a responsibility that may not be dodged with excuses about being "too old to change" or "too set in the old ways." Our task is to affirm the power of the gospel to break into and change human life, literally turning us around and setting us on a new way.

NOTES

1. On the Old Testament, see Phyllis Trible, "Depatriarchalizing in Biblical Interpretation," *Journal of the American Academy of Religion,* 41 (March, 1973), 30-48; on the New Testament, see Krister Stendahl, *The Bible and the Role of Women: A Case Study in Hermeneutics,* trans. Emilie T. Sander (Philadelphia: Fortress Press, 1966).

2. By *"the churches"* I intend to refer to those churches which admit hermeneutical principles and a view of tradition which encourage reconsideration of the role of women. This rules out churches which take a fundamentalist approach to scripture or, as in the case of the orthodox churches, an extremely inflexible view of the authority of traditional practices.

3. Lawrence A. Cremin, *The Genius of American Education* (New York: Vintage Books, 1965), pp. 9-11; John H. Westerhoff III, "A Changing Focus: Toward an Understanding of Religious Socialization," *Andover Newton Quarterly,* 66 (November, 1973), 118-29. Westerhoff makes a very helpful distinction between education and socialization.

4. C. Ellis Nelson, *Where Faith Begins* (Richmond: John Knox Press, 1967), pp. 101-2.

5. The churches that have begun ordaining women since the fifties are joining the Congregationalist, Baptist, and Unitarian-Universalist denominations, which have granted full ordination to women since the nineteenth century. The question of women in the Roman Catholic priesthood has been discussed favorably in two major recent works: Haye van der Meer, S.J., *Women Priests in the Catholic Church?* (Philadelphia: Temple University Press, 1973), and George H. Tavard, *Woman in Christian Tradition* (Notre Dame, Ind.: University of Notre Dame Press, 1973); an excellent ecumenical newsletter on the status of women in religion, *Genesis III,* is published by the Philadelphia Task Force on Women in Religion, P. O. Box 24003, Philadelphia, Pa. 19139.

6. Figures on the United Church of Christ and the Boston Theological Institute are from the Women's Theological Coalition of the Boston Theological Institute. The Episcopal figures are from Suzanne R. Hiatt, "Project Report on 'Women in Theological Education,' " paper, p. 2.

7. Beaver, *All Loves Excelling: American Protestant Women in World Mission* (Grand Rapids: Eerdmans Publishing Co., 1968). See also Alice L. Hageman, "Women and Missions: The Cost of Liberation," in Hageman, ed., *Sexist Religion and Women in the Church: No More Silence!* (New York: Association Press, 1974), pp. 167-93; "Retreat to Tokenism," *Genesis III,* 1 (May-June, 1971), 4; Florence V. Bryant, "Church Employed Women: Economy Class Citizens," *A.D.,* 3 (November, 1973), 19-23.

8. Removing barriers is often not enough. It might be appropriate to set up special training classes for lay readers, for example, which would give women an opportunity to develop confidence to take on new roles.

9. *Included Out,* a film distributed by Mass Media Ministries, 2116 North Charles Street, Baltimore, Md. 21218. A list of films on women can be obtained from Ms. Ellen Kirby, Room 1556, 475 Riverside Drive, New York, N. Y. 10027; see Sharon N. Emswiler and Thomas N. Emswiler, *Women and Worship: A Guide to Non-Sexist Hymns, Prayers, and Liturgies* (New York: Harper & Row, 1974).

10. See *Genesis III* for regular reviews and digests of publications on women and religion; Hiatt, "Women in Theological Education," p. 7.

11. Westerhoff, "An Understanding of Religious Socialization," p. 122.

12. Miriam Christ and Tilda Norberg, "Sex Role Stereotyping in the United Methodist Curriculum," app. I in Sarah Bentley Doely, ed., *Women's Liberation and the Church* (New York: Association Press, 1970), p. 119.

13. Women on Words and Images, *Dick and Jane as Victims: Sex Stereotyping in Children's Readers* (Princeton, N. J.: Women on Words and Images, 1972). For a survey of developments on women in secular education, see Judith Stacey, Susan Béreaud, and Joan Daniels, *And Jill Came Tumbling After: Sexism in American Education* (New York: Dell Books, 1974).

14. Diana Lee Beach, *Sex Role Stereotyping in Church School Curricula* (Richmond: John Knox Press, 1972), pp. 2, 4.

15. See Nelle Morton, "The Rising Woman Consciousness in a Male Language Structure," *Andover Newton Quarterly,* 64 (March, 1972), 177-90, and "Preaching the Word," in Alice L. Hageman, ed., *Sexist Religion,* pp. 29-46.

Chapter 9

ADMINISTRATION OF THE
RELIGIOUS EDUCATION PROGRAM

Allen W. Graves

Effective administration of the religious education program is directly related to sound theology and educational philosophy. Educational organization, facilities, and methodology should be designed as means to help the church achieve its basic nature and mission and its divinely assigned objectives.

The Nature and Mission of the Church as an Educational Organism

A church does not *have* an educational program, it *is* an educational program. The very nature of the church constrains it to be an educational organism. As James D. Smart expressed it, "The Church must teach, just as it must preach, or it will not be the Church . . . . Teaching belongs to the essence of the church and a church that neglects this function of teaching has lost something that is indispensable to its nature as a church." [1] The churches we observe in the New Testament era were actively engaged in teaching ministries. Jesus was himself known and addressed most often as teacher. The early Christian churches engaged in intensive instructional programs designed to help believers grow to spiritual maturity and to equip them for their ministries as Christians in the world. In Paul's letter to the Ephesians he describes how God gave leaders to the church, "apostles, . . . prophets, . . . evangelists, . . . pastors and teachers." "He did this to prepare all God's people for the work of Christian service, to build up the body of Christ. And so we shall all come together to that oneness in our faith and in our knowledge of the Son of God; we shall become mature men, reaching to the very height of Christ's full stature" (Eph. 4:11-13 TEV).

Paul began his own first major ministry as a Christian leader, after his enlistment by Barnabas, by serving with Barnabas as a teacher in

Allen W. Graves is Professor of Church Administration at the Southern Baptist Theological Seminary and Executive Director of the Boyce Bible School, Louisville, Kentucky.

the church at Antioch, equipping the hundreds of new converts in the Antioch church to live and function as Christians.

Gaines S. Dobbins suggests that a church

> is not a religious institution with a school attached; it is essentially a school. Christ is the Great Teacher, the Holy Spirit is his interpreter, the Bible is the chief textbook; the minister is the chief officer of the school, about him are gathered teachers and staff; every church member is an enrolled student, all others who can be reached are sought as learners to be led toward Christ and then to him and into church membership through conversion.[2]

Religious education then is a basic and essential function of the church. It has been a part of the Christian strategy from the first century onward.

Good administration helps the church to clarify its educational objectives and philosophy. One of the first responsibilities of the church educational administrator is to lead the church in rethinking and defining its basic objectives and philosophy and to develop an educational plan to achieve those objectives.

When the church has achieved a sound theology and educational philosophy, it is the task of administration to lead the church in evaluating carefully the educational opportunities and needs confronting the congregation and to develop specific objectives related to those items given highest priority. Church members and church educational leaders will be much more thoroughly committed and willing to work diligently in achieving those educational goals which they see to be related clearly to the basic objectives of the church which they understand and support. When educational priorities have been determined, plans can then be made for establishing the organizational structure and enlisting and training the needed leadership.

Identifying Educational Objectives

What are some of the educational programs needed in a typical church? This entire area of educational objectives is dealt with elsewhere in this volume. Certainly if the church through its educational programs is to enable persons to become aware of the love of God as revealed in Jesus Christ and respond to him in faith and love, the church must provide an adequate teaching ministry to interpret Christ's purposes for his followers and to assist each individual in growing toward Christian maturity. Knowledge regarding the nature of the Christian life is communicated through the language of human relationships, through the study of the Bible, through experiencing together Christian worship and Christian ministry.

Effective administration begins with clarification of objectives and a determination of priorities. The needs of a particular congregation and its community will indicate the kinds of educational organizations and programs to be established and maintained.

Leadership resources will need to be enlisted and developed to implement the desired programs. Consider the following probable educational needs in the local congregation:

1. a program of Bible teaching and Christian nurturing to lead children, youth, and adults into a vital relationship with God and toward continuing growth in Christian maturity and Christian discipleship;

2. a program of leadership enlistment and development to provide a continuing supply of effective leaders for all aspects of the work of the church;

3. group activities providing opportunities for Christian fellowship, for discovering community needs, and for ministering to others;

4. preparation for participation in meaningful corporate, family, and private worship;

5. preparing participants in church programs for Christian family life and for implementing the Christian way of life in every realm of human life such as business, politics, recreation, and the arts.

Establishing and Maintaining Educational Organization

Churches have found a wide variety of educational structures useful in achieving their educational objectives. Many rely on comprehensive organizations with specific responsibilities for a major segment of the church educational task. The Sunday school, under many titles, is an example. Grading and grouping of students may follow chronological age or, for school-age children and youth, the school grades. Adults may be grouped by age, sex, interest, congeniality, couples, or some other criteria determined by the leadership of the church.

Grouping and grading policies should be determined on the basis of the major objectives of the particular church-educational organization. If, for example, the Sunday school, by whatever title, is expected to be the chief instrument for performing more than the first of the five functions listed above, its component groups could be formed with these additional functions in mind.

Some denominations have found that if they are to succeed in their effort to enlist every individual resident in a given community in a program of Bible study, there is needed a comprehensive plan for—

1. identifying and locating the person to be enlisted;
2. enlarging or modifying the organization to serve the desired constituency;
3. enlisting and training the needed workers to provide adequate instruction and administration;
4. providing adequate space and equipment for an effective educational program; and
5. establishing a plan for communicating directly with and enlisting persons sought for participation in the church Bible-teaching program.

In addition to the traditional approach of Bible-study classes meeting in the church buildings on Sunday, the opportunities for Bible study may be expanded by use of vacation Bible schools serving all age groups, conducted morning, afternoon, or night on weekdays during the summer. Weekday Bible-study classes may be conducted in homes or in the church facilities for adults and for children and youth after regular school hours. Shut-ins and others unable to attend group Bible study may be provided guidance materials for independent home Bible study.

Preparation for Participation and Leadership

Each congregation needs an organized program for preparing its members for responsible participation in its worship, life, and ministry. New-member classes may be established annually or on a continuing basis. Some churches have found it beneficial to assign responsibility for seeing that new members are properly assimilated into the life of the congregation to specific individuals or families who maintain continuing contact, giving assistance, counsel, and encouragement.

Churches receiving large numbers of new members may find separate, ongoing group meetings useful for those in various age groups, providing instruction regarding the practice of Christian life, growth, and doctrine, organizations and programs of the church and denomination, and worship and service opportunities provided by the church.

All church members should be assisted in continuing growth to full spiritual maturity and in developing skills that will enable them to participate effectively in fulfilling the mission of the church.

Leadership Training

Any organization to remain viable must provide for an adequate supply of qualified leaders to guide the organization in achieving its goals. This means for most churches the establishing and maintaining of a program for discovering and developing those within their membership who have gifts, talents, and abilities that can be developed and utilized in church leadership positions.

Preparation should be made available, whether within the congregation or through denominational or interdenominational programs, that will develop increased competence for effective church leadership.

The curricula of such leadership-training programs should include basic understandings regarding the Christian faith, its beliefs, history, denominational structures, and means of providing for both mission outreach and organizational maintenance.

Leaders working with particular age levels or special groups in the church or community need to learn of the developmental characteristics and needs of such groups. All leaders will profit through better understanding of planning techniques, principles of group dynamics, communication skills, and effective teaching-learning procedures.

Most denominations offer to the local congregations extensive assistance and materials for leadership training. Church educational administrators should keep informed about such resources and available personnel to assist the church in its leadership training programs.

Supervising and Coordinating the Educational Program

Many different structures and plans are utilized by churches in supervising and conducting their educational programs. Staff leadership may be given by the minister or one of his associates. An associate with special training in religious education may serve as minister of education, director of Christian education, or educational director. Coordination of the several educational programs may be provided through a church education committee or a church council. Either would combine the resources of professionally trained staff members, when available, with key volunteer leaders from the congregation. In such a group the annual calendar of educational events for the congregation could be planned, guaranteeing a balanced program with a minimum of conflicts, whether in calendar dates or educational philosophy.

Planning

Good administration will provide definite times and leadership for organizational planning. Some very effective Sunday schools utilize a weekly planning session with all Sunday school teachers and age-group leaders meeting with others serving the same age group to discuss mutual problems, make lesson plans for effective presentation of the Bible lessons for the week, and handle any administrative matters. Such a leadership meeting may be held weekly following a congregational fellowship meal which all members of the church attend. During the planning sessions other members of leaders' families may be engaged in music groups, mission study and mission action groups, or other suitable activities for all age groups. By scheduling activities for each member of the family all on a single weeknight, repeated trips to the church can be avoided.

Consider the following as a suggested schedule for such a "family night at church":

> 6:00-6:45 P.M.—Church family-night dinner (may be prepared by paid staff, a caterer, by volunteer workers, or brought by families attending). Around the tables new members and new leaders may be introduced and special events and achievements in the lives of those present may be mentioned.
> 6:45-7:00 P.M.—Worship around the tables
> 7:00-8:00 P.M.—Activities
> 1. Sunday school officers' and teachers' planning meeting
> 2. New members' class
> 3. Task forces for selected mission action groups meet to plan
> 4. Youth choral-group rehearsal
> 5. Children's choirs

Some congregations find a monthly meeting of teachers and other educational leaders sufficient to provide coordination and direction for educational programs. A variation of the schedule above may be utilized if such a monthly educational leadership planning meeting is combined with other church activities.

If the church educational program is divided among several different specialized groups, then each group will need to have a planning and coordinating meeting for its leaders at least monthly. For example, leaders in the Bible teaching program will need such planning meetings as indicated above. Mission-action task forces will need leadership strategy-planning sessions. Training groups for leadership development, new member training, *et cetera* will need a leadership meeting for planning and coordinating their work.

Church committee chairpersons and members and other officials of the congregation will at least need annual sessions to review objectives and procedures for their work and prepare them for effective service.

Preparation for Religious Living and Service

The educational organization should provide activities and experiences that will enhance the religious maturation of each participant and prepare each one for involvement in ministries projected by the congregation. Members should be equipped to cross social, racial, economic, and geographical barriers to minister in all areas of spiritual need. Educational programs and experiences should aid persons in becoming helpful.

Church educational administrators have a responsibility for equipping each participant in the congregation's several educational programs for the living of a full and meaningful life in which one's concern for others is manifested in effective ministries to those with real needs, whether in the local community or elsewhere in the world.

A comprehensive educational program will require organization, leaders, curriculum materials, and educational plans for achieving desired goals in each of several areas. When basic skills of members are developed, task forces may be formed to assemble those with similar concerns and prepare for and engage in various forms of mission action as indicated by discovered needs.

Consultation with community agencies, surveys of needs whether local, regional, national, or international will identify specific tasks which individuals or groups in the congregation should be trained and equipped to perform. The development of interpersonal competence and skills in group formation and management should be included in the educational objectives.

Educational activities will need to be provided for congregational leaders to ensure institutional maintenance and effective organizational functioning. Good administration will help the congregation to keep a good balance between mission goals and maintenance goals. Some congregations have made the mistake of focusing exclusively on mission goals and have failed to maintain themselves. More frequently congregations have focused predominantly on maintenance and survival goals with concerns for keeping the organization functioning, the bills paid, and the building and facilities in good condition. Educational administration should always be concerned for individual maturation and group growth that is demonstrated in effective service to others.

Music Education

A significant aspect of the church education program in many churches is the music program. Church members find meaningful opportunities for spiritual growth, worship, and for the expression of their gifts through music.

In administering a church music education program several purposes may be kept in focus. The program may equip participants to sing, to play, and to direct music. The music education program may provide music for church and community events. Music is a means of worship and an aid to worship. Music involves members of the congregation in praise, adoration, confession, and communion with God and one another. It is appropriate therefore to include a comprehensive music education program as a part of the church educational program.

Rehearsal times for choirs involving some or all the various age groups may be scheduled as part of a comprehensive church family night mentioned earlier.

Securing and Maintaining Educational Facilities

Effective religious education is more likely to occur when there is an appropriate environment for learning and suitable learning aids are utilized. Those responsible for administering the educational program should be aware of the kinds of facilities, equipment and supplies that will encourage learning. Administrators should plan for the multiple use of facilities and equipment. Church buildings constructed at great expense should not stand idle for much of the week but should be used often, perhaps daily, in serving the spiritual needs of the congregation and its community.

Facilities serving preschoolers on Sunday may house a weekday child-care program. Clubs and activities for various age groups from the pre-teens to retirees may utilize church educational facilities every day in the week.

Before educational facilities are constructed or remodeled, the congregation should conduct a careful study of the total program needs of the church, both present and projected. Such a survey should identify the activities in which the church will be engaged during the foreseeable future and plan for buildings and equipment that can best serve those activities and that are within the limit of available financial resources. Often the "cost-benefit ratio" can be improved by designing facilities with the possibility of multiple use, serving the needs of activities scheduled throughout the week.

Construction should be planned for functional effectiveness, ease of maintenance, durability, safety, and security, as well as aesthetic beauty.

The building committee, or the architect it employs, should consult with local fire department officials regarding design, materials, and location of educational facilities to assure maximum safety from possibility of fire and related hazards.

Police officials can often advise regarding security plans and precautions that will reduce losses from vandalism, burglary, and other crimes and that will enable participants to come and go from church activities in reasonable safety.

Evaluation

At least annually the responsible administrative leadership group in the church should review and evaluate the adequacy and effectiveness of the educational organizations in the church and initiate needed changes to assure the accomplishment of church educational objectives.

Evaluation may include some kind of testing to discover what has been learned by participants in the various educational activities. Evaluation should review the stated educational objectives of the congregation and assess the progress during the year in achieving these specific goals. Leaders in each organization should evaluate the growth and effectiveness of each worker and determine leadership needs for the coming year. Budget requests should be submitted for literature, supplies, and needed equipment. Long-range plans should be updated annually and specific goals set for the coming year in terms of spiritual growth, outreach, and ministry to the community and the world.

Bibliography

Drucker, Peter F. *Management, Tasks, Responsibilities, Practices.* New York: Harper & Row, 1974.

Glasse, James D. *Putting It Together in the Parish.* Nashville: Abingdon Press, 1972.

Hersey, Paul, and Blanchard, Kenneth H. *Management of Organizational Behavior.* 2d ed. Englewood Cliffs, N. J.: Prentice-Hall, 1972.

CHRISTIAN EDUCATION IN AN ERA OF CHANGE

Mickey, Paul A., and Wilson, Robert L. *Conflict and Resolution.* Nashville: Abingdon Press, 1973.
Schaller, Lyle E. *The Change Agent.* Nashville: Abingdon Press, 1972.
————. *The Local Church Looks to the Future.* Nashville: Abingdon Press, 1968.
————. *Parish Planning.* Nashville: Abingdon Press, 1971.
Taylor, Marvin J., ed. *An Introduction to Christian Education.* Nashville: Abingdon Press, 1966.

NOTES

1. Smart, *The Teaching Ministry of the Church* (Philadelphia: The Westminster Press, 1954), p. 11.
2. Dobbins, *Building Better Churches* (Nashville: Broadman Press, 1947), p. 92.

Chapter 10

CHURCH EDUCATION AS AN ORGANIZATIONAL PHENOMENON

Robert C. Worley

The thesis of Michael Polanyi's book *Personal Knowledge* is that everyone takes a perspective or stance on the viewing process which is personal and prior to the actual seeing. His argument is: What we see is largely determined by a personal stance which has tacit dimensions that are largely unexamined. The tacit dimension has its source in faith communities, groups of people who habitually see realities from perspectives which are unexamined as to their trust, historical, and skill components. Each stance imposes constraints upon what a person sees so that seeing is always partial and personal. It is personal in the sense that the tacit dimension, while having its source in faith communities, is always internalized and operative in particular persons who have their own unique history and who, therefore, always personalize the tacit dimension.

Church education has been and will continue to be seen from different perspectives which, if exposed and made visible, have the possibility of informing and correcting the partiality of particular perspectives. The thesis of this essay is that church education can be seen from an organizational, holistic perspective which will help to clarify and develop a better understanding of some aspects of education in the church. It is not argued that this is necessarily a better or more accurate stance, but a *different* stance from which different phenomena become visible and comprehensible.

Traditionally education has been understood as a highly individualized activity typified best, perhaps, by the imagery of Mark Hopkins with the teacher at one end of the log and the student at the other, with both holding a curriculum book. The potency of this imagery is only enhanced when the psychological sciences undergirding educational theory and practice use individual rats, mice, pigeons, and persons in a program of individualized sensory stimulation. The major focus of both theory and practice is the programming of particular

Robert C. Worley is Director of the Doctor of Ministry Program and Professor of Education and Ministry at McCormick Theological Seminary, Chicago, Illinois.

stimuli irrespective of any larger context. From this stance one looks for and sees primarily the effects, or lack of effects, of particular pro-grammed stimuli through curriculum books, various teaching methods, activities of the teacher, and/or different media. Teacher, delivery of experience through a medium, and the student are seen through this lens. It is important to note that which is not seen through this per-spective. The impact of multiple environments, culture, and a wide variety of organizational variables are missed. Important variables such as climate, structure, norms, values, and communication and decision-making processes are ignored.

Protestant church educators have known for some time that this stance is imperfect and inadequate even though it is still the dominant perspective of those who are at the delivery point in local churches. More recently we have looked at church education as a group phe-nomenon. From this perspective we have seen the dynamics of the classroom as a transactional process between teacher, curriculum, media, and students in which all are in motion and in a context. John Dewey impressed us. Social psychology and group dynamics became new sources for both informing and confirming the validity of this per-spective. Through this lens the classroom became more complex, active, and the educational prescriptions became less simplistic and individualized.

More recently, church educators have begun to use organizational concepts, particularly those ideas from systems theory which depict the interrelation of educational systems, so that curricular resource systems and teacher support systems have been designed even if they have not become fully operative. It is evident that there is movement toward understanding church education through a different lens, through perception of education as an organizational phenomenon. This movement is related positively to events in the larger culture, the focus on the turbulence and ineffectiveness in most organizations such as schools, families, business, and industrial organizations. The studies of other organizations suggest a perspective for studying church orga-nizational behavior and particular aspects of church organizational life.

The question behind the writing of this essay is: What more can be seen by looking at church education as an organizational phenome-non in contrast to the traditional and historical individual and group perspectives? The most obvious point is that church education is indeed an organizational phenomenon. It is an expression of a huge bureaucratic organization composed of national agencies, middle-level church organizations (synods, districts, conferences, presbyteries, etc.), and local congregations. It is no longer a movement in any significant sense. The Sunday school movement is a matter of history. Today there is an ordered, structured, goal-seeking organization at every level of church life involved in church education. The interdependency of these organizational levels has not been studied, but it is necessary to point out the profound constraints which each level means for other levels. The ineffectiveness of any level is disastrous for the goals of the other levels. The tasks to achieve the objectives of church education at each level and in the special and particular environment of each organization, depend not only on the resources and support from that level, but from other levels. If for example, a national church-education program agency ignores the differing environments and assumes that the environments of all congregations and middle-level church organizations are the same, the results are indeed disastrous. The tools needed in a particular environment, ideas, and other resources will not be made available by a program agency. Effectiveness is measured in terms of how well the resources of one level enhance and facilitate the effective mission-goal achievement of another level in its environment. Ineffectiveness does not pertain only to the educational part of these different levels, but to the total organization. Human organizations exist so interdependently, and they have parts which are also interdependent, that ineffectiveness and dysfunction in any part affect every other part and the whole organization at every level.

This huge bureaucratic system has operated from an assumption that it is a closed system which need only respond to those environmental variables (teachers, students, church education committees, middle-level church education committees, and particular age-group or teacher-curriculum needs in the case of church education strategy) which are directly connected with achieving denominational goals in church education. It has attempted to achieve these goals with a closed-system approach through a monolithic central network by controlling resources and professional staff. The assumption has been that church education resources and strategy can be designed without regard to the congregational context of church education. The assumption is: Church education is a system which is not affected in any significant way by the environment external to the congregation or by the internal climate and characteristics of the congregation.

The assumption of such a closed system is a colossal error. All human organizations in Western culture are open systems varying in both the degree of openness and the number and kind of environmental variables which influence them. In viewing church organizations and church education as an organizational phenomenon through an open-system perspective, the impact of environment upon different levels and types of church organizations can be seen. The uncertainty which a turbulent environment such as ours introduces into church organization and education can be dealt with only when an organization assumes that such an environment will introduce uncertainty and indeterminacy into its life and then begin to search and discover those means for achieving more certainty in its life and program. It will not do this as long as it assumes that it is a closed system at all levels and hence can ignore environmental variables. Developing mechanisms for dealing with uncertainty as an organization while still focusing on the achievement of goals is a first-order activity for church organizations. Church education takes place in an organization which is affected dramatically by its environment. The debate of the sixties between national church educators who insisted that education in an urban church is achieved simply by adapting and/or modifying a single national church curriculum illustrates this point. The assumption that church organizations are essentially the same everywhere, with only inconsequential differences, led to an arrogance which has alienated many segments of denominations. Goals, methods, resources, abilities of personnel are all affected dramatically by the environments of each church organization. The assumption that all organizations, all environments, and all goals and tasks to achieve the goals of church education are the same is an incorrect assumption. Environmental effects alter the nature of church education at each level so that the old closed-system assumptions are outmoded with their strategies of educational program control. Instead, open-systems assumptions, which lead to the development of strategies of coping to achieve educational goals, must be adopted. This means a new noncontrolling relationship between levels of church organizations, if the necessary degree of positive interdependency and mobilization of human and other resources necessary to cope in at least minimal ways with the environment, is to be achieved. Church education in the classroom is affected by the ways in which church organizations cope or fail to cope with environmental variables.

We need to look more closely at church education as a part of each level of church organization, but for the purposes of this chapter the local congregation is the focus. The most independent variables of any church organization are the goals and primary tasks toward those goals. The goals may be explicit or implicit, examined or unexamined, and competing and conflicting.

In order to see the goals of any organization, budget allocations, use of time by staff and volunteers, agendas, and minutes of committees, processes for recruiting and incorporating persons into the church, processes for directing persons and other resources into different goal-task groups, and the messages and products made visible as output of a congregation should be examined. Church education as a goal-task area of congregational life is but one such area. It is in direct competition for resources with all other goal-task areas, and it is always within some implicitly or explicitly determined priority ranking. The perceived importance of each goal-task area determines the amount and kind of resources available. A major factor influencing the ranking in any goal-task area is how well the activities of a particular area enable the congregation to cope with the internal and external challenges. Motivation and intensity and degree of involvement are increased in a congregation when goals are perceived as appropriate and necessary to persons in the organization. Appropriateness and necessity relate to environmental conditions. The point is that church education is but one goal-task among several in any congregation. It may be given a quite low ranking among goals. If this occurs, apathy and/or alienative involvement may occur with nonachievement of the goals in this area. Effectiveness in achieving the goals of church education depends upon how these goals are perceived by the total organization and the implicit and/or explicit ranking of these goals among other goals.

The impact of the Human Relations School of organizational theorists has produced a tendency to ignore structural, political, economic, and environmental factors in church organizational behavior. There is no doubt that human relations and good leadership are important, but the explanatory power of this branch of organizational theory is low in light of the nature of church organizations as voluntary complex organizations. Nor do the most frequent prescriptions of individual and group growth join with the need for total organizational transformation. Effectiveness in achieving goals in any area of congregational life is influenced by the structure, the patterns of communication, the political (decision-making) system, the economic and the other resources available, the environment, and the health and effectiveness of other subsystems.

The role of structure in achieving goals has not been studied in church organizations, but some observations can be made which point to needed research. In a stable environment in which tasks are simple and known, a stable structure supported by a few standardized rules and procedures is adequate for goal attainment. Church education until the last few years took place in a relatively stable environment, and the tasks of teaching for educators were comparatively simple and known.

But today the environment is turbulent, the tasks of church education are increasingly complex, heterogeneous, multiple, and frequently unknown. Standardized curricula, teaching methods, and classroom procedures have become increasingly obsolete, or if not obsolete, they appear to be appropriate under only the most stable, traditional conditions.

Today, each congregation is invited to construct its own curriculum, to mobilize its own resources, and to establish its own goals. But the congregational structures still tend to be rigid—rather than flexible and modifiable—in order to reflect and facilitate goal achievement in a turbulent environment. Many congregations despair because the standardized rules and procedures are no longer viable, but the alternatives of more effective human communication, congregational goal-setting and planning, and a variety of feedback mechanisms have eluded them.

In many congregations, leaders and followers have been unwilling to find alternatives to traditional practices, rules, and methods. Alternatives in a turbulent environment with tasks that are complex, unknown, and multiple are bound to be costly in terms of human energy. The human communication necessary for effective consensus formation requires different patterns of communication. If the goals related to church education or any other goal area are to be known, understood, and supported with the necessary resources, then congregational communication about these goals is required. No elite group can announce the goals or tasks related to these goals and expect automatic support. Patterns of congregationwide communication through clustering or area grouping, telephone networks, effective congregational meetings, etc., are essential.

In many congregations elite leaders and goal-task areas are mismatched so that the elites do not reflect goal priorities of a congregation but are the product of a political process which produces nonrepresentative leaders who do not or cannot communicate with a constituency which must support the programs they approve. Or even worse, the elite leaders may approve programs, curricular resources, and teaching methods which are inadequate, inappropriate, and unresponsive to the needs of teachers and students. On occasion, leaders approve inconsequential goals which use a disproportionate share of resources. The goals they approve may create division, tension, and apathy which reduce the resources or the power of the total organization to achieve any goals adequately.

Goals, structure, communication patterns, and political processes are variables which function in every congregation. These variables influence one another in such a way that goals and tasks to accomplish goals suffer if structure, communication patterns, and political processes are not designed to facilitate goal attainment. This is obvious, but the focus in church education has not been on the nature of the organization which must accomplish the goal of church education, but on church education itself. Education is an expression of a total congregation, not just of those who find themselves in the church education program.

There is a need to question the effectiveness of church education in another way: What are the conditions in a church organization which make possible effective church education? There is an increasing body of literature which points to the relation between climates of church organizations and their effectiveness in achieving goals. Following the typology of climates used by Litwin and Stringer in *Motivation and Organizational Climate* (power-oriented, achievement-oriented, or affiliation-oriented climates), hypotheses can be stated concerning the relation of these climates and congregational behavior. From our experiences of research and development in a number of congregations, we conclude that the more achievement-oriented the climate of a congregation and the more coping mechanisms and resources exist in relation to the environment, the more effective the goal achievement in all areas of a congregation's life. If this can be substantiated, then a precondition suggested for more effective church education is that of an achievement-oriented climate. An important task then is the transformation of a congregation to this type of climate. This illustration is meant to suggest that we have been preoccupied with curricula, teaching methods, and teacher training and not sufficiently alerted to the church organization which must accomplish the goal of education. Sick congregations may not be able to accomplish any goal effectively. This is true even when we have adequate resources, teacher training designs, and all the rest of the church education apparatus.

In power-oriented climates there is a great deal of political struggle for control of resources and the direction of congregational life. Consequently, there is a loss of energy, persons, money, and other resources for focusing upon congregational goals. There is either struggle or apathy, depending upon the investment persons have in winning the power struggle. Under these circumstances no congregation is effective in achieving goals.

While the affiliation-oriented climate may appear more congruent with the words of Christianity, fellowship, koinonia, community, there is little evidence that congregations which tend to have this type climate are, in fact, able to achieve the goals of the congregation effectively. As a council of a Lutheran church concluded after a period of time in which they focused upon meeting affiliation needs, "We have grown to feel good about each other, but we haven't done a damn thing." They suggested that they would feel even better about one another, more motivated and more committed, if they worked together to achieve a significant goal effectively. Their achievement and affiliation needs would have been met.

The most vexing climate which is found in congregations and other church organizations is not mentioned in any of the texts on organizational climate. The goalless, or climate of anomie, is too characteristic of many congregations. The aimlessness, confusion, low level of energy, and involvement in these congregations affects every aspect of congregational life including the educational program. No area is effective. The climate dampens the mood and depresses the spirit of those few people who would like to see the congregation engaged in significant ministry and mission.

Teacher training and new curricular resources are largely irrelevant to effective education when the climate of a congregation destroys the motivation and commitment of persons. It is difficult to understand conceptually that congregations are more than a collection or aggregate of individuals. Congregations are an entity in and of themselves. They have characteristics which are different from the characteristics of individuals and groups. It is the congregation as an entity which educates. The climate of the congregation is a powerful influence on the goals, tasks toward goals, and organizational parts of a congregation.

Currently no discipline within theological education reflects about or focuses upon the congregation. We have specialists in worship, pastoral care, homiletics, community organization, church education, and polity, but no one really studies the whole entity, the congregation. Consequently, all goal-task areas, including church education, suffer from lack of understanding. The implication of this observation is that *no* curriculum or teaching methods or teacher training programs may be adequate for achieving effective church education. The problems of church education may not lie in the traditional areas or categories of church education, but in the problems of church education as an organizational phenomenon. When church education is viewed as an organizational activity, the tasks of creating greater effectiveness in church education will probably relate to total organizational behavior rather than church education behavior.

This thesis is set forth to suggest that many of the present frustrations of church educators, pastors, and church education committees can be better understood through looking at the influence of the congregation as a church organization on church education. If there is any validity to the observations shared in this paper, then church educators may be even more responsible to their enterprise if they study the relation of church organizational behavior to church education.

This may appear to be a gratuitous and hardly charitable remark to church educators, of which I am one. But increasingly as our work has progressed with dozens of congregations in revitalization processes for total congregations, we have found that the church educational needs of congregations are more wide ranging and profound than the traditional categories of curriculum, teaching methods, and teacher training suggest. The whole enterprise of church education has been tilted toward the Sunday school.

This selective tilting or focusing of congregational resources to the church school has allowed educators and other church professionals to ignore the educational needs of the total congregation. In the parishes with which we have worked to enable them to gain clarity about the goals and objectives which are important for the congregation, we and the leadership groups of these congregations are continually faced with the educational tasks which must be accomplished, if the congregation is to increase its effectiveness in ministry and mission. The educational tasks which are important for the congregation may be different from the educational tasks associated with the Sunday school. The Sunday school may be only one task area which is important in the congregation. It may suffer profoundly because the other educational tasks have been ignored or neglected. At any moment it may be more important to ignore or pay minimal attention to the church school while focusing maximally upon those educational tasks which will bring health and vitality to the total congregation.

Denominations through their national educational program agencies and the middle-level (judicatory, district, conference, synod) church education committees and programs exacerbate the problem. The habit of focusing on the church school while other educational tasks are virtually ignored is continued as long as Christian education or the church education program is the target and that which is resourced. The target is the congregation, and the congregation has educational needs.

Too long we have treated the educational committees of the congregation as the property of the national educational strategy rather than the congregation. As long as this continues, increasing frustration and ineffectiveness will continue.

We have hardly begun to understand congregations as entities which behave, but they do as any perceptive person can attest. This article is a statement urging that we seek to learn more about the complex and significant relation between education in the church and church organizational behavior. As we do learn more, the shape of church education will be greatly affected.

Bibliography

The following is a list of books which should be helpful for readers who desire further exploration of some of the concepts.

Etzioni, Amitai. *A Comparative Analysis of Complex Organizations.* New York: The Free Press, 1961.

Litwin, George H., and Stringer, Robert A., Jr. *Motivation and Organizational Climate.* Cambridge: Harvard University Press, 1968.

Maurer, John G. *Readings in Organization Theory: Open Systems Approaches.* New York: Random House, 1971.

Perrow, Charles. *Organizational Analysis: A Sociological View.* Belmont, Calif.: Brooks/Cole Publishing Co., 1970.

Thompson, James D. *Organizations in Action.* New York: McGraw-Hill Book Co., 1967.

Worley, Robert. *Change in the Church: A Source of Hope.* Philadelphia: The Westminster Press, 1971.

Chapter 11

CURRICULUM THEORY
AND PRACTICE

D. Campbell Wyckoff

The curriculum of religious education is the plan by which religious groups propose to carry out their educational responsibilities. Religious education is actually accomplished through a variety of methods which, when shaped into a plan, become a curriculum. Once that plan is set up, administrative devices (organization, management, and supervision) are employed to implement it. The curriculum thus occupies the strategic position between the varieties of educational possibilities (which need to be approached selectively and functionally) and the practical instrumentalities employed by the religious group to do its work.

Previous studies have provided technical reviews of educational objectives and plans, the scope of the curriculum, models of teaching and learning, curriculum organization, and the varieties of curriculum materials.[1]

The question that curriculum workers (whether at ecumenical, denominational, or local levels) try to answer is, "How may a responsible educational plan be designed and carried through?" The question requires that the dimensions of religious education be examined in specific detail and that recommendations be made for enterprises that promise to explore these dimensions satisfactorily with children, youth, and adults in and out of the church.

At the same time it must be recognized that the question itself has become problematical. While the usual curriculum discussion deals with the dimensions of religious education, as indicated above, the very appropriateness of the curriculum concept itself is being challenged. Does religious education need a plan? Is a plan really appropriate to an enterprise that should be in essence creative and that should be responsive to the unpredictabilities of personal and social experience? Can a plan take full cognizance of significant emergent experience?

There is no doubt about the urge for emphasis on the *now* among many religious educators, expressed in an impatience with prearranged educational systems. The life of the magazine *Colloquy* is a clear indi-

D. Campbell Wyckoff is Thomas W. Synnott Professor of Christian Education at Princeton Theological Seminary, Princeton, New Jersey.

cation of this urge and impatience. *Colloquy* replaced the more traditional "teacher's magazine" with treatments of current topics that were intended to open the religious educator to what was going on in the world around—tensions, crises, challenges, and opportunities.[2] The obvious point was that in such awareness the teacher would change the style, plan, and even the objective of religious education. Even so, plans were implied (and thus curriculum was implied). John H. Westerhoff III, the editor of *Colloquy*, in a key position piece, defined Christian education as "deliberate, systematic, and sustained efforts which enable persons and groups to evolve Christian life-styles."[3] The shift of focus in planning is significant, from a curriculum that is a plan for the transmission of a life-style (or something even more specific and limited) to a curriculum that is a planned process from which various appropriate life-styles may emerge. The premature demise of *Colloquy* does not invalidate the point that it was trying to make. Rather, it indicates the urgency of the next step—to move from awareness to planned action.

Indicative of this same trend, the bulk of the seminars included in the convention of the Religious Education Association in Chicago 1972 were issue oriented. The seminar on curriculum (one of thirty-six reporting) saw religious education as both cognitive and affective-social; relating in love to others; emphasizing joy, celebration, freedom, and kindred experiences; concerned with life *now;* using methods of stimulation, discovery, consultation, and discussion, particularly listening and dialogue; employing "poetic-simple," nonverbal language, the "language of relationships"; using multi-media and "secular" materials together with pupil experience; and set in a context of flexibility and a variety of groupings.[4]

Contemporary curriculum options, then, span a range that includes: (1) a curriculum plan for direct instruction and socialization within a particular religious tradition; (2) a curriculum plan that introduces self-determination and flexibility into the picture, but whose context is still that of particularized religious socialization; and (3) a curriculum plan that emphasizes self-determination and flexibility, together with an openness as to the context and end of religious education. All of these are more or less represented in the present curriculum situation.

The Curriculum Scene

Continuing curricula. Several Protestant curricula seem to be more or less permanently established. They represent attempts to meet a variety of needs, but their designs, while they do evidence important differences, tend to overlap. Each has involved a great deal of research, both in its establishment and in its continuing revision.

The curriculum of the United Church of Christ is outstanding in its dealing with the foundations and implications of Christian living at various age levels. Its preschool material has been adopted by other denominations, and certain units, like "Becoming a Christian Person" for the Middle Highs, have become almost classics. The theory and design of the United Church curriculum are set forth in Roger L. Shinn's *The Educational Mission of Our Church* (Philadelphia: United Church Press, 1962).

The curriculum of the Lutheran Church in America is noteworthy for its thoroughgoing research base, its clear design, and its functional utilization of a coordinated group of local church agencies (the Sunday church school, weekday church school, confirmation class, etc.). Studies leading toward its revision continue and have been spurred on by the cooperative work undertaken with the American Lutheran Church. The central objective of the curriculum was thoroughly scrutinized in C. Richard Evenson (ed.), *Foundations for Educational Ministry* (Philadelphia: Fortress Press, 1971). The psychological base for curricular sequence was reexamined in light of the Lutheran Longitudinal Study (a research in which ten thousand persons participated) in William A. Koppe's *How Persons Grow in Christian Community* (Philadelphia: Fortress Press, 1973).

Primarily a research program, but continuing to utilize a continuously revised curriculum as one of its research instruments, the Character Research Project publishes, in addition to the curriculum itself, a journal, *Character Potential, A Record of Research,* and a periodic newsletter.[5] Because it is a research program, close touch is maintained with teachers and participants through written reports and conferences.

The Cooperative Curriculum Project and Cooperative Curriculum Development, related to the National Council of the Churches of Christ in the U.S.A., have been definitive for a number of denominational curricula, those of The United Methodist Church, the Christian Church (Disciples of Christ), the American Baptist Convention, and the Southern Baptist Convention in particular. Some of the key elements in the cooperative design are as follows:

The objective. The objective of Christian education is that all persons be aware of God through his self-disclosure, especially his redeeming love in Jesus Christ, and they respond in faith and love—to the end that they may know who they are and what their human situation means, grow as sons of God rooted in the Christian community, live in the Spirit of God in every relationship, fulfill their common discipleship in the world, and abide in the Christian hope.

The scope of the curriculum. The scope of the curriculum is co-extensive with what God has revealed through his redemptive action and the implications of this redemptive action for man in the whole field of relationships—God, humanity, nature, and history.

Curriculum areas. The cooperative design refined the idea of curriculum areas so that each area provides an experiential vantage point from which to deal with the whole scope. The areas are identified as follows:

Life and its setting—the meaning and experience
of existence
Revelation—the meaning and experience of God's
self-disclosure
Sonship—the meaning and experience of redemption
Vocation—the meaning and experience of discipleship
The church—the meaning and experience of Christian
community

Learning tasks. The cooperative design sees learning taking place through the undertaking of certain lifelong learning tasks:

Listening with growing alertness to the gospel
and responding in faith and love
Exploring the whole field of relationships in
light of the gospel
Discovering meaning and value in the field of
relationships in light of the gospel
Appropriating personally the meaning and value
discovered in the field of relationships in
light of the gospel
Assuming personal and social responsibility in
light of the gospel

These and certain other definitive concepts have been the basis for the detailed development of curricular possibilities: meanings and experiences relevant to particular age levels, readiness for certain learnings, teaching and learning activities, and appropriate achievements. These were first detailed in a massive analysis in *The Church's Educational Ministry: A Curriculum Plan* (see Bibliography) and further developed in a document entitled "Specialized Resources for the Church's Educational Ministry," distributed to and used by the denominations involved in the project. An abbreviated form of this material, with only one sample of the detailed development, was published as *A Design for Teaching-Learning* (St. Louis: Bethany Press, 1967). Additional technical help was provided in *Tools of Curriculum Development for the Church's Educational Ministry* (see Bibliography).

Based on a "consciousness, communication, exploration, reflection-action" model, the United Presbyterian Church in the U.S.A.'s *Christian Faith and Action/Designs for an Educational System* intends to develop five abilities:

1. The ability to interpret intelligently the Bible as the unique medium through which God chooses to speak to men, thereby calling his people to active response in the worship and mission of the church in the present world.
2. The ability to understand the beliefs of the church in order to participate constructively in the community of faith through worship, service, and witness.
3. The ability to work for the unity and mission of the Christian church.
4. The ability to understand the implications and risks of committing one's personal life—in occupation, home, and all other situations and pursuits—as an offering to God in response to his call to faithful service in Christ.
5. The ability to deal with ethical issues and to work toward the solution of contemporary personal and social problems.

Christian Faith and Action provides a systematic, graded program for grades 1-10, mostly biblically oriented, with an elective system for grade 11 through the adult years. As a planning guide for this elective system, the manual, *Lay Education in the Parish,* provides an introduction to the situational approach that is recommended.

Urban curriculum. Some attempts have been made to meet the distinctive needs of urban people through Christian education, but most of these have been one-time studies and experiments that did not result in widely circulated curriculum plans. An exception is the preschool-through-grade-6 program called *Hey, God!* (Philadelphia: Fortress

Press, 1972). The Fortress Press has also published three volumes of educational resources for the urban church under the title *Educaid* (1972).

Joint Educational Development. Joint Educational Development is a consortium of six Protestant denominations, committed to doing their educational planning together. Its mandate calls for everything from basic research and study to the production of curriculum materials.

Reporting on JED's curriculum developments, Michael Leach writes:

> They have projected a four-faceted curriculum plan that they hope will meet the needs of at least 80 percent of their 11-million combined membership. The plan calls for four separate and complete educational systems, ranging from a more traditional system designed to serve churches dissatisfied with the national emphases on social action to a forward-looking system meant for churches wishing to be involved in social change. Broken down, the systems will look something like this:
> System 1: A strongly biblical, well-structured, simple, dated curriculum, similar to the Uniform Series.
> System 2: Undated curriculum of in-depth biblical studies that emphasize a contemporary and scholarly interpretation of Scripture. The present resources most nearly resembling this system are the Christian Faith and Action series.
> System 3: An experience-oriented curriculum suitable for creative teaching and learning activity. The most similar present resources are the United Church, Covenant Life, and Christian Life series.
> System 4: A curriculum to equip people for mission and to explore the issues that confront Christians in a changing world, such as the newly emerging Shalom resources developed by the United Church of Christ.[6]

The Shalom curriculum. The prime example of System 4, the Shalom Curriculum, is built on the concept of "whole community, liberation and justice, harmony and peace, fullness of life. In a sense it is a vision —the reign of God. In Jesus, the Shalom of God is present among us as a gift, for which we are called to respond and act." Various units are prepared for preschool through adults, with others for intergenerational use. The curriculum's fundamental concepts and implications are set forth in Edward A. Powers, *Signs of Shalom* (Philadelphia: Pilgrim Press, 1973).

Roman Catholic curriculum. Roman Catholic curriculum development takes place at three levels: (1) official decision on basic policy by the church itself through its bishops and councils, (2) analytical and critical work by scholars in universities and seminaries, and (3) design and publication of programs and materials by publishing houses serving, but not always related to, the church.

Among the scholars who are influencing curriculum development, Gabriel Moran and James Michael Lee are outstanding. Moran has published a series of books, both constructive and critical, relating theology to education and seeking to lay a firm foundation for the church's educational work in intensive religious education of adults combined with mass education techniques for the general laity. Lee is seeking to direct Catholic education theory away from theology toward the social sciences, and his curricular proposals are worked out in detail to accomplish this end. Key works of Moran and Lee are annotated in the Bibliography.

To take one large publishing house as an example of specific directions in Roman Catholic curriculum, the Paulist Press is a good choice. It pioneered in designing and producing materials that approached education in faith through contemporary concerns; their *Discovery* series opened up faith dimensions in art, film, news, prayer, and a series of other matters.

At the adult level, their GIFT (Growth in Faith Together) program is planned to involve large numbers of adults in a needs-based adult education enterprise, centered and developed in particular parishes. The program is one outgrowth of James R. Schaefer's study, *Program Planning for Adult Christian Education* (see Bibliography).

Most recently, the press has issued a curriculum entitled "Family: Parish Religious Education," an extended multi-media experience in which whole families participate together.

As a resource for putting together a variety of topics, *Designs in Affective Education* (New York: Paulist Press, 1974) provides units on scores of themes such as communication, freedom, happiness, life, peace, and love.

United Methodist "education futures." The United Methodist Church is one of the major denominations not officially a part of Joint Educational Development. Their work stays mainly within the context of the Cooperative design. At the same time they have undertaken a vast study of the future of church education under the title, "Education Futures." As a first step, 279 persons representing a wide range of experience and expertise were consulted on their visions and concerns for the future of Christian education. The purpose was to get direction in initiating and revising program and curriculum.

The over two hundred "visions" identified are "a collage of hopes for the future of church education." The topics of study include human concerns, concerns of the church, aims of church education, designing church education, various participants in learning, various congregations and parishes, models and methods of learning, settings for learning, leaders and leadership, and resources for learning. These topics are being investigated in detail by consultants, and monographs for study are being published. In addition, an "Education Futures Exchange" has been set up to promote dialogue among Christian educators on these matters. The result, in time, should be specific changes in curriculum and program, based upon good theory and shared experience and experiment.

Areas for Research and Study

What are the trends and needs in the present that should be developed through research and study, to the end that curriculum may be more functionally designed and effectively used? The United Methodist "Education Futures" study has identified a number of these areas; Joint Educational Development is working along these same lines; Moran and Lee have significant suggestions. Here, five areas are emphasized.

A difficulty in curriculum in the past has been that it is often designed at the top, to be used locally, yet without enough attention to effective communication. Participatory planning processes such as those used in the educational plan of the Church of the Brethren, centering in local curriculum planning but using a library of recommended materials—can be used effectively in curriculum development so that those whose responsibility it is to use curriculum plans are in on the making of those plans.

In the next decade millions of children and young people must be won to and become committed and active members of the Christian church. Christian education is essential to this if persons are to be intelligent and effective members. This is nothing new; it has been true for centuries. What is new is the urgency for decision on how this may take place in light of contemporary problems and possibilities. At this point curriculum plans have to come to grips with the questions of effective socialization and freedom and authority. This has been begun, but it needs to be fostered vigorously and decisively.

At the same time, the question of relevance is vital. The curriculum should reflect the needs and concerns that are felt by contemporary learners; it should also raise questions and press issues that are critical. Continuing studies are required to make these specific. Technical research is also required in the production of curriculum material so that the time lag between the emergence of a concern and its effective incorporation in the curriculum may be cut down.

To add to the knowledge of human development so that promising decisions on curriculum sequence may be made, studies in certain developmental areas are needed. The work of James W. Fowler III of the Harvard Divinity School on stages in faith development (stimulated in part by Kohlberg's study of stages in moral development) is indicative of what is needed.

A great many key concerns in curriculum development may be suggested by the term *alternative futures.* Through the exploration of alternative futures the general educator is beginning to be able to sift through past experience and projected innovations, to arrive at practical decisions on educational and curricular change. Christian educators are beginning to learn how to cooperate in this process and use it for themselves. The other option—which could become disastrous —would be to back into the future haphazardly and without plan.

Bibliography

The Church's Educational Ministry: A Curriculum Plan. St. Louis: Bethany Press, 1965. A total curriculum plan from which denominations, and conceivably local parishes, might build specific curriculum plans. A thorough analysis of curriculum design in theoretical terms (covering objective, scope, context, learning tasks, and organizing principle). Existential "areas" are delineated, each involving experience with all the elements of the scope. The areas are broken down by themes which are developed in detail for four age groups in terms of essential experiences, readiness, learning tasks, and possible achievements. Guidance is provided on administration and on the development of specific teaching-learning units.

Colson, Howard P., and Rigdon, Raymond M. *Understanding Your Church's Curriculum.* Nashville: Broadman Press, 1969. A general introduction to new developments in Protestant curriculum, with special reference to Southern Baptist curriculum. It includes broad theoretical and comparative material on the Cooperative Curriculum Project and discusses the rationale for Southern Baptist decisions of curriculum design. Strategic help for local churches is provided.

Evaluative Reviews of Religion Textbooks. Washington, D. C.: Department of Education, U. S. Catholic Conference, 1971. Analytical and critical reviews of twenty-five sets of religious education curriculum materials produced for Roman Catholic use. Included are detailed descriptions and criticisms, both objective and personal, of the content and method of each series.

Hyman, Ronald T., ed. *Approaches in Curriculum.* Englewood Cliffs, N. J.: Prentice-Hall, 1973. This symposium provides representative selections of eleven different approaches to the curriculum, from Dewey to the new humanistic emphasis. For the person trying to see what the curriculum alternatives are, this might be the place to start.

Lee, James Michael. *The Shape of Religious Instruction.* Dayton: Pflaum Press, 1971. Pressing for a "social-science" approach to religious instruction, the attempt is "to work out the principles of formulation, methodology of study, scope of content, direction of activity, and evaluative-corrective norms (for religious instruction), all within a broad framework of a systematized, taxonomic set of principles and procedures." These principles and procedures are further delineated in Lee's *The Flow of Religious Instruction* (Dayton: Pflaum Press, 1973). Third volume in the series is *The Content of Religious Instruction* (Dayton: Pflaum Press, 1975).

Moran, Gabriel. *Design for Religion: Toward Ecumenical Education.* New York: Herder and Herder, 1970. Incisive thinking on theology and education, leading to the conclusion that traditional religious education has actually lacked the essential religious quality and that, henceforth, it must be set firmly in an ecumenical framework, that is, with a concern for all that is human. The curriculum is redesigned in light of this principle, particularly with the parochial school and adult education in mind.

Phenix, Philip H. *Realms of Meaning: A Philosophy of the Curriculum for General Education.* New York: McGraw-Hill Book Co., 1964. The task of the curriculum of general education is to foster meaning in a world threatened by meaninglessness. There are six realms of meaning, each a disciplined way of knowing, all to be represented in the curriculum: symbolics (language and mathematics), empirics (the sciences), esthetics (music, literature, the arts), synnoetics (I-Thou), ethics, and synoptics (history, religion, philosophy). In light of this position, solutions to the technical problems of curriculum (scope, sequence, etc.) are suggested.

Schaefer, James R. *Program Planning for Adult Christian Education.* New York: Newman Press, 1972. The author presents a theory of Christian education and the curriculum worked out with breadth and precision, comparing a number of Protestant and Catholic approaches. The practical focus is on building a sound basis for adult work.

Tools of Curriculum Development for the Church's Educational Ministry. Anderson, Ind.: Warner Press, 1967. Contents are four curriculum-building aids: analysis (taxonomies) of motivations, methods, and appropriate outcomes; implications for leader development in the various curriculum areas; an outline of the teacher's character and role; and detailed suggestions of biblical materials basic to the various curriculum areas and themes.

NOTES

1. D. Campbell Wyckoff, "The Curriculum and the Church School," in Marvin J. Taylor, ed., *Religious Education: A Comprehensive Survey* (Nashville: Abingdon Press, 1960); Randolph Crump Miller, "The Objectives of Christian Education," and C. Ellis Nelson, "The Curriculum of Christian Education," in Marvin J. Taylor, ed., *An Introduction to Christian Education* (Nashville: Abingdon Press, 1966).

2. Published by the United Church of Christ and used by other denominations, January, 1968, through August, 1974.

3. Westerhoff, "Dear Ruth," *Colloquy* (March, 1972), p. 3.

4. Earl Gaulke, reporter, "Trends in Curriculum Development," *Religious Education* (March-April, 1973), pp. 233-34.

5. Union College Character Research Project, 10 Nott Terrace, Schenectady, N. Y. 12308.

6. Michael Leach, "The Future Came Yesterday," *Christian Century* (February 20, 1974), p. 202.

Chapter 12

THE STRUCTURE AND QUALITY OF CHURCH EDUCATION IN THE FUTURE

Robert L. Browning

A *systems approach* to church education may provide a guide to us for developing a church education adequate for our somewhat unpredictable future. Systems theory sounds and is somewhat complex. Yet its purpose is to provide clarity about overall objectives of a total system with careful identification of all subsystems involved in reaching objectives successfully. Each subsystem has unique and crucial functions to perform and standards of performance (quality) which make possible the reaching of objectives. Each subsystem has a basic structure which fits into the total structure in a dynamic but predictable way and makes it possible to reach the objectives desired and to do so with all persons, materials, methods, and time factors functioning in ways that are effective and personally rewarding. The human aspects cannot be overlooked.

To improve the quality of church education in the future calls for much more than the identification of individual problems—a better curriculum, new methods, better teacher preparation—or any one thing. It calls for consistency and high quality within several interrelated systems fundamental to church education. More especially, it calls for clarity and agreement about our central objectives. When we know where we are going, we can get all the subsystems working in line with these objectives. Moreover we need teams of persons who trust and respect one another to work cooperatively in each subsystem, persons who realize that evaluation of their effectiveness is normal and crucial in order to reach the objective. It is because of the systems approach that we were able to put men on the moon. The objective was clear. All subsystems—spaceship, rockets, propellant systems, communications, training systems, and management which put it all together—had to check out in relation to the objective.[1] The *quality* of the functioning of these systems was absolutely crucial. The way the systems meshed, the timing of the interaction were of

Robert L. Browning is William A. Chryst Professor of Christian Education at The Methodist Theological School in Ohio, Delaware, Ohio.

critical importance. Also anticipation of all possible problems and failures had to be faced and backup systems designed. Human frailty was anticipated through the use of simulation training and theoretical understanding so that the astronauts could think creatively and solve problems on the way.

Likewise in church education there are systems with certain basic structures and functions which can be brought together in order to achieve our objectives. Each subsystem must function in accordance with certain standards (quality) in order for the objectives of church education to be reached in an ongoing way—not mechanically, but personally—admitting our mistakes, making corrections, celebrating our meanings.

A systems approach tries to take advantage of all the knowledge we have from research and previous experience so that we do not repeat too many mistakes for which we already have workable answers. For instance, in relation to the future of church education we should base our work solidly upon what Jean Piaget calls an emerging "science of education." [2] We say *science* because there is now available a body of research findings and tested practice about the structures and capacities of persons in their mental and personality development, a body of findings about the basic structures of knowledge and how core ideas can be structured for persons at different age levels, a body of research concerning patterns of teaching and learning which are effective at different ages and stages of growth. Church education in the future cannot ignore these findings. Some of the key elements in the system and their interrelationships follow.

1. *The structure and quality of the development of the person*—from birth to death—the stages of mental and personality development which must be kept in perspective if we are able to communicate the faith without distortions and waste.
2. *The structure and quality of the core ideas and experiences* within the Christian faith which guide objectives and ground church education biblically, theologically, and historically.
3. *The structure and quality of the learning environment*—the way teachers, learners, resources, facilities, and methods are interrelated in order for persons to appropriate the Christian faith and relate it deeply to their lives in society.
4. *The structure and quality of local church educational planning,* which brings together needed persons, resources, training designs, evaluation procedures, and management systems for the local church.
5. *The structure and quality of general church curricular and program resources*—developing denominational and ecumenical curriculum materials, leadership patterns, in the light of clear objectives.
6. *The structure and quality of the church (local to international),*

the way the church speaks to or against objectives through its preaching, liturgy, building, budget, and actions in the community and the world.

7. *The structure and quality of overall society*—the values which come to us and are built into our governmental, educational, and legal institutions and their support or negation of our objectives.

I

The first three of these key elements are central. They are included to some degree in every approach to Christian education, although often not interrelated or balanced well. Some approaches have emphasized the child and his/her development as central and deemphasized biblical, theological, and historical grounding necessary for faithful response within the faith community. Other approaches have stressed the content of biblical faith but in ways insensitive to where persons were in their capacities to think about concepts to which they were being introduced. Other approaches have been enamored with new teaching methods and innovative learning patterns, often to the point of forgetting what the purposes were and sometimes not challenging persons to grow and make decisions about the Christian faith along the way. Any approach to church education which does not interrelate and balance these three systems and bring them together in realizing a central objective will be, to that degree, ineffective.

The fourth subsystem is crucial because it is the local church management system. These local educational planners help keep the first three systems interrelated and functioning well as they make plans, review materials and resources coming from various sources, evaluate the results of new learning environments, recruit and develop leaders who themselves understand persons, the core ideas, and experiences of the faith. Without this team of local leaders we will not know how well we have reached our objectives, where or when corrective measures are needed, and how church education is related to the local community and the whole life of the church. Also, with many more options for the curriculum and learning patterns, this group has many more decisions to make. While this is a heavy burden, here is where most denominations place primary responsibility. Composed of laity and clergy, it is something like a local board of education, with many of its strengths and pitfalls.

The fifth subsystem is the national program/curriculum system. By that I mean the curriculum materials, programs, and leadership patterns which provide both content and process guidance for local church education. The national committee tries to be responsible to the task of interrelating all of these key elements with clear attention to the nature and purpose of the church and the needs of wider society. After spending three or four weeks annually for eight years on such a body, I can testify that this representative group tried very hard to be clear about the objective of church education, responsible about the stages of development of persons, clear about the five core areas and experiences seen to be central to the Christian faith (as delineated by the Cooperative Curriculum Project), and how these could be interrelated well in the teaching-learning situation with persons at differing stages of development. In the future this task must be continued at a much higher level. Because of our increasing trust, and frankly also due to the high cost of developing, publishing, and training persons to employ new resources, we will increasingly be working ecumenically. Already we are doing this. Sixteen denominations worked together in the Cooperative Curriculum Project in planning the curriculum design which was the foundation of many of our present resources. However, each group tended to do its own publishing. We must also cooperate in joint publishing, with a wide range of optional resources available to local churches.

The sixth subsystem is the structure and quality of the church (local to international). Church education recognizes that there must be some consistency between what goes on in a classroom and what is happening in the whole life of the church. John Westerhoff has emphasized the great teaching power of the actions, budgets, rituals, preaching, building designs, attitudes of members, and outreach or lack of it. He calls it the socialization process in which there is a powerful hidden curriculum which reinforces (or undercuts) stated curricular aims.[3] The most powerful education is informal appropriation of values, attitudes, and understandings of what a Christian is and does, which comes through participation in the Christian community. Also, of great concern is whether or not children, youth, families, men, women, persons of different races, single persons, and older persons are *structured in* instead of *out* of these wider experiences.

The seventh element in the system is the structure and quality of society as a whole. It is a society in great pain and travail today. Its structures have been challenged, tested, changed in some cases, and under severe attack in others. It is a society which is communicating some values which accord with our Christian understanding of life and other values which are dehumanizing, sensate, even sick. Major issues about the quality of life (work, leisure, ecology, social justice, medical practices which extend life but cause new moral problems related to death) must be confronted by the Christian faith. In many ways the church gets a large part of its agenda from this wider social scene. Moreover, if we believe God is acting in the world today, we will look to these wider issues to discern God's creative, reconciling actions, point to them and celebrate them. Church education in the future must anticipate new issues and work with others to bring purpose and meaning into our common life.

One of the realities about this wider social setting is the prophecy by persons such as Robert M. Hutchins that we are going to move from a work- or fun-oriented society to a learning society. Changes will come so fast that learning will have to become a way of life. This means that increased leisure may be used to probe the deeper meaning of life, to find purpose in *being* as well as in *doing*. Futurists such as Harvard's Emmanuel Mesthene predict that persons in the future will hunger for a religious quality to their personal lives and a moral responsiveness to ethical dimensions of their faith.[4] This may mean that we will get much more support from the movements in society for learning in the church context than we have thought. In other words, any decision we reach about the direction of church education must be made in relation to these systems within a wider system. The systems must reinforce one another.

II

A closer look at the first three systems is now possible. Let us examine more fully the structure and quality of the development of the person. Fifty years of careful research by Jean Piaget and countless follow-up studies, including those of Jerome Bruner and his Harvard associates, reveal that within the first few days of life the child develops characteristic and unique structures within the mind by which he/she assimilates experience from the outside. The child is a very active learner from the beginning. The child's mind develops structures which are actively transforming and restructuring the experiences coming from the external world. This is done, says Piaget, in a way which consists in "an organization of reality, whether in act or thought, and not in simply making a copy of it."[5] A central finding then is that the mainspring of learning is the internal activity of the learner. The primary source of motivation for the learner is his/her internal state of equilibrium or disequilibrium. When the child is in a state of disequilibrium and is motivated, he/she learns very quickly what will bring equilibrium again. In the process he/she assimilates characteristic ways the mother responds, and his/her mind builds new structurations by accommodating itself to what has been assimilated. He/she moves from states of disequilibrium to equilibrium as he/she faces new problems and experiences fresh needs to grow and control the external world. This is the genesis of individual differences.

There are several characteristic stages in the development of the person. The following brief summary reflects the work of Piaget, Erik Erikson, and Ronald Goldman, a British religious educator who has applied this research to religious development. From birth to two years is a *sensory-motor stage.* It is characterized by reflex activity, first motor habits, the beginnings of perception, language, emotional fixations. The development of trust plus a feeling of trust via the parental relationship is crucial and is the seedbed of faithful responses to life. From two to seven may be called the *preoperational-intuitive stage.* Its elements are spontaneous interpersonal feelings; language development related to perceptions, since conceptualization remains quite limited; intuitive behavior; egocentricity; religious thought tending to be prereligious. Goldman suggests that this lasts in reference to religion in most children to nine years. Ages seven to eleven might be called the *concrete operational stage.* Mental operations are possible when related to concrete experiences; the child can check the accuracy of his/her thought in relation to objects, does not think abstractly very well, moves out socially, developing self-consciousness and self-confidence based on skills attained. This is still a subreligious stage, tending toward anthropomorphism. Ages eleven/twelve to adulthood are called the *formal operational stage;* included are the formation of personality of the affective and entry via intellect into the society of adults. Characteristics include the ability to translate concrete operations into propositions, make logical connections; and do symbolic thinking.[6]

Goldman tested Piaget's work with respect to religious education and discovered that there may be an even greater lag in religious thinking than in general thinking capacity. Intuitive, preoperational thinking about religion lasts for some children until age nine. He calls this "prereligious" because the child's thinking is anamistic, fantasy oriented, and highly egocentric. Ideas about God, Jesus, or the Holy Spirit are only intuitively received and cannot really lead to faith responses in a transcendent God but rather to faith responses to parents and teachers who become Godlike to the child. As Kierkegaard painfully discovered, he had to be weaned from his dependency upon his father in order to surrender himself to God. While this autonomous decision is appropriate for the adolescent period, many youth and adults as well do not seem to have reached this formal stage of thought because they are emotionally tied to securities which are related to their previous experiences in early or middle childhood.

While Piaget's stages of development are somewhat controversial, there is little disagreement that we should base religious education on a solid understanding of the structures of mental and emotional development from stage to stage. In the light of this research it becomes crucial for methods and learning to be *individualized* in relation to where individual learners are in their growth; *interactive* in terms of socialization and testing of learnings with others; and *active,* since learning proceeds best when the learner is invited to act on the learnings being undertaken. Although religious education has utilized learning-by-doing quite often, frequently the activities are not inquiry or discovery oriented and do not really open up core ideas or relationships basic to the Christian faith. Furthermore, often persons do not reflect on the meaning of the discovery and seek to order their lives in accordance with this meaning. Activity which is dumb and merely time filling is not what Piaget and Bruner propose.

Bruner identified three levels of learning: *enactive,* as discussed above; *iconic,* communicating through visual images; and *symbolic*— use of verbal symbols and signs to point to abstract meanings. All three are important at each development stage, but each stage will emphasize a different one.[7] Young children need the enactive, using their own bodies through play. Use of pictures and visual images (iconic), while helpful, is less effective, unless the pictures have been created by the children. The young child cannot translate the concepts portrayed visually nearly as well as he/she can discover meaning through the manipulation of the environment. Therefore to teach through lecture or catechetical propositions and right answers is really contrary to all that we know about how young children learn. Even older children are unable to deal with symbolic approaches which employ hypotheses and methods which rely on abstract concepts or propositional truth. Thus those in the seven/eleven category are usually not ready for educational methods beginning with statements of truth and concluding with processes of proof, whether mathematical or theological. Persons in the formal operational stage can be taught effectively with symbolic, abstract methods. However, most youth and many adults learn much better if they first experience a core idea enactively or iconically. The level of symbolism is very important, because it allows persons to move beyond literalization and concretization of ideas and increases the ability to think without having to manipulate the objects for which the symbols stand. Persons working in the vast worlds of mathematics, biology, philosophy, linguistics, and theology are dependent upon the power of symbolization to forward their thought and apply their insights to concrete situations. Piaget reminds us well that the learner will be internally very active as he/she progresses from intuitive preoperational through concrete operational to formal operational symbolic thought. Becoming a faithful, loving, just person is certainly not only the result of thinking. It is also caught in a faithful, loving, just community. Yet, sensitivity to the ways persons think is also important to a mature faith that can sustain persons throughout life.

III

Now, on to discussion of the structure and quality of the core ideas and the Christian faith. For a long time we have thought about teaching in terms of collecting and selecting a great deal of information for transmission to students. Now we know that this approach is rather costly in terms of freeing the intelligence to understand and interrelate the various aspects of knowledge. Jerome Bruner has been the chief American proponent of an alternative methodology. It emphasizes the structuring of a discipline so that its internal relationships, principles, and basic ideas are arranged clearly and in sequential steps that are consistent and can be discovered through inquiry by students at different stages of development and experience. He thinks that the structures of a subject are important because the discovery of the basic relationships and the resultant grasp of basic principles can be transferred to new learning situations later. To grasp a *fundamental idea* makes a subject more comprehensible. In addition to learning fundamental ideas, emphasis on the structuring of a subject aids human memory. "Unless detail is placed into a structural pattern, it is rapidly forgotten." Also, by focusing on the structures of a discipline in terms of both basic principles and relationships within the discipline as a whole, including what the most advanced thinkers and latest research present, we are then better able to find a consistent and meaningful sequence of learning for persons at different places in their mental development. By being clear about the structure of a discipline, various core ideas and relationships can be explored by learners in accord with a spiral theory of curriculum whereby Bruner believes that "any subject can be taught effectively in some intellectually honest form to any child of any stage of development." [8] To become clear about these structures is just as important as one's ability to communicate with the learner and get inside the way the learner views things and acts upon and transforms the core idea for his own experience.

In the area of religious education it seems imperative that we become much more conscious of and define much more precisely the core ideas, basic understandings, and relationships which our best minds conceive to be fundamental to the Christian life and beliefs and their relationship to actions and attitudes. Then we must discern what consistent understandings, facts, ideas, and attitudes most appropriately can be discovered and internalized by children, youth, and adults at various ages and in varying life situations. These core ideas and attitudes can then be put into a spiral of learning experiences appropriate to the internal structures within the learner's mind and in relation to his personal and affective life within the family and the community of believers.

IV

Structuring high-quality learning environments is the next task. Quality learning environments can result only when we keep in mind what we are trying to accomplish, who the learner is, and what resources, methods, and facilities teachers and students need to discover afresh the meanings intended. Frustration and disappointment inevitably follow decisions to try new methods or materials without regard for objectives. Too often we hear, "We have a learning-center approach this summer." When asked, "What are your purposes?" often only a long pause is the answer.

Clarity of learning objectives is a prior issue. If, for instance, our goal is to develop persons capable of telling others in what ways they center their lives around values/commitments reflected in Christ's life, we must be concerned about where each person is in his/her pilgrimage of faith. This calls for individual attention and sensitive nurture. It also requires teachers knowledgeable in ways for helping persons identify where they are in relation to the central ideas and experiences of the faith. If one of our goals is to equip persons to become conscious members of the Body of Christ in corporate ministry/mission, we are called to structure learning environments which bring persons into depth relationships with one another and the wider community. We can neither affirm individualization nor community at the expense of the other. There are values in both which must be discerned and sustained. Today when some youth don't want to identify with the church youth group, we tend to write them off as having let down themselves, the church, and God! Quite often their resistance is fully justified. There must be alternative ways for them to grow and serve. I believe that we have quite literally lost thousands of youth because of our limited ways of relating to persons. The issue should be "Where are you in your pilgrimage?" Where can we work with you? How can you participate in the community of faith?" It should not only be "Will you come to youth group next Sunday evening?"

If we are to work closely with individuals and help them to relate to and affirm the church in its ministry, several changes will be necessary. We will require an increasingly rich bank of well-designed, theologically sound learning resources which are capable of meeting the needs of individuals at different places in their development. For every possible learning interest there is some potential activity with which the child can interact until he or she has mastered the learning. Without a rich bank of resources, individualization is defeated at the outset. Learning modules (books, tapes, experiences) must be designed and produced for those who are ready for them. We will need a new view of the teacher who, while competent, is still a learner; one who is trained to relate to individuals within a group; who has learned to plan group experiences which move persons toward overall objectives while at the same time helping individuals discover their strengths/needs and plan their own learning goals/activities. Thus the teacher becomes a knowledgeable facilitator of learning rather than an information giver. Teaching teams make possible more careful work, balancing individual attention with group communication.

We will also need a view of the learning arrangements which make possible the interaction of all elements in the system. If we move in the direction of open classrooms/ungraded learning pods/ learning center approaches/intergenerational groups/family clusters/ learning at home, etc., let us have sound reasons for doing it. Temporarily "turning people on" is surely inadequate. Whatever we do must have clear objectives which relate the core ideas/experiences to the persons involved (their mental and personality development) and to the wider values and commitments of the church.

Both teachers and students will also need a much higher expectation of learners. Some teachers expect very little, especially in church education. Yet it is clear that children who are goal oriented and have future-focused images of themselves have much higher expectations. Benjamin Singer in *Learning for Tomorrow* says that we should be helping children to project themselves into the future, to go beyond the "now" education. In his research, students without this future-focused image tend to get lost in peer-dominated activities and develop "behavior which is self-destructive as well as socially harmful."[9] Within reason a future focus appears to promote personal health and to help persons have higher expectations (if grounded in reality). What is true for persons is also true for institutions. Scientific studies of teaching procedures and teacher attitudes reveal a major block in the minds of most teachers concerning the ability of their students to learn. Most have much too low expectations. Research provides convincing evidence that 95 percent of learners can be expected to have the learning capacities for the tasks before them, rather than the 15–20 percent we tend to expect. This is true, provided instruction is individualized, personalized, and the learners have available the time needed for mastery. Benjamin S. Bloom's research was on public school education, but his findings have deep meaning for church education as well. Both teachers and students normally assume that learners fall into three groups: a large group of average achievement; a small group who will master the learning; and another small group who will do poorly. It is the normal bell-shaped curve. This is often the pattern of achievement in group teaching contexts where all students are provided exactly the same instruction. If the teaching is individualized and personalized in relation to the learning patterns of particular students and the student is brought into the objectives for the learning along with the teacher, and the student is given the time he/she needs to master the subject in a supportive environment where feedback is given quickly and the student can make corrections soon, 90–95 percent of the learners can *master* most subjects, with some variation in terms of special talents or special limitations.[10] Research has discovered that only 5 percent have special intellectual gifts, and 5 percent have genuine intellectual difficulty. This means that 95 percent can master a subject (to 90 percent accuracy). Of course the time factors are much greater when the learning is more advanced and the learner has had a poor learning history and a poor self-image concerning his ability to learn. Also, gifted students can learn in much less time than we often assume.

The research also says some things of great significance about what this higher expectation does to the student. Those who master learning tasks tend to develop a positive regard for the subject they have mastered. We can stand positive regard for Christian content on the part of more students. To do well in a subject tends to open up other questions and encourages students to further exploration of the subject. Students desire some control over their environment, and the mastery of a learning task gives them just such a feeling. Students are motivated to learn more because of positive regard for the subject and even more by the positive regard for themselves which they get by public affirmation received for mastery of learning and the objective indications derived therefrom that they are developing persons. Church education has been plagued with an image of persons who have spent twelve to twenty years in church schools and know very little about their beliefs, very little about the biblical sources of their faith, very little about the church's history and the major personalities who have influenced them.

We now have increasingly proven ways to help children, youth, and adults identify where they are in their knowledge, understandings, attitudes, and skills, and also where they need to grow. Moreover, we have approaches to learning through a combination of group and individual instruction in which students can come to master learning tasks appropriate to their mental development and to their self-development. Bloom and his associates have tried many patterns, from one-to-one tutorials to nongraded patterns in which students move at their own pace with different tracks or streams, to regular group instruction being supplemented by diagnostic procedures and alternative instructional methods and materials, geared to individual differences in the group. The most functional for church education is a group instruction base with individual options. With this pattern the teachers were able to increase their effectiveness so that 90 percent of the students were able to master the subject instead of the 20 percent achievement when everyone has the same instruction.

A rich bank of learning resources, prepared with interesting and engaging formats (from carefully identified reading materials, tapes and slides, films, video tapes, games, person-to-person contacts including lecture/discussion), all can be employed to improve the quality of church education provided we have clear objectives, a good management team, and effective ways to evaluate where persons are. This means that national program/curriculum resources will have to be designed to support individualization and personalization along with group communication and group consciousness.

The crucial issue in the attempt to structure higher quality individual and group learning experiences is *evaluation*. It is impossible to individualize and personalize learning without providing ways to evaluate the differing levels of knowledge, understanding, attitudes, and abilities present in the group members. Most of our evaluation has been informal and oral. We have wanted to know if the learners liked the class session, if they reacted vigorously to the discussions, if they read the materials. We have avoided testing approaches because they would be too much like school! Our views of evaluation must be changed if we are to help individuals know where they are in their understandings of the faith and themselves. The church is really fortunate in this respect. As a voluntary organization it does not provide reward or punishment in the form of grades. A pretest can be interpreted as a way for students to discover what they really understand and what their needs actually are. This discovery by itself has some power of motivation. A posttest, or "evaluation points along the way," provides immediate feedback which again motivates, encourages, corrects, and eventually leads to mastery of the learning task. It also leads to a more positive regard for the subject as well as more positive regard of the learners for themselves as persons. Of course, evaluation must also be focused on our honest assessment of our corporate, relational life and the quality of our realization of the purposes of the faith community.

Recently I studied several new approaches to learning—self-instruction, individualized instruction, open classroom, learning center and learning pad, programmed instruction, and education through technology. In all these newer patterns there is the danger of following the individual's agenda into a series of cafeteria-like learning experiences geared too much to the whims of student or teacher; or developing learning centers or resource books which are not clearly related to the core ideas and experiences being communicated; or developing learning experiences which "turn on" students rather than challenge them to mastery. The only effective structuring of group or individual learning is that which is tied directly to clear objectives which focus solidly on core ideas and experiences. It must utilize ongoing instruments and procedures for evaluating student achievement, problems, attitudes, and growing self-understanding. When the evaluation is effective, the newer approaches to learning environments can be of a high quality.

These facts all present a very great challenge to church education in the immediate future. Already many churches are experimenting with alternatives to the graded Sunday church school. They are moving to learning center, intergenerational grouping, family cluster, home communications center, house-church patterns, and individualized approaches via cassettes and guides. These efforts are often exciting, but also eventually disappointing unless they are a part of an overall system of church education which has clear purposes, sound concern for the structures of persons' development, deliberate concern for the structure and quality of the core ideas and experiences of the faith —and means to evaluate whether the new approaches are actually helping persons to become knowledgeable, faithful, competent Christians as individuals and committed members of the Body of Christ in corporate ministry.

NOTES

1. C. West Churchman, *The Systems Approach* (New York: Dell Books, 1969), pp. 6-7.
2. Jean Piaget, *The Science of Education and the Psychology of the Child* (New York: Orion Press, 1970).
3. Westerhoff, *Colloquy in Christian Education* (Philadelphia: Pilgrim Press, 1973), pp. 80-90.
4. Emmanuel G. Mesthene, "Technology and Humanistic Values," in *Technology, Human Values, and Leisure,* Max Kaplan and Phillip Bosserman, eds. (Nashville: Abingdon Press, 1971), pp. 54-56.
5. Piaget, *The Science of Education,* p. 29.
6. See Erikson, *Identity: Youth and Crisis* (New York: W. W. Norton & Co., 1968); Goldman, *Religious Thinking from Childhood to Adolescence* (New York: The Seabury Press, 1964); Piaget, *The Child and Reality* (New York: Grossman Publishers, 1973); see also chapters 4 and 5 in this volume in which developmental theory is discussed.
7. Jerome Bruner, *Toward a Theory of Instruction* (Cambridge: Belknap Press, 1966).
8. Bruner, *The Process of Education* (Cambridge: Harvard University Press, 1960), pp. 24, 33.
9. Singer, "The Future-Focused Role Image," in *Learning for Tomorrow,* Alvin Toffler, ed. (New York: Random House, 1974), p. 27.
10. Bloom, *Evaluation Comment* (Los Angeles: The Center for the Study of Evaluation of Instructional Programs, University of California at Los Angeles, 1968), pp. 2-3.

Chapter 13

SIMULATION-GAMES THEORY AND PRACTICE IN RELIGIOUS EDUCATION

Paul M. Dietterich

There has been an explosion of educational simulation games. In 1960 only eight educational simulation games were copyrighted. By 1973, Zuckerman and Horn's *Guide to Simulations/Games for Education and Training* listed more than six hundred. Churches have contributed to this explosion. Church curriculum writers invent and/or refer teachers in local churches to educational games for use in church school classes, vacation church schools, summer camps, and conferences. Games have been invented for use by pastors and church administrative leaders. In 1970 Dr. Martha Leypoldt of Eastern Baptist Seminary in Philadelphia made a survey for the Association of Professors of Religious Education and received reports of a surprising array of simulation games being used in theological education. The churches are obviously beginning to make wide use of this educational innovation.

Educational simulation games have come out of two different theoretical traditions.

1. A *simulation,* broadly defined, is a "condensed representation of reality, a simplified model of a real-world system." A simulation has adequate detail and includes quantitative fidelity to the dynamic behavior of the system. A system could be, to name a few, a vehicle, a social process, an organization, or a group. In the last two decades— or mainly since World War II—modeling has most often been done by computers programmed to provide solutions to the basic mathematical equations describing the behavior of the system being simulated. The computer is then said to *simulate* the system, and the computer and its program constitute a *simulation.*

Simulation makes it possible to work with and draw useful conclusions from one system, usually a computer, instead of another less tractable system. Simulation is often the most effective way of testing a system, far preferable to having the system itself be the testing

---

Paul M. Dietterich is Co-Director of the Center for Parish Development in Naperville, Illinois.

ground. For instance, simulation has been used to predict the runaway behavior of a nuclear reactor, violent maneuvering or crashing of a vehicle, the consequences of subjecting a human body to intolerable environmental or internal physiological conditions, the effects of imposing a drastic change of policy upon the management of a company, the effects of wind conditions on airplane wings in a wind tunnel, and the long-term results of introducing large amounts of radioisotopes into a populated region. A well-known simulation is *World Dynamics,* developed by Jay W. Forrester of Massachusetts Institute of Technology. This simulation attempts to show how the behavior of large systems results from an interplay of demographic, industrial, and agricultural subsystems. It is a way of enabling several diverse disciplines needed for problem-solving to have a precise representation of what they are talking about. *World Dynamics* was used as the basis for *The Limits to Growth* study.[1]

During the last two decades there has occurred a remarkable increase in the variety of systems which have been simulated successfully and an even more remarkable improvement in the computers which became available for simulation. From the Link Trainer, there evolved more elaborate and realistic man-in-loop flight-simulation equipment, including G-seats to produce actual motion of the pilot. Trainers have been developed for automobile drivers, industrial process operators, submarine helmsmen, and other human operators. Similar equipment has been developed for engineering purposes. Through television, the general public has become aware of the use of simulation for training astronauts and for presenting simulated docking and other space maneuvers. The use of analogue and digital computers for simulation of flight vehicles has spread likewise to other vehicles, to most industrial processes, structural dynamics, human physiology, watershed management, military operations, electrical systems, and an ever-growing variety of applications in the social sciences, politics, and economics. Simulation now accounts for several percent of the multibillion-dollar investment in computers and of the approximately three hundred-thousand persons who work with computers in the United States alone.

2. *Games* are characterized by reciprocal actions and reactions among at least partly independent entities having different objectives. "A game may be defined as any contest (play) among adversaries (players) operating under constraints (rules) for an objective (winning, victory, payoff)."[2]

At least three kinds of games have been identified:

1. *Showdown games:*   Each player exhibits his/her best physical or mental performance or

	luck without interference from any other player, and the results are compared. Examples include golf, track and field, poker, charades.
2. *Strategy games:*	Opposed players interfere with one another's exhibited performances. Examples include bridge, chess, checkers, boxing, wrestling.
3. *Combination games:*	Players use strategic exchanges preliminary to showdowns. Examples include football, soccer, hockey, basketball, baseball.[3]

Games perform many functions in people's lives, in addition to providing entertainment and exercise. Informal games of young children, for instance, appear to be important means for learning about life and experimenting with life. Jean Piaget, carefully observing children playing the game of marbles, has concluded that, for children, games are more than a caricature of life; they are an introduction to life. Through games, children are introduced to (1) the idea of rules which are imposed on all alike; (2) the idea of different roles; (3) the idea of aiding another person and of knowing that one can expect aid from another; (4) the idea of working toward a collective goal; and (5) investing oneself in a collectivity larger than self.[4]

Georg Simmel in his essay on sociability maintained that the games which people play over and over again are those which mirror important real-life situations or problems so that in playing a game a person can "practice" real life but without having to pay real-life consequences for his actions. Simmel believed that games are important because they help people actually "play" society. In fact, the reason people play games as if they are a matter of life and death is that games are in fact a model or simulation of real life.[5]

Educational simulation games combine these two different techniques: *simulation* with its creation of the key elements of the outside or future world, and *game structure* with rules of play and methods for determining winners. The result is players operating in a simulated environment, making decisions according to certain rules, filling certain roles or functions, in order to "win" in this environment.

There are many categories of simulation games. There are those which have been developed primarily for research purposes. Others have been created for projective analysis. Simulation games can be categorized as computerized and noncomputerized, scenario versus role-playing games, fictional versus historical, physical object-oriented with emphasis on objects to be manipulated versus people-oriented with the moves of people receiving most emphasis. Nearly all simulation games are based on the issues arising from the allocation of limited resources, the problem being how to divide the resources.

In the early years of creating and using educational simulation games, since one of the major goals of the creators was to facilitate the use of the games in schools, the emphasis was upon cognitive learning. The early research done by Project Simile of the Western Behavioral Sciences Institute explored the use of simulation games with social studies classes in junior and senior high schools. The High School Geography Project was another research effort to discover if and how simulation games increased the cognitive ability of the students studying high school geography. The Nova Academic Games Project conducted by Johns Hopkins University dealt with the integration of academic simulation games into the school curriculum and included evaluating the effectiveness of games in helping students comprehend, recall, analyze, and synthesize the subject matter.[6]

Many people recognized that simulation games could also be used for several other purposes: affective learning, developing skills (including negotiating and mathematical skills), values learnings, and insights into social systems (games which pluck a circumscribed arena out of social life, economics, politics, or business and attempt to reconstruct the major rules by which behavior in this arena is governed and the principal rewards that it holds for the real participants). The original emphasis upon cognitive learnings may have been caused by fear that emphasis upon other areas would not be accepted in school systems.

As a result of the rather skimpy research which was done in the early days of simulation-gaming, many gamers began to emphasize games as ways of increasing interest and motivating students to want to learn cognitive matters in other, more traditional ways. After all, anything with the name *game* attached to it should not be expected to "teach" anything! Boocock and Schild call this attitude "inverse puritanism." When they speak of *puritanism* they mean the belief that "learning is a very serious business; games are fun; therefore students cannot learn from games." This old-fashioned view still dominates curriculum committees in some public schools and churches leading people to draw the conclusion that games, like other new-fangled frills, have no place in education. "Inverse puritanism," on the other hand, asserts that schools ought to allow for play and games because they provide morale-building relaxation from the real (and inherently unpleasant) business of learning. But one should not expect children to learn anything from them. Boocock and Schild maintain that such thinking is erroneous. They believe that games in themselves teach, that players learn from their very participation in the game.[7]

Sprague and Shirts approach the problem of resistance to educational games from a different direction by examining the assumptions of traditional education. They assert that the main trouble with schooling in America is that it is designed to support information flow from adults to kids to produce learn*eds* instead of learn*ers*. "Given the rate of change in most important aspects of life, such a system will produce carriers of an obsolete culture, instead of viable, renewing individuals." They challenge the school establishment to accept other goals for education: (a) to help students become excited about learning, growing, and new experiences; (b) to assist them in learning how to learn; and (c) to provide learning resources and aids which fit the students' individual styles. "The test of success for an educational system is whether the learners are 'turned on' about learning, know how to learn, and are working with the best learning tools for them."[8] Educational simulation games, say Sprague and Shirts, can help people become these kinds of active, renewing learners.

Games Constitute a New Educational Technology

A purpose of simulation games is to help people enter the historical process as *subjects* who know and act and shape history rather than as *objects* which are known and acted upon. Most simulation games enroll people in the search for self-affirmation and in the struggle for humanization and overcoming alienation.

In traditional education the teacher is seen as an information bank, filled with ideas, concepts, and knowledge which can be imparted by teacher to student through classroom procedures which the teacher dominates. The teacher judges and evaluates students; rewards and punishes them according to their ability to "learn" the information; certifies them; selects the curriculum; determines the methods of instruction. Heavy emphasis is upon orderliness: courses, units of study, schedules, tidy classrooms. The educational systems of many schools and churches are run by a self-certifying group of adults, often for their own rather than the students' goals. The present system is designed to support information flow from adults to youth, teacher to student. The teachers themselves are products of a training program which is practically identical to the one they perpetuate.

Students are relatively uninvolved or at best inactively involved in much of classroom work. Only one person talks at a time; the others are to listen. In a word, in traditional education, the students are *objects* to be acted upon rather than *subjects* who know, act, and shape the historical process.

Educational simulation games are being introduced into this setting, carrying a very different educational technology, including—

1) the active and simultaneous participation of all students in the game;
2) the teacher in the role of aid and facilitator of the learning process rather than the judge;
3) the internal rather than external locus of rewards so that learners are motivated by identifying and achieving their own goals rather than the goals set by someone else;
4) the linking of the student to the outside world through the simulated environment which, by reproducing in the setting of the classroom a slice of the conditions of outside life, allows students to practice taking the kinds of roles and making the kinds of decisions which they will face outside the classroom.[9]

Simulation games provide a new technology. They provide a bridge between talk and action. Learners are provided with the opportunity to move from theory to practice, as they see it. After studying theory, through simulation games learners can actually try out their theory. Inconsistencies between words and action are likely to decrease when the simulation games have been used as a teaching method. Persons can make a rapid, effective transition from the point where they intellectually understand a new kind of group, social, or international behavior to the point where they act on the basis of their new understandings.

Simulation games provide a safe learning environment. In those simulation games where emphasis is on human behavior, persons can try out, without fear of punishment or failure, new forms of behavior. Since the person's role or function is being discussed and evaluated rather than his/her real-life behavior, she/he is more likely to feel free to experiment with new actions. Mistakes can become fodder for personal or systems improvement rather than threatening to be dangerous or costly errors. To this extent, the "not-for-keeps" atmosphere is unlike real life, although in a very positive way.

Simulation games make actual behavior available for study, analysis, and improvement. They are highly action-centered and provide learning members with a focused, common experience which they can talk about without falling into semantic traps. The group has immediately available data on human and structural relationships, data which are ordinarily rather difficult to collect.

Simulation games can be used at several stages of problem-solving and planning.

1) *Increasing insight into human relations situations.* Many human relations problems are made more complex because neither party to the situation can transcend his/her own private understanding of what is wrong. Failure to understand the perceptions and feelings of others almost inevitably leads to partial, distorted views and the deepening of problems. Simulation offers an excellent opportunity to "stand in another's shoes." Whether it is a model United Nations General Assembly which is being simulated or a one-to-one situation such as *Prisoner's Dilemma,* persons find themselves in circumstances which enable them to see a human situation from another's point of view.

2) *Diagnosing situations.* Students are helped through simulation games to differentiate themselves from their world. They are helped to objectify their own activity. They can begin to locate the seat of their decisions within themselves, in their relations with the world, and with others. They can begin to recognize the relationships among various aspects of their situation, a kind of systems analysis. Through simulation games, a complex situation can be made available for study and analysis. The complexity of human relations problems can be dramatized. A group can replay the situation in order to help people see vividly the complexity of the many different relationships. The group is helped to become more analytical in approach. Persons can begin to get in touch with power relationships and other political dynamics in their situation, an aspect of education that has been largely neglected or ignored.

3) *Pretesting solutions.* In problem-solving, many possible approaches for solution are usually identified. By making use of simulation games, often designed on the spot by group members, the validity of alternate solutions can be assessed before they are tried out in an actual situation.

4) *Practicing needed skills.* Simulation games are especially helpful after members of a learning group have a clear idea of what action is most likely to be effective in a situation but are still unsure of their ability to carry it out. The use of simulation games as a dry run can be very helpful in improving skills which are to be used in actual future situations.

People come to think of themselves as subjects, not objects. They become learn*ers,* not learn*eds.* They begin to develop the skills which will be essential in this world of rapid change.

Theoretical Assumptions

Simulation games grow out of some rather clear assumptions which are in sharp contrast to the assumptions made by many educators today. For the sake of emphasis, these assumptions are outlined below in crisp, abbreviated style. There are, of course, exceptions to all these generalizations, but even though stated in broad strokes, they are basically accurate.

A. *Assumptions about human motivation.* Many traditional educators make the following assumptions about the motivational forces that are at work in people:

1) Persons have an inherent dislike of learning and avoid it if they can.
2) Because humans are characterized by resistance to learning, most people must be coerced, controlled, directed, threatened with punishment in order to get them to put forth adequate effort toward the achievement of educational objectives.
3) The average human being prefers to be directed, wishes to avoid responsibility, has relatively little ambition, and wants security above all else.[10]

In contrast to these assumptions, educational simulation games consider persons as—

1) eager to learn. There is nothing more natural about human nature than learning and growing. People are directional; they want to grow. They do not need to be coaxed or bribed into learning if they can see that what is to be learned meets their goals for themselves and their needs at that moment;
2) need oriented. Human needs are organized in a series of levels. As soon as needs of one level are satisfied, persons immediately move to the next level. Beginning with basic physiological needs (food, rest, exercise, shelter, sex), persons move to the second level of safety needs (protection against danger, threat, deprivation). Once these needs are met, persons move toward meeting social needs (belonging, association, acceptance, giv-

ing and receiving friendship and love). Once these needs are satisfied, persons begin attempting to satisfy psychological needs (self-esteem, autonomy, achievement, competence). And when these needs are satisfied, persons move toward self-actualization (self-fulfillment, fully realized potential, continued self-development, being creative in the broadest sense). And when these needs are satisfied, persons continue to grow in their desire to know and understand;[11]

3) subjects, not objects. A person's vocation is to be a subject, to act upon and transform the world, and in so doing, to move toward ever new possibilities of fuller, richer life individually and collectively. Every person, no matter how ignorant and submerged in an oppressed condition, is capable of looking critically at the world, analyzing it, and making judgments about it.

B. *Assumptions about the future.* Many traditional educators make certain assumptions about the future which contribute to their understanding of the educational task:

1) The world is static and closed, a given reality which in the future will be much the same as it is right now.

2) In the future, the best procedure will be to adjust to the world, to accept it as it is.

3) Education in the future should be an instrument to indoctrinate persons into the logic of the system and increase conformity to it. Since we know what it is that persons need in order to thrive right now, we also know what it is that persons will need in order to thrive in the future: mathematics, science, English, social studies, and their particular theological interpretation.

In contrast to these assumptions, educational simulation games are based on the following assumptions about the future:

1) Change will be the constant. Almost every aspect of the physical and social world will follow a line approximating the exponential curve.

2) Jobs and work will change in form and quantity to such a degree that they will no longer be dependable means of alleviating our Protestant guilt or increasing our feelings of self-esteem and well-being.

3) Cybernation, the integration of computers and automatic

machines, will change our lives in many ways. Machines will do even more of the work that people used to do. Chances for dehumanization will increase.

4) Leisure time will be abundant. Long periods will be available for self-development and recreation. The other side of this will also be available: opportunities for boredom, ennui, and neurosis.

5) Much of our biological, physical, and social life will be controllable. "Personality-affecting drugs, weather control, laboratory creation of life, widespread understanding of human motivation will lead us to control important aspects of our future." [12]

6) Education in the future will become the practice of freedom, the means whereby persons deal critically with the reality of their world and discover how to transform it.

7) In order for people to thrive in the future, they will need to know how to learn, grow, change, and find new experiences. They will need capacities for self-renewal. They will need to have ways of clarifying their goals for themselves and for their world. They will need to know what strategies and tactics will enable them to live most joyously and effectively in the world.

8) A partnership will be created between teacher and student, both of them engaged in a process of problem-posing and problem-solving, co-intent upon seeing reality critically. They will begin to develop diagnostic, analytical skills to differentiate themselves from their world, capable of recognizing relationships among various aspects of their situation, a kind of systems analysis. They will get in touch with power relationships and other political dynamics in their situation. [13]

Educational simulation games begin to move the educational process in the direction of these assumptions about the future. Of course no one game does all this, but simulation games taken as a whole tend to demonstrate how the educational process of the future will operate.

Basic Elements in a Simulation Game

Although not all simulations will have all of these elements, most educational simulation games will have many of the following:

A scenario. A history or story is written up to the point where the participant takes over. The participant learns through the story how many points she/he has, her/his status, role as a citizen, legislator, pirate, etc. This is usually presented graphically. *Dangerous Parallel* presents its scenario with a sound and full-color filmstrip.[14] Most games introduce the scenario with readings. The scenario is like lining up the runners at the starting line, up to the point where the gun goes off and they take over and begin running the race.

Goals. The goals for the game must be clearly identified. Sometimes teams can define their own goals. As soon as the goals are accepted, the simulation game has begun. Goals must be real in the sense that they must overlap with goals of players. Realistic goals lead to realistic role-taking by the players. The more players can see that they will fulfill some of their own personal goals by playing the game, the more they will invest themselves in the experience.

Decision units. Every educational simulation game needs some kind of decision units, something that is valuable in the game and that leads to the game outcome. Sometimes it is play money or real money. Sometimes it is points or chips, votes, energy units, military units, time, space.

Consequences. The consequences are usually tied to the decisions which people make in the simulation game. Common consequences are economic advantage, luck, good management, highway construction, stock market rise, war stopped or started, social advantage, prestige, number of arrests, status in the community, personal growth, self-esteem, intellectual gain, political or other form of power.

Conflict. In most educational games, groups are set up with opposing interests and with a limited supply of the resources which the game considers valuable. Conflict may be between teams, between the individual and the system, between self and the community, between groups of teams, person with person, person with model. Opposing interests are established and the conditions are created in which people have wealth as their only goal, or else in games with a "double bind" with wealth and several other conflicting goals to keep players from going single-mindedly after any particular goal without suffering severe consequences.

Teams. Five or more persons in a group bring greater variety and make educational games more animated and exciting for players.

Sequencing. The best educational games have tempo, plot, style, timing, mood, conflict, pacing. (Creating an educational game is far more of an art form than a science.)

Feeling of open-endedness. It is important for players to have the feeling that the game is open-ended, that they are not in a closed, predetermined system. The more open-ended the game, the more the element of reality to it and the more the game contributes to helping players develop a futures-orientation and increase their problem-solving skills.

Use of chance. Chance as an element in games is easily abused. Some games use chance to handle all sorts of strange things. The game that uses chance should use it carefully so that even the use of chance is realistic. Chance as an element in an educational simulation game is a valid ingredient. We do not live in a surprise-free world. Many things occur by chance—a surprise chain of events, an unexpected and unplanned meeting of people, an accident, an assassination that makes serious changes in the course of history. Chance is realistic to use, but it must be used carefully for best effect.

How to Select a Game

In selecting simulation games for use in education, several questions need to be kept in mind:

(1) *What are the educational objectives for this group?*

Is the objective to promote the growth and development of the group as a learning community? If so, then a game should be selected which leads to those outcomes.

Is the objective to help group members increase skills in decision-making and planning? If so, then a game should be selected which will enable the group to get some immediate feedback on its decisions and plans.

Is the goal to increase the group's substantive knowledge of a particular moment in history, say during an international food crisis or a national political crisis? If so, then the leader will want a game that enables students to get into the shoes of the persons who had to make decisions during those crises, to feel what they felt, to make the decisions that had to be made, to consider the options that were available, and to deal with the values at stake, all with a sense of urgency.

If I am interested in helping the group explore the meanings of certain biblical concepts such as "reconciliation," I might select a game in which there is alienation and the possibility of reconciliation.

The educational objectives must be clearly in mind before selecting the game.

(2) *Who is the game for?*

Games have been created for persons of different ages and skills. They should be selected on the basis of the group that will use it.

(3) *When will it be used?*

Some games take approximately fifteen minutes. Others take more than a week to play. It is important to have the time parameters clearly in mind before selecting a game.

(4) *How many people can play it?*

Some games are for four players. Others can be used by more than two hundred people. Others are created especially for classroom use. Select a game that fits your group.

(5) *How flexible is the game?*

Flexibility is important in most games. Can the game be played in part as well as in full and the participants still get important learnings from it? Is it an analogue game that permits persons to put different meanings into it? Can slight adaptations be made in it so that it emphasizes the kinds of things you need to have emphasized?

(6) *Does the game have a stimulating and realistic framework within which moral and political dilemmas can be played out?*

The artistry of the game designer is revealed in the answer to this question. The realism contributes to stimulating play. The dilemmas must be felt. They must not be overdrawn. It must relate to the concerns of the group and be the kind of game in which group members can become invested.

(7) *Will the game take you deeper into the area you are studying?*

Does the game bring something new to the group: new perspective, new information, new feelings, new opportunities to explore a situation or circumstance?

How to Use Games

Several steps can be followed in leading an educational simulation game. Games usually can be thought of as having four parts: introduction, play, debriefing, and reflection. Not listed here but certainly an important step in using any game is the leader's own preparation. Some games are quite simple to lead and take little preparation. Other games are quite complex so that the leader, to be effective, must prepare with great care.

a. *Introduction.* In introducing a simulation game to a group, it is helpful to mix explanation with group activity. As soon as possible, have the group begin to walk through the steps of the game. Some leaders like to begin a game by saying, "We're going to use a simulation game today to help us increase our skills. In order to play the game, we'll need five teams with six people per team. Take about thirty seconds to form your teams. Go!" Such an introduction immediately sets the tone for the rest of the game experience. People will be taking action with little information or direction from the teacher. In this illustration, the teams had to self-select, allowing for natural groupings of the class. From the outset, decision-making was in the hands of the learners.

Some leaders prefer to arrange the room ahead of time so that as people arrive they find that they are already seated in teams or at tables with certain materials spread out before them or in some other arrangement. The room itself and the "hardware" of the game catches the interest of the group immediately.

Some games require considerable reading of background material and learning of rules prior to playing. In some games it is possible to distribute the rules to a group the evening before the game is to be played and instruct players to study the rules so that the first round can begin without any further introduction as soon as the group meets the next day.

Depending upon the complexity of the game, as well as its objectives, the leader may need to give more or less help to the players in the introductory moments. Because games take off so rapidly, it is often helpful to the group to be as clear as possible about what they are expected to do, so some explanation is necessary—but avoid overdoing it.

b. *Play.* Many games are played in rounds. Such a design enables a teacher to use the technique of "stop action." Here the leader discusses with team members their behavior in the preceding round.

> "Why did you take this action?"
> "Why didn't you do that?"
> "What options do you see for yourself right now?"
> "What do you think other teams see as their options?"

Questions such as these can be asked to help people look at the ways their teams are making decisions. This often leads to more effective team functioning later in the game.

c. *Debriefing.* Debriefing is one of the more slippery aspects of using simulation games. Players become invested in their game, often taking roles in which they tend to feel quite comfortable. Some people become so comfortable in a role that they find it difficult to lay the role aside and return to themselves again. Depending upon the game, it may be useful for the group members to engage in a discussion of what it felt like to be in a particular role. By dealing with this question, players are helped to put some distance between themselves and their simulated role. This allows them to begin to put the role aside. Debriefing is often a process of de-roling. It is important to do, for it allows people to begin to objectify their game experience so that they can learn from it.

d. *Reflection.* Reflection is a touchy and dangerous time in the game process, and yet it is usually the most fruitful part of the entire experience. The purpose of the reflection period is to help participants identify their learnings and generalize upon them. Some forces may be operating in the group which will tend to block effective reflection from being done:

1) Participants are tired, physically and emotionally, from the game. This is especially true if they invested themselves in the game for several hours.

2) Some are embarrassed. They may not have played well or may be disappointed in their performance. They may have lost their cool or done something of which they are ashamed. In the heat of a game, players often surprise themselves with the amounts of their investment in the game and the exuberance of their play. I have seen Quakers resort to violence while playing *Starpower,* and clergy steal money in *Powerplay.* Some players were embarrassed or defensive about it. Others were only surprised.

3) Some are already working on some deep insights into themselves. These persons may try to participate in a reflection process, but in the middle of the game they receive some sharp insights into themselves which they need to work through, so they may appear to be withdrawn. They are actually working on some important inner concerns.

4) Some may be angry. The debriefing process was not sufficient for them and they feel that they have been ripped off or otherwise demeaned by other persons or teams. They are in pain because of this and may be sitting in the room, filled with anger and frustration.

The wise leader, therefore, can expect some things to occur in the reflection process. Some people may attack the game: "This was a lousy game!" Some may attack the leader: "You didn't give us enough help!" Some may withdraw. Some may have "died" in the game, not played well, and suffered some ego damage. In these cases the leader can accept the person's pain, but for the sake of clarity ask others in the group to share their perceptions of the game, saying, "I can see how you might feel like that, but I wonder how others saw it." This way the person can have his/her perceptions checked by others and be made aware of the divergent perceptions in the room. It is always helpful for persons to have their feelings accepted as being OK. Later they may be open to looking at the feelings which were generated by the game as a way of increasing their self-understanding.

Do not tell a group what they should have learned from a game. If the game is any good, they will tell one another *and you* what they have learned. All you will need to do is introduce the process that helps them categorize and organize their learnings. Everyone will have a story to tell about the game. Through small groups, mixing people up across the former teams, using group-on-group and other processes, players can have this important opportunity to tell their story.

A further step can be taken in the reflection process—theological reflection. Some persons see theological reflection as a work of rationalization, giving pseudotheological justification for doing what is decided upon or forced upon people, e.g., identifying a few Bible verses which appear to apply to certain actions. Such an understanding is inaccurate.

Theological reflection, if done well, enables persons to increase their ability to make theological meanings in the face of concrete social settings presented in the simulated situation.

In the process of theological reflection, the learner asks such questions as: "What does this special aspect of the human condition mean to us?" and "As vast and complex a social problem as this may be, how are we to respond to it in faith?" Such questions penetrate to the ultimate issues which are at stake in a given situation.

Three theological reflection steps may be used in reflecting on a simulation game.

The ethical task. Questions can be raised which deal with ultimate issues, enable people to explore meanings, and build social visions:

> "What ultimate issues are at stake in this situation?"
> "What are the quality and meaning of life to persons in this situation?"
> "What conditions might exist here?"

The symbolization task. The concern here is to help persons who are involved in efforts to change the social order form and reform their symbols and rituals. The process includes identifying the symbols of the faith which give meaning to experience and clarifying their meaning in a particular situation. For instance:

"What is the meaning of reconciliation in this situation?"
"What does the concept of redemption mean here?"
"What does liberation mean in these circumstances?"

The confessional task. Persons can identify, clarify, and own their personal commitment to changing the social order. They can face the question, "What is the nature of my commitment to changing the social order in this situation?" Such an approach as this leads to deepening one's understanding of the Christian faith and its demands upon those who follow it. It also leads to using simulation games as a way of increasing the theological depth of the players.

Some Issues in Using Simulation Games

The person making use of simulation games in religious education needs to be aware of and take into consideration at least the following three issues:

The reality issue. How "real" must an educational game be in order to justify its use in a learning situation? Critics of educational simulation games often stress the simulated nature of the process as a liability. A game may ignore, oversimplify, underemphasize, or overemphasize some factor in a complex social situation. The fear is that students will acquire an erroneous, naïve, or inadequate view of reality. The teacher, although intending to instruct, may actually mislead the students.

These fears are well founded. All simulation games oversimplify some aspects of reality. They are not reality, but simulations of it. Games are a caricature of social life.[15] This does not necessarily diminish their usefulness. Although the reality question needs to be faced, and although any person intent on using an educational game should examine carefully the assumptions that the game makes about reality, other important factors need to be considered:

(a) Is the game relevant for the study at hand? Do the key concepts of the game help persons learn the key concepts the leader wants them to learn?

(b) Can the game's departures from reality be used as a springboard for helping persons understand social processes by comparing the game with reality?

(c) Can the participants, after playing the game, redesign it to make it more "real"? Many game designers maintain that the best learnings about a subject are found in the process of designing a game rather than in only playing it. Through game design a group can engage in the process of building social theory.

The learning-unit issue. Very few simulation games are intended to be complete learning units. Most games need to be used in conjunction with additional resources—readings, discussions, lectures, films, interviews, etc. The teacher may make the mistake of assuming that a game stands alone and use it improperly.

In selecting a simulation game for group use, the teacher must recognize the need to build the game into a larger unit of study. Since games are fun to play, many leaders mistakenly assume that they are entertainment. They therefore select a game for use, say, on a given Sunday evening with a group of youth. There is little preparation for the game, little discussion of it except on the level of how much players "enjoyed" it; the game is not related to other deeper learnings, and several excellent learning opportunities are lost.

In contrast to this approach, a teacher should ask:

(a) What is it that I want this group to learn? What are my teaching-learning objectives?
(b) What different learning experiences will help the students achieve these objectives?
(c) If I decide to use a simulation game, how will it be used? With what other resources will it be used?
(d) What plans do I have for helping students enlarge on their learnings from the simulation game?

The values issue. All simulation games reflect the values of the game designer. Sometimes these values are implied, sometimes they are explicit. An important part of using any game is discovering and making explicit the values assumptions of the game designer.

It is possible for a group to identify and reflect on the designer's values. These values assumptions can be part of the learning process for the group. They can ask: "Do I share these values?" "What other values might I seek?" "Which values are most important to me?" Such questions lead into the process of ethical reflection mentioned above.

Since the church deals in values, a major contribution of simulation games can be in helping persons identify the values operating in the game and the values operating in real life. It is a mistake to use a simulation game and not take advantage of the opportunity it provides for identifying and dealing with values.

Educational simulation games are a useful innovation in education. If used with care and skill, they can contribute to the growth, empowerment, and development of persons and groups.

NOTES

1. Forrester, *World Dynamics* (Cambridge: Wright-Allen Press, 1971); D. H. Meadows et al., *The Limits to Growth* (New York: Universe Books).
2. Clark C. Abt, *Games for Learning,* Occasional Paper, no. 7, The Social Studies Curriculum Program (Cambridge: Educational Services, Inc., 1966).
3. *Ibid.*
4. See Piaget, *The Moral Judgment of The Child* (Glencoe, Ill.: The Free Press, 1948), and *Play, Dreams and Imitation in Childhood* (New York: W. W. Norton & Co., 1962).
5. Simmel, "Sociability: An Example of Pure, or Formal Sociology" in Kurt Wolff, ed., *The Sociology of Georg Simmel* (Glencoe, Ill.: The Free Press, 1950).
6. Hall T. Sprague and R. Garry Shirts, *Exploring Classroom Uses of Simulations,* Project Simile, Western Behavioral Sciences Institute (October, 1966); Alice Kaplan Gordon, *Games for Growth* (Palo Alto: Science Research Associates, 1970); Sarane S. Boocock et al., *Simulation Games Program: Annual Report* (Baltimore: Johns Hopkins Press, May, 1968).
7. A leading game designer, Clark C. Abt, even titled his book *Serious Games* (New York: Viking Press, 1970); Boocock and E. O. Schild, eds., *Simulation Games in Learning* (Beverly Hills: Sage Publications, 1968).
8. Sprague and Shirts, *Exploring Classroom Uses of Simulations; ibid.*
9. Boocock and Schild, *Simulation Games in Learning.*
10. Douglas McGregor, *The Human Side of Enterprise* (New York: McGraw-Hill Book Co., 1960).
11. A. H. Maslow, *Motivation and Personality* (New York: Harper & Brothers, 1954).
12. Sprague, *Changing Education in America* (Western Behavioral Sciences Institute, 1966).
13. Paulo Freire, *Pedagogy of the Oppressed* (New York: Herder and Herder, 1970).
14. Roger Mastrude, *Dangerous Parallel* (Chicago: Science Research Associates, 1968).
15. James S. Coleman, "Introduction: In Defense of Games," *American Behavioral Scientist,* vol. 10 (October, 1966).

Chapter 14

WORSHIP AS CELEBRATION AND NURTURE

Ross Snyder

Celebration and Education

"Really and truly" education always has within it celebration. First of all as a style of aliveness in which our effective world hums with the do-mi-sol triad of a tuning together of creation, covenant, and the coming of a not-yet and often-defeated kingdom.

In contrast, what often passes for "education" is a motley of people long dead in trivia, circling in a well-enclosed paddock, in careful control so that they will never change but only grow fatter and more stable, forever dismounting at the point they entered.

But to nurture and be nurtured is to:

Sing the Lord's song in an ever strange land
And walk with a truth that is ever before.

To nurture and be nurtured is to again and again improvise, from materials at hand, huts of meaning through which the stars can shine, where we and our neighbor-near can dwell celebratively in the midst of our sowing and cultivating and harvesting.

So if we ask Can there be nurture without abundance of meanings? the answer is no. Can we have nurture without celebrative flair? No. Can *human* beings even survive in families and institutions that are impoverished in appreciations and celebration?

Celebration Contains Indispensable Ways of Knowing

Religious celebration enlarges us in two ways of knowing often neglected both by persons and by our educational systems. The ultimate degradation of Christian education is to insist that its genius is fact-imparting, disconnected "happenings," trainings to be an instru-

Ross Snyder is Senior Professor at Chicago Theological Seminary, Chicago, Illinois.

ment that can manipulate one's-self and others in the clichés and habits of pop and establishment culture, frosted with the latest fad in "therapy."

Rather in celebration we are dealing with two fundamental ways of knowing. The expressive sensitivity of the poet-artist is one of these primordials. For it allows the othernesses of the world not to be afraid of revealing themselves to us. And how can we ever know a person unless he chooses over a period of time to reveal to us the architecture and expectancy which he is to himself? And by the keenest excitement of our imaginations together create the powerfully right symbol by which we can understand and build? Further we do not know what we see or think or can innovate until we have before us a work of our hands and mind—and all that happened while we were doing it. We discover only as we celebratively create.

To art is to clarify the architectonics and depths of what we are involved in, to intensify them, and to put them into significant form. Arting is to form compellingly fascinating worlds in which we live, and so is what meaningful work has always been. Expressive spontaneity which says and does the sensitively relevant, marks the art style of consciousness. So, also does a prevailing climate of appreciative consciousness. "Revelation as the meeting of event with appreciation" is a forming concept and style of religious celebration.

But, finally the heart of Christian education and our major contribution to civilization is the religious mode of knowing. But what is the religious mode of knowing? to intuitively approach all things from within a creative fidelity to the growth of an ecology of spirit in which we are all first-class citizens; to participate in this ecology, perhaps particularly through trials and tribulations; to utter a "nevertheless" to the world monstrosities even as they run over us; and thus know man's nature and destiny—"To this end was I born, and for this cause came I into the world, to bear witness to the truth." The religious mode of knowing is also the willingness to be birthed by the God "whom to serve is perfect freedom."

So a most important function of religious education is to emphasize these two ways of knowing—the knowing which distinguishes the poet-artist within each of us, the knowing which distinguishes the trothful mystic who risks beyond what he can presently prove and so pulls unexpected life out of the endless potential in which we live and move and have our being. These two modes of "knowledge of" rather than mere "knowledge about" should characterize the church.

If we developed with some completeness "worship as celebration and nurture," our churches could establish in many people the conviction that these two modes of knowing precede in importance and sequence all other modes of knowing, particularly since education is so much more than what we usually mean by *knowing*. Education is *a world becoming meaningfulized*. Education is persons emerging, persons participating at ever-fresh levels in the developmental enterprise of a span of life.

This *developmental* enterprise is what a church is about, what the Body of Christ is about. If generations of ministers who really believed this could be raised by their congregations and the theological seminaries of the country, religious celebration would be a potent sector of their ministry. And they would have an identity.

> We are the shapers of symbols
> That tell of the tuning man is
> The thirst for unrationed meaning
> The flair for celebrative life.

Celebration Is a Consummatory Phase of Every Complete Act

Characteristically, American educators have been concerned with experiencing, with the complete moral act. Every complete act has a consummatory phase. This fact has great grounding and implications for worship as celebration and nurture. The human mind is so constructed that, even while we are acting, some past memories and feelings are a part of the act. Every act also has "feed forward" content; a stretching toward some expectation, some momentary world in which some hope can be realized. Further, these residues from the past and valuings toward a future do not stay separate, they mix. These two also combine with our very immediate report of what is now happening to us. Thus, mating, they create a fresh world to be lived.

Such valuing is going on all the time, in every split second. At least, if the act is meaningful it is. But a completed act includes a period when this three-way mix and constructing of world is a period in itself. The action is over externally, but the internal flow of energy, of continuing discernment of the act's significant structure and the most desirable future we can now possibly project, keeps going on.

When all three time contents (past, present, future) cumulate, build an image greater than any of them, intensify one another to the speed of light, the act is in this consummatory phase. Shared with others, the act fills out into its celebrative phase. The crucial insight here is that the consummatory phase and the communal celebrative phase are not added on to action. They are *inherently part of the action.*

Without them the act is aborted; it never has a chance to become human. Its faint significance-stirrings in consciousness are lost, the act adds nothing to the riches and depth of our inner-personal region. For it is a nonpersonal act.

Some acts are more potent in felt significance than others, and it is these that we particularly invite to give birth to fresh meanings. And upon them we center our communal celebration and worship. Without such lived moments, experiences, events active within us while we talk and think and pray, our "worship" is wordy, abstract, nonpresent. And unless we bring the great words of our people into the consummation and celebration, we may leave our action trivialized, permanently immature, centered and bounded by our selfish self.

Time for consummatory "work," time for the flaming of spirit in celebration is often the most important part of an act. Particularly for those who live educationally, who nurture their experiences toward the developmental leap and the earth-filling chord of "Gloria in excelsis Deo." There are a number of time-honored religious forms of such consummations—healthy "conscience work," prayer, contemplation, meditation, expression in poetic imagery and memorable phrase, singing, witnessing, "hearing" a sermon, etc. Today we would add the "creative brooding" which, in silence and without determination, allows that which is struggling to be born from within and without, a chance to emerge in an inscape beauty.

Two further implications would seem to follow. Congregational worship moves more vigorously when a fairly large number of the worshipers have individually some personal competence in such creative and consummatory arts. The second is the centrality of lived moment as the ground of every celebrative worship. What if there is no act in motion to be completed with celebrative consummation? Then our words and songs and prayers are but pollutions of God's breath. Lived moment consummation would seem to be celebrations distinguishing character, particularly if we call it *contemporary* celebration—contemporary with the history-making of our time, contemporary with the boys and girls, men and women with whom we must somehow make a viable world, contemporary with Christ as God-in-the-world, and contemporary with the language with which we choose and value.

Dwelling—Indwelling

Again and again man builds lived space. He dwells in this meaning-fulized world in relationship with those who have helped create it with him, with those who "indwell" him.

Joyfully affirmed indwelling is therefore a major enabler of worship as celebration. *Dwelling* refers not just to a geographical location, but to a net of life in which we participate; not as a sojourner or stranger, but as one who intends it as home place "where none can make us afraid," where we *place* our life for a destiny. The celebration must help us discover such a participatively meaningful world of a size we can make good in. For "to dwell" is the given nature of human beings. To dwell with one another requires that we *in*dwell one another. That something of "where *we* live" is respectfully taken into other persons' consciousness and taken account of in their decisions and feelings and self-identity.

Religious celebration deepens our understanding of the indwelling that may happen. The second chapter of Ephesians declares to Christians, "You are no longer aliens in a foreign land, but . . . are being built with all the rest into a spiritual dwelling for God" (2:19-21 NEB).

We are to build a possible dwelling place (situation, meaningful joint world) for God. And if we do not joyfully will to do this, we handicap the coming of the Holy Spirit with enlivening power. To be either man or the Christian God, we must be "indwellers." And man must do his part to put together such a world—in particular, a gathered *congregation* as of that particular time.

What are some of our relevant actions in helping constitute a "dwelling for God?" "Total person" singing by all; strenuous and exultant praying; honest access to the inner speech of all present (and particularly some few of spontaneously fresh vitality who utter "speaking words," not borrowed and stale); a spreading conviction that we are all grasped by a common destiny, talk the same language, have intense experiences, inhabit together a clearing in a night *and* day wilderness that is at least partly colonized by us, filled with our yet-to-be-completed trails, tuned by the melodic line of our song and the bark of our anger. And in this our "meaningfulized" world, there is indestructible inner sanctuary, arenas of struggle in which we taste some victories, significant others who have preceded us and will follow. And they too "indwell" us and encompass us in an ecology of spirit.

With such events happening in a celebration, at times God surges with power and a consummation flares out of the very depths of our everydayness and despairs and half-triumphs. The great prayer of the Eucharist seems a possibility "that we may evermore dwell in him, and he in us." We know that we are an *expression* of something, not a self-referenced entity pervaded by the mediocrities of pleasure and circumstances. We are *spirit*.

175

Dwelling—"indwelling" is primordial for celebration. Let us give it the time it needs and not trivialize it with gimmicks.

The Kind of Theologizing We Find Ourselves Doing in Celebrative Worship

We are doing theologiz*ing*. Our understanding of what God and man have to do with each other is emergent. Theologizing is not an easy clamping down onto our live experience of categories previously finalized.

We theologize partly because we find ourselves needing a wide range of symbols and epic stories—perhaps more so than any previous generation. We are part of a worldwide search for new imaginative metaphors and concepts with which to organize life rather than death. And we do not wish to be tricked into the bad faith of seeming to give unearned assent to hereditary statements. The record of the past is not altogether positive support for its stock of religious symbols. And surely there are nuances and symbols yet to be formed by another generation of mankind. But chiefly we theologize because we are driven to do so by the day-to-day struggle to survive (though sometimes also by the startle of amplitude). If anyone hears the rustle of the coming of the fresh winds of God, let it be communicated—and in situation!

At celebration's best, we are doing *realization* theologizing, i.e., at some moment we become conscious—with unusual clarity and out of the story of our lives—of an inmost founding of our lives. Realization of what has been going on (the story within the obvious story) hits us sometimes with staggering force. Those who celebratively theologize are on journey in a precarious, yet many-potentialed world, focused in finding a yes to participate in. I find the energies of such people beginning to cluster around the term *spirit*.

Spirit

The term *spirit* brings with it an expectancy of quickening power, of glad thrusting and communicating beyond ourselves, of a truth that penetrates and discerns the false from the authentic, of the immediacy of presence and communion. *Spirit* is a particularly important idea for the reason that we apply the word to both God and man (though not to equate them). Therefore, we have expectation that there can be transmission of power, there can be communication and communion between the two. We are not so *wholly* other that God's nature is irrelevant to our lives, except as an external judge. Freedom and an ethic are both possible.

Spirit is life-forming, creative power, a burning to become. Spirit "makes live" humankind and gives rise to history and meaning. It is primeval in man in that out of it develops many powers so that it is not merely energetic power, but it becomes *wisdomed* power, a power *mighty in love*. Spirit moves us beyond the actual and holds the person together in the face of the slings and arrows of outrageous enemies.

By the religious person, spirit is felt as that within him which makes possible immediacy with other persons and with potentiality for being. And it is a participative immediacy, not a walled-off inwardness. In the Gospel of John we read, "'God is spirit, and those who worship him must worship in spirit and in truth'" (4:24 NEB).

God is spirit, and those who tune into his true nature will find themselves awakened into the activities we have been describing. Perhaps particularly as they wholeheartedly participate in religious communal celebration.

Ultimately, spirit is a corporate phenomenon, active in intersubjectivity. And the movement is into humankind worldwide, on into a transcendence of the wilderness of woe and threats which this world is. Spirit is the tremendous, fascinating numinous which shows through the veil of our consciousness in such a way that the deeply hidden is partly revealed.

God as spirit is suprapersonal, i.e., not less than a person, but certainly more than a person. We can speak of God only in metaphors —all of which are only partly adequate. He is transhistorical Depth, the Ur-Ground of our life pilgrimage, the ocean of Potential which emerges all that is, the Presence with which we commune. He is Shaping Power, but not a shape.

From time to time—in peak and in valley—we feel such a God as a flowing underground stream which the roots of our consciousness touch. Once in a while we hear news that there is a Power capable of handling the destructiveness and opportunities that keep coming at us in our moment on earth. The human scene is not only drought earth, of which I am a tumbling fragment.

In addition to understandings of God which come from heritage, long used and treasured, the mood in celebration today is to expect that from time to time each of us does his best to put together a statement compelling for us, in words and imagery memorable for us. So the other summer, as a wife and husband drove toward the west, they put together this address to God—cadenced by memories of the tune of a hymn a great-grandmother used to sing.

CHRISTIAN EDUCATION IN AN ERA OF CHANGE

> O God of our spirit
> Our joy and our fulfillment
> Whose service is freedom
> Enduring through time
>
> Our hope within struggle
> Our Spring in Weary Valley
> Our peace within tension
> The newness we seek.

Since the point of celebration is not idolatry, but participation in transformation, the Creator of the immense evolutionary journey into humankind lures us toward being little Christs to one another and our common world. Meister Eckhart stated it thus: God yearns the birthing within us which occurred at one point of time and will occur throughout time—the birth and growing up of a Christ.

In celebrative living, it is helpful to think of Christ as the transforming mode of being-in-the-world. Christ is a personal consciousness of such love and creativeness and overlap with God's spirit, that in particular situations it takes into itself the joy and agony, the good and evil of that situation. And in conjunction with others, that creativeness and love transforms the situation into new possibility which it makes manifest to those involved and, often in varying degrees, is crucified for it, but "resurrected" by its enduring troth to the God "whom to serve is perfect freedom." Such is the personal existence which we celebrate.

In understanding the functioning of Christ, we can also use the language of social psychology. For the Christian, Jesus Christ becomes the indwelling Significant Other, the personal consciousness with whom we carry on internal dialogue in the crisis and triumph events of our life. And in corporate celebration these three—Spirit, God, Christ—are the classic words and lived-moment realities which we encounter in Christian life. They point to otherness with which we must come to terms, which can endow us with energy and enable us to live with tenacity in the face of adversity so that we mature until, "come hell and high water, this is the life I choose to be. Even though powers of darkness do surround me to the point of invading me, for such a life has foundations."

We can possibly escape the arrogance and festering loneness of self-referenced "modern man" who feels that it is up to him to spread over the earth taking whatever he needs and then moving on to the next devastation and brutality, forming pseudomoralities out of his power to have dominion and Dionysian pleasures. We know now that this story is "played out."

For we live in its consequences. We are uncertain, frantically anxious, feeling that the hand of unknown "Everyman" is lifting against us. With the loss of sensing a founding Otherness, we point our "primal scream" in a direction from which no durational help can come.

Our salvation lies in Otherness with which we can intersubject. In a most immediate way we hunger for a group of people who believe in one another and in something together, who have symbols and ways of making sense out of life. Whatever we might name it to ourselves, we hunger for the body of Christ. Out of both deprivation and realization, we come to worship in order to re-experience first-class citizenship in such a life-giving body.

The Body of Christ

Why don't we just say *church* and be done with all this care about which symbols best express what we mean? Because church seems to be an institutional term rather than from the realm of spirit. Because having our name on the membership roll of a parish church is quite ambiguous in its meaning, it does not necessarily mean that we are members of an organismic corporateness. In contrast, *body* speaks of a "dwelling in." And finally we like to use the term in worship because the Body of Christ embraces more than the churchly organized. It is fatally easy to become a segregated and named elite rather than humankind.

Existing as Person

Having an *unusual* experience of being person (which includes theologizing about existing as human) is a significant worldishness of communal celebration. Most intimately, each of us has a special concern for our own "inner-personal" region. This above all, we are constantly sampling and liking or disliking. Its tone and quality and content is *us*. It is also our internal milieu. So we are concerned. Every worship service is filled with persons who are in some degree raising the question "How endure myself—just one more day—to be an aliveness? With a livable rather than a numbed internal milieu?"

Too often religion has emphasized in its worship mainly negative answers about the nature of "person," as if God were our enemy and all morality religiously originated is external and alien to man's fundamental makeup and so must be rebelled against before we can become adults. We have not done as much as needed on constructive theologizing for the artist and for the builders of civilization. We are still only in the beginning stages of considering—all over the world—everybody as person, and not just a select few. So a rushing momentum of establishing new discoveries of what that concretely means is called for. If people are to be liberated, into what freedom and fulness of being are they to liberate themselves? Which burgeoning potential of persons must the institutions of our society nurture and govern themselves by?

Hopefully, celebrative worship significantly practices us in the offering of the *creative* work of our minds and hands and in the respectful receiving of God's and fellowman's creations. Creative expression of significant form is one of celebration's generative themes. For God is concerned about a world, and not just our sins. Celebrative worship is a charter to do theoanthropologizing, discovering *simultaneously* the elemental nature of God and human being. Historically there has been no other kind.

Currently we need to work on "human potential." Is there a core in human beings that is trustworthy enough to bring off the good? Are all culture and culture norms a murdering of that good potential? Obviously, people as we know them have in them potential to murder and to maim, to lie (even to themselves), to deny guilt, to repress their impulses of concern for others, to drive insatiably to power over others, to demand that the world be directly controlled by their feelings and mindings, else they will throw a temper tantrum of terroristic dimensions. Just anything anybody feels like doing is no answer to the fundamental question we must work through if we are to be a communion and a civilization and bringer off of enterprises, rather than a surrealist anarchy.

If "spirit" is not the main answer to the nature of man, then what is? Or if it is, what total constellation of meaning and reality do we refer to when we say *spirit?*

Celebrative Worship Is Constituting and Experiencing a Religious Culture

Corporate celebration (at least implicitly) presents a total culture all put together in its most vivid essentials. In celebrative worship we learn more of what People we belong to and its distinctive ways of being in the world. We engage in a totalizing learning of its systems of meaning and modes of treasured existence. And partly to the degree we put ourselves into its making and ordering, and some of our lived moments into its content, we accept this world of meanings and vision as also our culture. It becomes indigenous in our interiority, and not just as bits and pieces, but as a livable whole, a whole which unites us with fellowman in history and world space and also in actual immediacy with those present in the celebrating congregation, so that (to borrow from George Herbert Mead) we have mind, self, and society.

So corporate religious celebration may well be the supreme art form of all art, a valuable mode of nurture, and an indispensable phase of education. In support of such a hypothesis, we can recall Whitehead's and others' insistence that effective learning is always learning *a whole,* rather than just isolated fragments. And Kurt Lewin's hypothesis that any learning which is to endure and be productive must be anchored in some fundamental social belonging. (To avoid the pitfalls against which the Hebrew prophets acted, however, we must keep clear that the whole which is to be learned is "meaningfulized world-to-live," and not merely the ritual which points to it.)

This view of celebration as presenting religious orientation all put together is in contrast to the mutilating and crippling which occurs when worship is interpreted as giving God the honor and praise which he craves, or as merely the place where our conscience pangs are forgiven, or where the exact ways of the past are perpetuated while the glory is hidden by accreted details. Using the word *celebration* rather than *worship* is one means of keeping alive connections with living experience and the present world-making activities of God. These connections and meanings cry out to be put into the most significant forms we too are capable of. Our best convictional arting must be offered and added to that of past believers. For in religious celebration we are about the development of a long-term culturing of humankind.

Looking now upon communal celebration from the standpoint of it as an occasion when the religious culture of our people is presented, enjoyed, developed, used as access to the immediacy of God, we are driven to ask What are the *components* of a culture? What is the full orb of any culture, not just some parts?

With insights answering such questions, we can understand better existing liturgies and worship services; we can focus and purify the materials used. We will be more able to participate and to create. We will have some outline of the next stage in the worship education of leaders of our congregation. For we would have a picture of the arenas of expression and invention which together could be a "celebrative arts lab" in which many people could participate, both for their own growth and our life together. We could have a guide to the range of materials they could create for cultivation of contemporary interiority.

In order to point these up most sharply, I am writing a statement of them in the form of—

Culture-Content Questions to Be Put to Every Celebration

1. What contemporary lived moment was made memorable . . . developed into *meaningfulized world-to-live* and religious conviction? Until everybody present understood it in about the same way? Partly because it established connections with a paradigm which has made us a people.

2. What spirit-awakening impact of "who my people is"—the stream of history-making, its distinctive symbols, my fresh membership in it?

3. What new structuring of time began to happen? A fresh imminence of a new future-past-present for some part of humankind. Its time has come and we are specially relevant to it.

4. What indwelling took place? Of one another and of significant authentics in other place and time? What awareness arose of an ecology of spirit which sustains our spirit? Pentecost?

5. What experiencing of how "new man" comes about? What for us, now, is our image of a potent, desirable person which is to be released into the world?

6. What discovery of "home place?" Of territory to colonize, fill with our song, our trails, our enterprises?

7. What immediacy of the numinous Holy? How symbolized in a familiar yet spontaneous way?

8. What offer of expected life story for an individual?

9. What story of the universe encompasses the whole celebration? A story which has been developing and made further development in this particular celebration together, a vision in which it all got put together, the plot and working pattern of God and man once more appeared?

10. A newsworthy report of some victory God and man just now brought off and of the continuing battle.

11.   What new experiencing of the self, particularly as spontaneity?

12.   Was the celebration multilanguaged, multiplet, multituned, dimensional?" The communication style dialogic and participative? The communication a mixture of "face-to-face village in situation," spoken and written words, significant art forms, electronic media?

Training Enterprises

What enterprises of developing worship that celebrates and nurtures can we set in motion so that it can happen well in the local congregation?

Perhaps first of all is a total attitude which encourages people of all ages to be creative, ranging from the Old Testament professor in a theological seminary who encourages students in a course on psalms to write six of their own, on to open "celebrative culture labs" for periods of time in a local church—not art for art's sake but for discovery's sake, for transformation's sake. Creativeness must be received at some depth by at least a small group (and some of it by a congregation) so that one is bound into a matrix of communal life rather than further alienated or feeling that what one does is trifling and actually outside a people moving through time with a destiny.

If (as is true) such worship enlarges greatly the function of the pastor—and at the same time opens worship ministry to lay members in a large and fresh way—a second priority is the work of seminaries with pastors in location, perhaps with a few pastors who are already in motion. For with such mutual learning we will best develop worship for the church and strengthen seminary education. Students find professors convincing if they can point to some pastors and say, "That's what an artist-teacher-leader of communal celebration looks like—and what also his congregation visions a minister being." Such working situations would be part of the continuing education of ministers and one specialized area for work toward a doctor of ministry degree.

In the meantime, there is widely in motion short-term training conferences for all kinds of purposes which climax with "a celebration"—which to some degree flowers out of what has been taking place, and invites the Holy Spirit to be spontaneous through these assembled. Ministers and lay people are learning celebration by being in special situations outside the set routines.

The church also now needs programs for growing-teaching a number of church members in making forms and contents of celebrative worship and in helping some of them think of themselves as an apostolate. This would be in addition to the most necessary beginning of mobilizing teams for special celebrations. A pastor (or preferably a group of pastors) could design training each year of eight or ten people in his church through mini-courses linked with celebrative enterprises in the congregation's encounters with the world. Such courses would train (1) in theologizing lived moments; (2) in communication into intersubjectivity about things that matter most; (3) in improving the language and art of poetic expression, of short spontaneous dramatization of the human cry (some video taped, some put into movie short), of a vocabulary of music which enspirits celebrative powers, of phenomenological photography and painting, of never-to-be-forgotten description of a great way of being-in-the-world, of recording cassettes and tapes of writings of significant others or of one's own (interspersed with music to add to its dialogic powers), of how to order a celebration so that it moves within an epic story and is consummatory.

Let me briefly describe a beginning we have made at the Chicago Southside Cluster of Theological Schools in what we call a "celebration concentration." For one quarter, students gave most of their time to this one effort. The concentration was led by a team of Catholic and Protestant professors. The students were also of both Catholic and Protestant faith. This mix was some of the excitement of the course.

We began by having *lived moments,* freshly experiencing the impact of two great elements of human life—birth and death. Each of us spent a night in a hospital with a mother who was giving birth to a child. As a group we listened to Dr. Kübler-Ross talk with a terminal cancer patient and a mother of a son who had only a short time to live. In small groups of four to six, we talked out the momentums and meanings of life that were stirred in us and then tried to put our own into significant form. We also listened to how such experiences had been interpreted by other people through memorable phrase or music.

We spent a whole "founding week" together doing such things. Away from school, we did nothing else but have these experiences, expressing and combining them and ourselves as best we could. Ultimately we put it together in a two-hour closing celebration of the birth-death structure of human life.

In between times, in order to understand something long important in each of us, each person produced a ten-minute cassette from the sayings of someone who was a significant other for him and then did a second cassette (a mixture of words and music) of some one thing he very much wanted to say to the world. Each time we took a whole morning, in groups of about six people, to receive these cassettes, develop further the thought, and make connections with other meanings.

Each week thereafter, each of us put in some art form a stirring which was awakened within us by what was happening, sometimes after exposure to someone who did that particular art form excellently. The most memorable of these was an artist who did murals of a people's struggle for a just order. Often a small group of us worked together in constructing a celebration for a larger group to which we belonged outside class, and what we did was a basis for further development of theory and practice through discussion in the class.

By the end of the quarter we each had considerable experience in interpreting and putting into beautiful form the significance of our own lived moments—through dyad conversation, through dramatic improvisation, in music and song, in photographing, in painting, in multi-media mix, etc. Each had worked as a team member in at least two or three celebrations for our own class. We had also reported and mulled over the celebration worked up with the larger group in which we were "interned."

One morning each week was devoted to theory construction. What is celebration and the celebrative style of life? What contents are in a lived moment? How do we understand what makes this particular one what it is, relates it to a larger frame of life? How do we design the pattern of a celebration? What theology and theologizing informs the celebrations we find most meaningful? What is the essence of liturgy and ritual? Of a rite of passage? What are the developmental epochs of a person's journey through life which may be celebrated?

When would you say you have really communicated? How do we experience what contemplation is? Prayer? Let's look at the doctrine of Spirit that is developing today. What is the genius of the Pentecostal, the charismatic groups, the black congregation folk preaching within celebration? What do we mean when we say *symbol?* What are the meaningful symbols which Americans really live?

"Creator of culture forms and artist of communal celebration"— is this a welcome part of your identity? The image—"the church as a celebrative institution, a convictional congregation with celebrative flair"—does it have wings for you?

Chapter 15

PUBLIC EDUCATION
RELIGION STUDIES
SINCE THE *SCHEMPP* DECISION (1963)

Nicholas Piediscalzi

I

The United States Supreme Court ruled on June 17, 1963, that public schools may *neither require* teachers and students to read selections from the Bible for devotional purposes nor to recite prayers.[1] Such practices, according to the Court, are in violation of the First Amendment. Unfortunately the mass media seriously misrepresented the *Schempp* decision in their reports and thereby created much confusion in the public domain. Most headlines and news reports announced that God, the Bible, and prayer had been banished from the public schools. Justice Tom C. Clark recalls one headline proclaiming "God Pushed Out the Front Door and Communism Let in the Back."[2] This misunderstanding still exists today for many citizens.

Actually the Supreme Court did not ban God, the Bible, or prayer from the public schools. The Court rather prohibited the schools as agents of the state from requiring the recitation of prayers and reading from the Bible for devotional purposes. Moreover, several legal scholars contend that the Court did not outlaw voluntary prayer in the classroom. Professor Paul G. Kauper of the University of Michigan law faculty holds that voluntary prayers, conducted without the school's stamp of official approval and conducted by others than teachers, possibly may be legal and permissable "in the interest of religious liberty."[3]

Furthermore, the *Schempp* decision contains significant dicta affirming the importance and legality of studying about religion in the public schools. Justice Clark, in the majority opinion, noted that education is not complete without a knowledge of history of religion, comparative religion, and Bible. He added, "Nothing that we have said here indicates that such study of the Bible or of religion, when presented objectively as part of a secular program

Nicholas Piediscalzi is Professor and Chairman of the Department of Religion and Codirector of the Public Education Religion Studies Center at Wright State University, Dayton, Ohio.

of education, may not be effected consistent with the First Amendment." [4] Both Justices Brennan and Goldberg expressed similar judgments about the importance and propriety of religion studies when conducted properly.

Despite these absolutely clear statements on the place and legality of religion studies in the public schools, many educators and school systems, because they misunderstood the *Schempp* decision and feared causing controversy, either eliminated their religion studies programs or resisted recommendations that such be introduced. However, as the decision was examined more carefully and its contents clarified and as conferences and studies were held to ascertain its implications, citizens, educators, and professional organizations realized that the Court actually encouraged the public schools to include religion studies in their programs.[5] As a result of this and other factors, such as the evident new interest both on the part of teachers and pupils, religion studies materials are being published, teacher education and certification programs are being inaugurated, and innumerable new courses are being introduced throughout the United States.

In late 1965 the Pennsylvania legislature, reacting to *Schempp*, enacted legislation providing "for a secondary course in the study of religious literature," thereby legalizing the study of the Bible and other religious literature on an elective basis. The Pennsylvania Department of Public Instruction invited Pennsylvania State University to produce the courses mandated by the legislature and to establish a training program for the teachers who would introduce this course. A teacher training institute was conducted in the Summer of 1967 and, that fall, thirty-one selected schools offered the pilot course "Religious Literature of the West," developed by the university curriculum project team. Today more than one hundred schools offer the course, and thousands of students are involved in other religion studies programs which were stimulated by the introduction of this initial project. A second pilot course, "Religious Literature of the East," was field tested during the 1974-75 academic year for introduction in the fall of 1975.[6]

Florida has been similarly engaged. In 1965 its State Department of Education established a State Commission on Study about Religion in the Public Schools. This group "set out to explore creative possibilities for the relationship of religion and education," [7] one result being the formation of the Florida State University Religion-Social Studies Curriculum Project. Between 1968 and 1971 it developed religion studies curriculum materials for inclusion in social studies classes at the secondary level and conducted training sessions for teachers.[8] In 1972 the university instituted The Religion in Elementary Social Studies Project. This group is in the process of producing multi-media instructional packets (with extensive teachers' guides) for the elementary grades.

A group of ecumenical scholars published in 1969 *The Bible Reader,* a special edition of the Bible for use in public schools.[9] This volume contains key biblical passages in various translations with introductory articles, essays, and notes from the Catholic, Protestant, and Jewish traditions. Special references are made to art, literature, history, and the social problems of contemporary life. An accompanying teacher's guide was published in 1970.

All of these projects were in direct response to the *Schempp* decision. In addition, other efforts underway before *Schempp,* e.g., The Educational Research Council of America's Social Science Curriculum Project[10] and the Nebraska Curriculum Center's English Curriculum Project,[11] which were seriously considering including religion studies in their materials, were given greater impetus by *Schempp* to fulfill their plans along with the mandate to be academic and objective in their presentations.

Both the Florida and Pennsylvania projects included teacher education programs. They are only two of many which have emerged since 1963. Drake University introduced a Summer workshop and course on public education religion studies in 1968. In 1970 Indiana University began the Summer Institute on Teaching the Bible in Secondary English. At the request of local teachers from the Dayton area, Wright State University in Ohio offered two workshops, "Teaching About Religion in the Public Schools" and "The Bible and Literature," during the 1971 summer term. These workshops have been repeated each summer since the introduction. The University of Alabama inaugurated a summer institute, "Teaching of Comparative Religion in the Secondary School," in 1972. During the summer of 1973 the University of Iowa conducted a comprehensive institute, "Teaching About Religion in the Public Schools." Altogether more than twenty such summer programs operated by 1974. They varied in length from just a few days to as long as six weeks. Many of them covered the entire field of public education religion studies, while others were limited to specific subjects, e.g., teaching about the Bible, the Bible and literature, comparative religion, and religion and values.

Union Theological Seminary in New York, in conjunction with Columbia University, introduced in the fall of 1972 two experimental courses: "Religion and Education" and "Teaching Religion in the Secondary Schools." Student enrollees had the opportunity to practice teach in New Jersey high schools. In the fall of 1972 Harvard's Divinity School and Graduate School of Education inaugurated an experimental course of study entitled "The Secondary School Teaching Certificate Option." The program included courses in the philosophy of education, adolescent psychology, methods, and religion, as well as student teaching. According to one of its leaders, the Harvard program operates "on the assumption that religion can be taught meaningfully in a number of ways; the most important criteria are that the method be comfortable for the teacher and relevant to the students." [12]

Since 1971 four states (Wisconsin, Michigan, Vermont, and California) approved certification programs in religion studies. The University of Wisconsin at Whitewater, Edgewood College at Madison, and Marquette University in Milwaukee are all authorized to offer major and/or minor teacher preparation programs in religion studies. Michigan's State Board of Education approved Calvin College, Michigan State University, and Western Michigan University to provide an academic minor in the field. The State of California provides certification in religion studies for the elementary and secondary levels under the Diversified Option for Elementary Subject Credential and Single Option Credential in the Academic Study About Religion, respectively.

At the 1973 Wright State University Consultation on Teacher Education Programs, Frank L. Steeves, Dean of the School of Education at Marquette University, summarized and characterized this extensive activity in the following way: State-approved curricula are interdisciplinary in nature, and their orientation tends to be quite clearly nonsectarian. The purpose is "to deal significantly with religion as a significant factor in man's interpretation of reality." Programs reflect the same concerns for general education and preparation of teachers which characterize other subject fields, with special attention being given to be certain that teachers are aware of the problems and restrictions involved in religion studies. Most state programs share these elements and emphases. Steeves also found some differences. Michigan and California have produced "definitive standards" to guide the approval of programs, each of which is published in some detail. In contrast Wisconsin, which was the first state to identify religious studies as a certifiable area, has published no such specific guidelines, acting rather on the basis of written applications which provide the details for programs under consideration. Teacher preparation in academic majors varies from thirty to thirty-six semester hours, with minors ranging between eighteen and twenty-four credits. Steeves also noted a clear distinction between "religious studies" as a certifiable subject area for teaching religion and theology as an academic discipline.[13]

Although no official or thorough surveys have been conducted and published, there is growing evidence that religion courses are increasing at a rapid rate in public schools. Informal reports from many sections of the United States support this generalization. Thomas Love of California State University, Northridge, reported that at least eighty religion courses were introduced within a sixty-mile radius of his campus during the period 1968-72. He also noted that "many units on various courses, and many enrichment programs, also are offered in religious studies." [14] At least fifteen new religion courses have appeared in the area of Dayton, Ohio, during this same period. Fifty-nine of ninety-six Michigan high schools responding to a survey conducted by L. J. Ponstein, Hope College professor, reported that they had introduced such courses since 1970. The number of students studying religion in Pennsylvania schools has increased from only seven hundred in 1967 to twelve thousand in 1974. New programs were begun in high schools in Oxford, Medford, and Needham, Massachusetts, as well as Stowe, Vermont, in the fall of 1974. These are merely illustrative of the nationwide growth in religion studies. The Bible as literature and world religions courses are proving to be popular elective options in public high schools.

II

The events, developments, and programs reported above obviously have been both piecemeal and uncoordinated. This situation made it evident to concerned individuals and groups that the expanding area of public education religion studies would benefit from the establishment of a center to coordinate, encourage, and facilitate these many and varied efforts. Thus the Public Education Religion Studies Center (PERSC) was founded at Wright State University in September, 1972.[15] This author serves as its codirector. PERSC's goals are to encourage and facilitate increased and improved teaching about religion within constitutional bounds, mainly in elementary and secondary schools and where applicable in relevant areas of postsecondary education. PERSC emphasizes the natural inclusion of the study about religion within regular curricular offerings such as history, art, English, music, and geography; the addition of specific courses or units, such as "Religious Literature," "World Religions," and "Religion and Literature"; and the improvement of pre- and in-service training of teachers. The Center is dedicated to a comprehensive and nonsectarian study about religion as one of the significant areas of man's life and thought. To achieve these goals PERSC holds conferences and workshops; serves as a resource center for curriculum materials and a research center for scholars studying this phenomenon; provides consultative services; publishes a quarterly newsletter; and encourages and commissions responsible review and evaluation of existing curriculum materials and the development of necessary new materials.

In the light of PERSC's conversations and work with educators, teachers, and citizens, there are seven problems and issues which have become evident to this author as requiring special attention during the coming years. First, there remains a need to clarify the legal issue. Large numbers of individuals and groups continue to believe that the Supreme Court banned the study about religion from the public schools. Therefore, ongoing concerted efforts are required to inform the public of the actual content of the Court's decisions.

Second, many individuals confuse the *practice* of religion with *study about* religion and oppose the introduction of religion studies in the public schools because they believe that students will be indoctrinated in one faith, viz., Anglo-Saxon Protestantism. This confusion is the result of three factors operative in American history: (a) the domination of the public school system by the Protestant model developed in the Massachusetts Bay colony; (b) the founding of our first universities for the purposes of training men for the Protestant ministry and governmental service and fostering Protestant Christianity; and (c) the ensuing and continual conflict among the proponents for preserving the Protestant hegemony over public education and non-Protestants and secularized intellectuals. This conflict led to the founding of parochial schools, where once again religion studies were limited to confessional training in a particular faith, and the exclusion of academic religion studies from land-grant colleges and secular universities.

The battle between secularized intellectuals and "defenders of the faith," according to Guntram G. Bischoff, produced "an almost simplistic, two-dimensional development of thematic attitudes toward religion. The traditional, seminary-cultivated theology of church and synagogue found itself in a kind of permanent and progressive confrontation with its great debunkers who, more often than not, spoke from the rostrum of colleges and universities." Moreover, the debunking process prevented Americans from discovering and utilizing a new approach to religion studies which "found its way into the universities of Europe as early as the 19th century where it became variously known as *Comparative Religion, Science Religieuse,* or *Religionswissenschaft.*" [16] The goal of such study is neither to indoctrinate nor debunk religion but, rather, to understand, appreciate, and evaluate religion as a given dimension of human existence—both for good and ill.

American colleges and universities, on the whole, now have religion departments organized around this approach to religion studies. However, many members of the intellectual community, public school educators, and citizens are not aware of their existence or significance. For this reason, it is especially important, as John R. Whitney has stated, for individuals dedicated to public education religion studies to help secularized intellectuals, educators, and other citizens understand the difference between the profession of and the academic study of religion, and "the appropriateness of the academic study of religion as the study of one of the basic institutional realities involving people in general and Americans in particular." [17]

Third, there is need to clarify what is meant by "objective study of religion." A large number of individuals believe that objectivity means either a cold, detached, and boring recitation of historical facts or a "scientific" reduction of religion to a meaningless and nonproductive activity. Both approaches, in their minds, misrepresent religion to students. These persons are not aware that objective study includes an open, empathetic, and appreciative study of religion. Phillip H. Phenix of Columbia University has made a valuable contribution toward clarifying and redefining objectivity. He wrote:

> No teaching, no educative activity, in any school ought to be indoctrinative, but should be based upon evidence and fair-minded inquiry rather than upon subjective opinion or special pleading. Knowledge in education properly conceived is everybody's knowledge, in the public domain. But "objective" does not mean value-free, abstracted from the domain of human interest. It is better interpreted as *disciplined intersubjectivity.* To be objective is to enter into the subjectivity of persons other than oneself in a disciplined way. It betokens a person's capacity to enter imaginatively into the position of another. This is the fundamental mark of human intelligence. We are humanly intelligent to the degree that we are capable of getting inside points of view other than our own, in a way that is genuinely appreciative. [18]

Building on this contribution, it is necessary to add that objectivity, in the words of Margherite La Pota, includes "a plurality in the presentation of interpretations, attitudes, and materials; . . . [encouragement of] free pursuit of related information; and [maintaining] reciprocal respect for contrary positions." [19] In addition, objectivity entails an appraisal of the positive and negative contributions of religion to human history. Any study about religion which ignores either is not objective. An objective study about religion also includes fair consideration of the atheistic and secular faiths by which human beings live. Since one of the goals of religion studies is the understanding of how religion functions in human life it is important to help students learn and understand the many and diverse forms of theistic, atheistic, and secular religions which operate in human history.

Robert A. Spivey recently suggested that one should avoid believing that one knows and understands thoroughly the phenomenon of religion once one has studied all of its manifestations and positive and negative functions. According to Spivey, objective study also should include the attitude that, no matter how thoroughly one studies religion, the religious dimension of human existence remains a mystery, and it should also cultivate an appreciation of this mystery. [20] Finally it must be admitted that no human being can be totally objective about the subject he teaches. The teacher about religion—as any other teacher—can make his own and his students' biases a teaching tool by pointing out his and their lack of objectivity and inviting them to join him in discovering (a) where he and they are not objective in their study about religion and other subjects and (b) the biased opinions they bring to their studies. Ideally, developing such awareness is a major goal of education.

Fourth, criteria need to be developed by which competent teaching about religion can be evaluated. PERSC has been engaged in the development of such guidelines, and a summary of them follows: (1) competent religion studies teachers, like all other teachers, should be professionally qualified, emotionally mature, and pedagogically sound; (2) competent religion studies teachers should also be well versed in the legal issues surrounding religion studies in public education, academically qualified in religion as an academic subject, and nonconfessional in approach. Full details about these criteria are available in the PERSC *Guidebook* listed in the footnotes.

Fifth, criteria need to be developed for evaluating and improving curriculum materials. PERSC has utilized a Professional Advisory Council in making an initial contribution toward the accomplishment of this goal. Stated in the form of questions, a brief summary of these criteria follows: (1) Is the material educationally sound and pedagogically effective? Is it appropriate in terms of subject matter, of the abilities of the students, and of the competence of the teachers? (2) Does the material reflect an academically responsible approach? Is it based on sound scholarship, which is pluralistic, balanced, and comprehensive? Does it combine the scholar's "outside" view with the adherent's "inside" view? (3) Is the material sensitive to the religious and political problems of pluralistic American society? Does it balance scholarly analysis with sensitivity to the views, beliefs, and concerns of religious minorities? Does it seek understanding and appreciation of the values that lead to different religious commitments, especially with the object of breaking down the stereotypes that lead to religious prejudices and discrimination? (4) Does the material reflect a nonconfessional and interfaith perspective? (5) Does the material reflect and has it been written within the parameters of the major Supreme Court decisions? Is it nonproselytizing? Have many positions and beliefs been presented so as to achieve a balanced view? (6) Has the material been field tested? Did this involve teachers and students of varied backgrounds, abilities, and faiths? In summary, "these general criteria imply material that is appropriate as to subject matter, age level of students, and teacher competence; material that is pluralistic, balanced, and comprehensive in content; material that employs objective data and an analytical but empathetic approach; and finally material that encourages awareness of and respect for each person's religion whether traditional or secular." [21]

In addition, a great deal of careful consultation needs to be conducted with publishers concerning the content and quality of curriculum materials. For the most part, religion is ignored or grossly misrepresented in curriculum materials. Moreover, when religions are presented, minority religions, e.g., Judaism and Islam, are presented inadequately and often unfairly. Likewise, when Christianity is studied, many groups, e.g., Eastern Orthodoxy, Fundamentalism, the Church of Jesus Christ of Latter Day Saints, and Jehovah's Witnesses, frequently are not mentioned or are misrepresented. Therefore, it is important to call the attention of publishers to these omissions and errors and to demonstrate how the correct application of the criteria presented above will improve the treatment of religion in their textbooks and nonprinted materials.

Sixth, pre- and in-service training of teachers and certification programs in religion studies must be expanded and improved. PERSC suggests several criteria for achieving these goals. Among them are the need for such teacher education programs to be a joint project of religion and education faculties, with the same educational standards required of public school religion teachers as are placed on instructors of other subjects. Teachers will also need guidance in becoming aware of their own attitudes toward formal and informal manifestations of religion and the ways that these attitudes influence their teaching. The importance for teachers of the curricular criteria noted above should also be a central element in any teacher education program.

Seventh, graduate schools of theology and seminaries need to avoid the temptation to institute teacher education programs in religion studies to solve their enrollment problems or accommodate the needs and/or requests of students who desire training in theology even though they do not plan to serve in the professional ministry but think that "they might be happy" as teachers of religion. Those who are selected for teacher education programs in religion studies, for the integrity and advancement of the discipline and profession, should be dedicated to teaching as a vocation and not as an *ersatz* professional ministry or vocational "moratorium" on the route to establishing a new identity.[22] Furthermore, persons in the process of leaving the professional ministry or religious orders who believe they can "make a valuable contribution" to religion studies in the public schools should not be hired as teachers until they are certified as *bona fide* public school teachers and demonstrate beyond any reasonable doubt that their commitment is to the purposes and goals of public education and the academic study of religion.

The data presented in the foregoing essay documents the fact that public education religion studies courses and programs are increasing in the United States. It is not clear at this writing whether religion studies will continue to expand and become a new element in public education. However, it is absolutely clear that the present moment demands that all concerned with this new dimension in the public schools must devote their energies and attention to improving the quality of existing programs and curriculum materials, expanding and upgrading teacher education and certification programs, and establishing sound criteria for evaluating programs, materials, and teacher education.

NOTES

1. *Abington* v. *Schempp; Murray* v. *Curlett*. The Supreme Court chose to hear these cases together and to issue one decision for both because each entailed similar constitutional problems. The cases have become popularly known as the *Schempp* decision.

2. "Personal Reflections on the *Schempp* Decision," an address delivered on June 13, 1973, by Justice Tom C. Clark at the Public Education Religion Studies Center Symposium I and published in *Public Education Religion Studies: Retrospect and Prospect,* 1963-1983 (Dayton, Ohio: Public Education Religion Studies Center, September, 1974).

3. Kauper, *Religion and the Constitution* (Baton Rouge: Louisiana State University Press, 1964), pp. 94-95.

4. *Abington* v. *Schempp; Murray* v. *Curlett,* 374 U.S. 219 (1963).

5. For a survey of the conferences held since the *Schempp* decision, see John W. O'Brien, "Religion in Public Education: The Implementation of an Idea," *The Living Light,* 10 (Fall, 1973), 433-65. In 1964 the American Association of School Administrators' Commission on Religion in the Public Schools stated in their report, *Religion in the Public Schools* (New York: Harper & Row, 1964), p. 56: "A curriculum which ignored religion would itself have serious religious implications. It would seem to proclaim that religion has not been as real in men's lives as health or politics or economics. By omission it would appear to deny that religion has been and is important in man's history—a denial of the obvious. As an integral part of man's culture, it must be included." Since 1968 several professional organizations, e.g., the National Council of Teachers of English, National Council for the Social Studies, Association for Supervision Curriculum Development, and National Education Association, have supported this position by including sessions on public education religion studies at their regional and national meetings in addition to publishing articles in their journals. See, for example, *Social Education,* 33 (December, 1969), 909-34, and *Today's Education: The Journal of the National Education Association,* 63 (January-February, 1974), 50-54, 77-79. Also it is important to note that the 1971 *Social Studies Curriculum Guidelines,* position statement of the National Council for the Social Studies (p. 17), states: "The program [social studies] should provide intensive and recurrent study of cultural, racial, religious, and ethnic groups, those to which the students themselves belong and those to which they do not." And the 1972 NCSS House of Delegates selected religion studies as one of eight priorities to submit to its membership for emphasis in program development.

6. John R. Whitney, "Introducing Religious Literature in Pennsylvania Secondary Schools," in *Religion in Public Education: Problems and Prospects,* David E. Engel, ed. (New York: Paulist Press, 1974), p. 111.

7. Robert A. Spivey, "A New Shape for Religion and Public Education in Changing Times," *Journal of Church and State,* 14 (1973), 441.

8. These materials are being published in a three-volume series entitled *Issues in Religion* by Addison-Wesley Publishing Co. (Menlo Park, Ca.). The separate titles are: vol. 1, *Religious Issues in American Culture;* vol. 2, *Religious Issues in Western Civilizations,* and vol. 3, *Religious Issues in World Cultures.*

9. Benzinger, Bruce, and Glencoe, *The Bible Reader* (Beverly Hills, Ca.), 1969.

10. *K-12 Social Science Curriculum* (Boston: Allyn and Bacon), 1971.

11. *God-and-Man Narrative: The Religious Story,* nos. 73-76 (Lincoln, Nebr.: University of Nebraska Press, 1968).

12. *Harvard Divinity Bulletin,* 3 (May, 1973), 1.

13. This material is summarized from a report prepared for the Public Education Religion Studies Center by Frank L. Steeves.

14. March 19, 1973, letter from Thomas Love to PERSC.

15. Another national organization, the National Council on Religion and Public Education (NCRPE), was founded in December, 1971. NCRPE is a coalition of national organizations and individuals whose purpose and

functions are: (1) to create public and professional awareness and support for the objective study of religion in public schools; (2) to establish liaison with other professional and lay educational religious and civic organizations; (3) to provide a forum for continuing dialogue on issues, programs, and projects which deal with the academic study of religion in public education; (4) to serve as a referral center for information about resource persons, programs, projects, curriculum materials, teacher education opportunities, legal decisions related to religion and public education. See below for the NCRPE address.

16. Bischoff, "A Call for the Study of Religion as an Academic Discipline," in *Religion and Public School Curriculum,* Richard U. Smith, ed. Proceedings of the National Council on Religion and Public Education, published in *Religious Education,* 67 (July-August, 1972, pt. 2), 101.

17. Whitney, "Religion in Public Schools: Some Pluralistic Arguments for Religious Studies in the Public School Curriculum," *The Council on the Study of Religion Bulletin,* 3 (June, 1972), 19.

18. Phenix, "Religion in Public Education: Principles and Issues," in Smith, ed., *Public School Curriculum,* pp. 18-19.

19. La Pota, "Religion: 'Not Teaching' but 'Teaching About,'" *Educational Leadership: Journal of the Association for Supervision and Curriculum Development,* 31 (October, 1973), 32.

20. Professor Spivey offered this suggestion in a presentation at the Catholic University of America, June 20, 1974.

21. Peter Bracher et al., *Public Education Religion Studies: Questions and Answers* (PERSC *Guidebook*) (Dayton, Ohio: Public Education Religion Studies Center, 1974), pp. 13-14.

22. *Moratorium* is used here as defined by Erik H. Erikson.

Organizations to Write for Assistance

Florida State University Religion-Social Studies Curriculum Project, 426 Hull Drive, Florida State University, Tallahassee, Florida 32306.

Indiana University Institute on Teaching the Bible in Secondary English, Sycamore Hall 201, Bloomington, Indiana 47401.

National Council on Religion and Public Education, Ball State University, Muncie, Indiana 47306

Public Education Religion Studies Center, Wright State University, Dayton, Ohio 45431.

World Religions Curriculum Development Center, 6425 West 33rd St., Minneapolis, Minn. 55426

Chapter 16

EVANGELICALISM
AND CHRISTIAN EDUCATION

Edward L. Hayes

Evangelicalism in America is currently enjoying a relatively high state of health. Measured by church growth, the state of its institutional expressions, and its appeal to the populace, evangelicalism is on the rise. Whether or not this is a short-lived phenomenon remains to be seen, but indicators point to an emerging alliance of quite diverse groups willing to be labeled "evangelical" or "conservative." An analysis of the theological mood and educational stance of evangelicalism reveals no monolithic structure, no hard-core integrative style. Rather, a somewhat loose affiliation which is characterized by a resurgent revivalism, some religious privatism, and always the threat of schism mark the movement.

The fact that evangelicalism may now be called a movement is a point of history. Some would prefer to call it a recovery of orthodoxy in American Protestantism, while others would see it as a cultural addendum to an already fragmented and pluralistic religious voice in America. While its organizational expression, the National Association of Evangelicals, claims slightly less than three million adherents, the tentacles of evangelical influence spread far beyond that body. Evangelicalism is to be found in nearly every Protestant denomination. For instance, at least two of the larger denominations not attached to the NAE continue almost totally conservative in theological stance —the Southern Baptists and the Missouri Synod Lutherans. Smaller bodies such as the Christian Reformed Church relate evangelical principles to their own distinctive existence.

Kelley, in *Why Conservative Churches Are Growing,* notes the fact that in the late sixties at least ten of the largest Christian denominations lost members.[1] The effects of this upon Christian education are enormous. On the upsurge side stand other groups including the Assemblies of God and various holiness groups. Even many smaller evangelical denominations are showing a rise.

The term *evangelical* is a rather inclusive term embodying con-

Edward L. Hayes is Academic Dean and Professor of Christian Education at Conservative Baptist Theological Seminary, Denver, Colorado.

servatism and some elements of fundamentalism. The latter term presents special problems because of connotations relating to the fundamentalist-modernist controversy of the early twentieth century. Bruce L. Shelley, in *Evangelicalism in America,* refers to evangelicals as "Christians who are concerned with that personal experience of Christ that results from the preaching of the biblical gospel." [2] Evangelicals, according to him, are orthodox Christians in the sense that they accept the cardinal doctrines of historic Protestantism. With all its shortcomings, the term does point to a revitalized inter-denominational mood and movement in America.

The Theological Stance of Organized Evangelicalism

Credally, evangelicalism is marked by a rejection of theological liberalism with its denial of supernaturalism, of theological neo-orthodoxy with its view of scriptural authority, and of historical fundamentalism with its denial of social action. Perhaps the simplest way to describe evangelicalism is by quoting the doctrinal statement of the NAE which was adopted in 1943 by representatives of some fifty denominations:

1. We believe the Bible to be the inspired, the only infallible, authoritative Word of God.

2. We believe that there is one God, eternally existent in three Persons: Father, Son, and Holy Spirit.

3. We believe in the deity of our Lord Jesus Christ, in His virgin birth, in His sinless life, in His miracles, in His vicarious and aton-ing death through His shed blood, in His bodily resurrection, in His ascension to the right hand of the Father and in His personal return in power and glory.

4. We believe that for the salvation of lost and sinful man regeneration by the Holy Spirit is absolutely essential.

5. We believe in the present ministry of the Holy Spirit by whose indwelling the Christian is enabled to live a godly life.

6. We believe in the resurrection of both the saved and the lost; they that are saved unto the resurrection of life and they that are lost unto the resurrection of damnation.

7. We believe in the spiritual unity of believers in our Lord Jesus Christ. [3]

The primary evidence of evangelicalism's vigor, however, does not lie in its credal affirmation, but in its twin thrusts of evangelism and missions. Because these action moods overshadow educational concerns it is a difficult task to sketch out the components of evan-gelical education.

A Basic Educational Outlook

Evangelical Christian education suffers from lack of a coherent theology, but probably no more than Christian education in general. One thing, however, does characterize its stance—a tenacious hold to a literal biblicism. God is viewed to be at the center of education. Authority resides in God, and all truth is subjected to scriptural scrutiny. This recovery of a reformed viewpoint has been articulated by two of evangelicalism's leading educators, Carl F. H. Henry and Frank E. Gaebelein.[4] Holding that there is unity to truth and that the truth claims of the Scripture are self-evident, these evangelicals, along with others, have developed educational ideals and some rudiments of a style. Gaebelein recognizes the problems posed by the orthodox position on the Scripture—problems relating to literalism particularly.

> This is not a plea for a wooden literalism that believes all words of Scripture to be equally important, that fails to distinguish between what is symbolical and poetical, doctrinal and practical, and that considers the writers of Scripture mere automata rather than human beings whose talents God sovereignly used. On the contrary, it is still possible to recognize the human element in Scripture and at the same time hold with intellectual integrity a high view of the Bible as the infallible, authoritative Word of the living God and the indispensable sourcebook of Christian faith and practice.

Authority thus resides in God and truth is an objective reality. This in no way precludes investigation because until the external truth becomes internalized it is of little value to the educative process. Evangelicals have sought to follow Sara Little's suggestion that Christian education be "a servant and not a master of revelation."[5]

Such a rejection of process theology does not negate creativity and investigation, and does not overlook the learning process. Evangelicals have attempted answers to the problems of a relational theology, creativity, and application of learning theory. These attempts, however, have not always been definitive and well enough developed to afford an investigator opportunity to see a consistent design to evangelical educational strategy.[6]

The futility of modeling an educational stance on a subjective theology is recognized by evangelicals. The shifting posture of theology has been a perplexing problem to church educators. Carl Henry observed in *Frontiers in Modern Theology* that theologians often outlive the influence of their own theologies. It was J. Gordon Chamberlin who once wrote, "The practical steps required to develop educational programs on the basis of any particular theological position take many years. Usually by that time the theological posture of the church has shifted." [7]

Evangelicals would prefer a conservatism which purports to have some answers at least to the questions of meaning. They would prefer an element of dogma to what Kelley refers to as a "dilute and undemanding form of meaning." [8]

The question of indoctrination haunts the evangelical. Fundamentalism has never had a problem with it, but many evangelical educators feel that a valid education must allow for investigation.

A hard look at indoctrination reveals some rather startling characteristics. It is persuasion without recourse to questioning assumptions. It is inculcation of a doctrine declared in advance to be so good as to justify no need for critical comparison with alternative viewpoints. It is coercion which demands uncritical acceptance and threatens the student with sanctions. Education patterned after these tenets presupposes that the teacher is the repository of a body of unassailable truth. Evangelicals reject this caricature of an educational style.

Evangelical educators, on the other hand, seek an adequate methodology to fit an adequate theology. God must be at the center. Authority rests in the Scriptures. The Holy Spirit progressively illumines the mind of the learner. Both teacher and learner are candidates for truth. Each person must individualize truth and make it his own. This internalization process calls for faith and some commitment to assumptions. There is no merit, evangelicals contend, in the absence of a point of view. Berkson, in *The Ideal and the Community,* declares that good teaching will include the two aspects of communication of accepted principles along with an analysis of issues still unsettled. Whereas some theologians would contend that everything is up for grabs, the evangelical would agree upon some assumptions pertaining to God, authority, the purpose of man, the church, and Christian hope.

Another distinctive of an evangelical stance in education is its relationship to Christian conversion. Evangelicals, in general, would reject the Bushnellian principle of an organic link between parent and child when it comes to the faith-building effort. Yet, they would seek to build upon the natural spiritual climate of the home and Christian community for inculcating faith in children. Evangelicals begin their explanation of true religion where Jesus began, "Repent and believe the gospel" (Mark 1:15). It emphasizes man's need for spiritual rebirth. Evangelicals are more concerned about inner personal depth than they are about external religious conformity. This tradition of Wesley, Whitefield, and others is rather central to evangelical church life and thus pervades the educational program as well. Shelley points out this genius of evangelicalism. "For these reasons, evangelicals, while holding to orthodox beliefs, insist that Christianity is more than theological orthodoxy and religious conservatism. It is a spirit, a concern for sinners, a way of life. Its master motif is the salvation of souls; its guiding image the redemptive gospel of Jesus Christ. All other considerations are subordinated to this standard."[9]

A final emphasis in evangelical education is the element of relationship. Education centered in God attempts to reach the inner self, to build strong relational dimensions. This ideal is only achievable by way of love. A proper "I-Thou" relationship, "I'm OK, you're OK" attitude is essential. "Education without love," asserts Jan Waterink in *Basic Concepts in Christian Pedagogy,* "is nothing more than the issuing of commands. But commands do not educate, they only drill; they can make of the human being a clever creature, which knows all . . . but they do not form personality."[10] Evangelicals contend that genuine faith must be active in love. Love finds its expression in relationships both inside and outside the classroom.

The Greening of Evangelicalism

Since the emergence of organized evangelicalism during the third through the fifth decades of the twentieth century, Christian education has passed through several discernible stages. Reeling from the theological controversy of the nineteenth century and early decades of the twentieth century, evangelicals tended to reject the new religious education fostered by such groups as the Religious Education Association (1903) and the International Council of Religious Education (1922). Evangelicals tended to reject the educational progressivism that was predominant in the early religious education movement. The philosophy of John Dewey (Dewey keynoted the first convention of the Religious Education Association) was seen as a threat to orthodoxy. The marriage of religious education and Dewey's progressivism was never understood by fundamentalists. Thus, educational attempts of fundamentalist denominations were more a reaction against progressivism and theological liberalism than they were positive attempts to construct a whole educational endeavor. Even the term *religious education* was rejected, and Christian education enthusiasts who were evangelical were suspect. For the most part, early educational efforts by evangelicals were privatistic and reactionary. Were it not for the efforts of Clarence Benson, evangelical Christian education prior to World War II would have suffered from substantive thinness.

With the emergence of new forms of evangelical cooperation in the mid-forties, Christian education gained new impetus. Riding the crest of a new enthusiasm for Sunday school expansion, the National Sunday School Association (NSSA) was formed. Its first convention was held at the Moody Memorial Church in 1946. For nearly two decades this organization attracted increasingly large convention crowds. Grass roots evangelicalism was showing enthusiasm for church education.

The revival of Sunday school conventions, which were once a driving force in nineteenth century American Protestantism, served to direct attention to evangelicalism. Despite the fact that the NSSA has failed to attract the support of the two largest unaligned evangelical church bodies, Southern Baptists and the Missouri Synod Lutherans, it may safely be claimed that NSSA has served to create a new educational awareness among evangelicals. Its influence, however, is being replaced by more localized conventions in major cities of America.

Another phase in evangelical church education may be under way. The patterns of evangelical allegiance are shifting. The emergence of renewal literature is reflecting and, in some cases, directing new models for church ministry. Roots of a renaissance, or "greening of the church," reach deeply into a theology of the laity. The appearance in the decade of the sixties of a spate of books dealing with lay renewal met with a responsive note among evangelicals. Oddly enough, the polity of many evangelical denominations was congregational to begin with. The reformed ideal of a ministering congregation has been very much a part of evangelicalism. What Hendrik Kraemer was saying (*A Theology of the Laity*, [Philadelphia: The Westminster Press, 1958]) began to be echoed and amplified by others. The recovery of the laity became a seedbed for evangelical church change.

An analysis of the shift in evangelicalism is difficult because of the pluralism within it and the emergence of proliferated programming. One thing can be said, however. Mainline denominations had been over much of this before. Evangelicals, because of inherent conservatism, were only discovering "new" educational styles previously tried in the early religious education movement—creative use of the arts, open classroom teaching, team teaching, use of audiovisuals, group dynamics.

Apparently evangelicals are building solidly on renewal efforts, and they may succeed where the religious education movement failed. One element may spell the difference—support of the large number of grass roots Christians.

A wide continuum of church education styles is evident in evangelicalism. On one hand we are seeing the phenomenon of the large church and its Sunday school attracting five thousand to ten thousand people, and on occasion even many more. *Christian Life* popularized this development in its ten largest Sunday schools in America contest (Elmer Towns, *The Ten Largest Sunday Schools,* [Grand Rapids: Baker Book House, 1969]). In 1971 this same publication listed one hundred large Sunday schools, eighty-four of which were Baptist. A high percentage of these are to be found in the South. The Sunday school is their major educational effort.

Another style within evangelicalism reflects disenchantment with the Sunday school. A kind of underground church is to be found where evangelicals are reacting to emphasis upon numbers and to strong, central pastoral leadership. The Faith at Work renewal group is an expression of this, although there is little discernible pattern. David Mains, in *Full Circle* (Waco, Tex.: Word Books, 1971), calls evangelicals to find expression of learning more in the worship and fellowship of the church than in the traditional Sunday school. And, of course, the emergence of the Jesus people in the late sixties meant that a conservatism somewhat devoid of systematic study and learning was touching large numbers of the young.[11]

The great bulk of evangelicals are to be found in small to moderately large churches with rather traditional educational programs. But some "greening" is taking place among them. The Sunday school is not being deserted. It is being surrounded by an active program of weekday, as well as Sunday, educational efforts. Notable educative ventures still attracting growing numbers include vacation Bible school, Christian camping, special boys and girls weekday programs, family-life education, home Bible classes, and children's church ministries.

Many churches are taking their educational tasks seriously. This is best illustrated by the growth and influence of the evangelical publishing houses. One of these, Gospel Light Publishing Company, through its International Center for Learning seminars attracts thousands of lay teachers annually. Well-attended local Sunday school conventions sponsored by evangelicals in the cities of Detroit, greater Los Angeles, Chicago, and Denver bring practical training within the reach of many.

An aggressive and effective black Sunday school organization, Urban Ministries Incorporated, headquartered in Chicago, is helping to shape church education within a wide cross section of American black denominations, although its appeal is nondenominational. Melvin E. Banks, its director, calls attention to the bibliocentric approach.

Perhaps this tradition developed through the zeal of the original white missionaries, or the need for something about which slaves could be certain in the midst of oppression, or a strong God-given conviction that God has spoken in the Scriptures. In any case the

Bible is almost universally recognized as the sole authority in the black Sunday school, and that is very significant.[12]

The growth and expansion of private Christian education reflects another of evangelicalism's educational expressions. Without doubt the legal climate for integration, desegregation, and busing for racial balance has contributed to the rise. Some denominations, however, are promoting Christian schools for sane theological and philosophical reasons, namely the various Lutheran and Christian Reformed groups. These schools do not seem to exist out of reaction to societal and cultural developments so much as out of a desire to present an integrative faith among the young. In the decade of the seventies there apparently is no diminishment of evangelical and conservative vigor to create private institutions, primarily at the preschool and elementary levels. While Catholic schools decline in America, Protestant schools are growing. Fiscal problems are being met, but not solved, by missionary zeal for private Christian schools where children are "safe" from the evils of society at large and the public educational system. Just what the loss of evangelical influence will mean to public education no one knows. Presently, at least, a growing number are opting for dissent in the form of desertion of the public system.

Organizations Active in Evangelical Christian Education

Within mainstream evangelicalism certain organizations have emerged to service Christian education ministries. The number of these is extremely small compared with organizations serving world missions and evangelism. Only the prominent agencies or institutions are mentioned here.

Evangelical Teacher Training Association. The Evangelical Teacher Training Association, the ETTA as it is called, provided for leadership training at both the professional and lay level. Begun in 1930 by Clarence H. Benson of the Moody Bible Institute, the ETTA was formed to offer an option to the Standard Leadership Training Curriculum of the International Council of Religious Education. Active membership includes both United States and Canadian schools of higher learning, for the most part small Bible colleges, Christian liberal arts colleges, and some theological seminaries. Affiliate status is granted lay training schools of adult education.

The ETTA provides three courses of study: (1) The Standard Training Course, offered to qualified students in member schools. A teacher's diploma is offered for completion of specified Bible and Christian education courses; (2) the Preliminary Certificate Course, granted by local churches and community lay schools; and (3) the Advanced Certificate Course for work beyond the preliminary certificate in ETTA prepared courses. A series of manuals and textbooks are available through ETTA.

The independent publishers. The influence of the independent Sunday school literature publishers cannot be minimized in the growth of evangelical Christian education. Leaders in the field are Scripture Press, with its All Bible Graded Sunday School Program and other related materials; Gospel Light Publications, leaders in closely graded non-denominational materials; and David C. Cook Publishing Company, an innovative publishing house offering a wide range of literature and learning materials. These three largely compete for a similar evangelical market and, because of their diversification, their materials are widely distributed in many mainline denominations as well as to independent churches. An early developer of Sunday school materials, the American Sunday School Union, now the American Missionary Fellowship, continues both as a publisher and sending agency for Christian workers in rural and urban settings. Formed in 1824, the ASSU was responsible for the effective spread of Christianity in the American frontier. It has retained its missionary and evangelistic posture despite a diminished influence in local churches.

Other publishing efforts for children and youth markets include Child Evangelism Fellowship and Success with Youth, Inc.

The National Sunday School Association. When the NSSA was formed as an affiliate organization of the NAE, evangelical church education programs were weak and poorly serviced. Since 1945 many Sunday schools have been revitalized and national conventions of size have attracted a cross section of denominationalists and independents alike. The NSSA still publishes uniform Sunday school lessons. However, they are not in widespread use at the present time. The influence of NSSA is larger than its services. Presently in a state of decline, its offspring are prospering—area conventions and Sunday school associations and the National Association of Directors of Christian Education. A loosely affiliated National Association of Professors of Christian Education attracts professionals from Bible college, Christian liberal arts college, and theological seminary faculties.

The Future of Evangelical Christian Education

The decade of the seventies promises a continued debate on the nature of the church. Evangelicals feel the tensions between the renewalists and revivalists. The revivalist tradition has provided a great impetus to evangelical church expansion. Reliance upon the Sunday school as an educational and evangelistic arm of the church is still very strong and undoubtedly will continue. Probably the two streams of church life will coexist, the renewalists turning more and more inward in their quest for religious vitality and the revivalists with their Sunday-school-oriented vigor turning outward toward the community.

Evangelicalism will not occupy itself with theological faddism, although it will develop its apologetic. Hopefully, a theological astuteness will blossom to help serve as a corrective to the inherent activism of evangelicalism. Hopefully, the soul of evangelicalism will continue to foster some of the dawning efforts of social action, long dormant.

Churches of size, and evangelicals claim them, have wielded power and influence in the past upon the American conscience. Perhaps the decade of the eighties will see a vibrant church life salting the American scene with authentic Christian discipleship.

NOTES

1. Dean M. Kelley, *Why Conservative Churches Are Growing* (New York: Harper & Row, 1972), p. 1.
2. Shelley, *Evangelicalism in America* (Grand Rapids: Eerdmans Publishing Co., 1967), p. 7.
3. *Constitution of the National Association of Evangelicals,* pp. 1-2.
4. The writings of Henry are extensive along these themes. His editorials in *Christianity Today* from the inception of that journal have consistently defended biblical authority. See also Gaebelein, *Pattern of God's Truth* (Chicago: Moody Press, 1968).
5. Gaebelein, *A Varied Harvest* (Grand Rapids: Eerdmans Publishing Co., 1967), pp. 188-89; Sara Little, *The Role of the Bible in Contemporary Christian Education* (Richmond: John Knox Press, 1961), p. 175.
6. See Lois LeBar, *Focus on People in Church Education* (Westwood, N. J.: Fleming H. Revell Co., 1968); Allan Hart Jahsmann, *Power Beyond Words* (St. Louis: Concordia Publishing House, 1969); and Martha Leypoldt, *Learning Is Change* (Valley Forge, Pa.: Judson Press, 1971).
7. Chamberlin, *Freedom and Faith* (Philadelphia: The Westminster Press, 1965), p. 45.
8. Kelley, *Conservative Churches,* p. 175.
9. Shelley, *Evangelicalism,* p. 17.
10. Waterink, *Basic Concepts in Christian Pedagogy* (Grand Rapids: Eerdmans Publishing Co., 1954), p. 56.
11. See also Larry Richards, *A New Face for the Church* (Grand Rapids: Zondervan Publishing House, 1970), and Findley Edge, *The Greening of the Church* (Waco, Tex.: Word Books, 1971); see Edward E. Plowman, *The Underground Church* (Elgin, Ill.; David C. Cook Publishing Co., 1971).
12. Banks, "The Black Sunday School: Its Strengths, Its Needs," *Christianity Today,* 18 (July 5, 1974), 9.

Chapter 17

EDUCATION IN THE
WORLD ECUMENICAL MOVEMENT

William B. Kennedy

The term *ecumenical movement* refers to the convergence of Christian interest and activity pointed toward unity of the churches in structure and work. Largely of the twentieth century, its roots go back into all previous Christian movements toward unification of church structure or action. In that history, the "movement" side of organized Christian life has always played a large part. Because the more official ecclesiastical side of the story has dominated the interpretation of the movement, there has been a certain tension in the ecumenical advance between the "order" and the "movement" sides. In this discussion of education, several "major allies" of the World Council of Churches (WCC) are included: the World Student Christian Federation (WSCF), the World Alliance of Young Men's Christian Associations (YMCA), and the World Young Women's Christian Association (YWCA). It also includes the World Council of Christian Education (WCCE) which in 1971 voted to integrate with the WCC and thus brought its lay "movement" work into the more formal ecumenical stream. (For introductions to these ecumenical bodies see *A History of the Ecumenical Movement 1517-1948.*)

The World Student Christian Federation

Student Christian groups have long pioneered in education in the ecumenical movement. Ecumenical efforts have been necessary on university campuses because the problems and specialized ministries needed have made denominational programs inadequate. Christian work with students and faculties has attracted a continuing fellowship of committed scholars and workers who have studied developments in education. Since the early sixties the WSCF has made education a major part of its work. In 1965 it published *Studies in Education* which included essays from all over the world. The range of interests was

William B. Kennedy was formerly Executive Secretary in the Office of Education, Program Unit Education and Renewal, World Council of Churches, Geneva, Switzerland. He is currently Director of the Atlanta Association for International Education, Atlanta, Georgia.

wide: articles related Christian anthropology and theology to education, analysed the pros and cons of schooling, studied the pressure of technology and secularization upon education, and challenged the idea of "neutrality" of methods. A study of education and community raised the question of individualism, spoke of the relation of education and revolution, and called for schools to produce more mature citizens and "a more humane social order." The book ended with a call to the churches to raise such questions and to work with Christian and other educators to find answers to them.

In 1968 the WSCF published another major study book on education, *Christian Presence in the Academic Community,* which analyzed educational developments in different continents. Special program activities included work with university students, secondary school students, and foreign students. A new theme, internationalization of the university, was discussed as "education beyond the nation—ethnocentrism, pluralism and cultural exchange in higher education." Throughout the book politics gained conscious attention.

In the 1968 WSCF General Assembly in Finland these themes reappeared. From the working group on the future of the university came this analysis:

> During many centuries, the development of education, universities, and science in the industrialized countries has benefitted from conquests, expansion of geographical frontiers, and exploitation of colonialized areas, as well as from the continuing multiple dependence of "independent nations" in the Third World on scientific progress in the industrialized nations. In the divided world, education has more often implemented a policy of social control and continuation of the *status quo* than a policy of basic social change and emancipation. Therefore, a concern for the "educational world" must address itself to the political, economic, racial, and ideological factors involved. (General Assembly *Minutes,* p. 33.)

The Assembly called for a restructuring of the university and society—and, in the light of the challenges, of the WSCF itself.

The Twenty-Sixth Assembly of the WSCF met at the end of December 1972 in Addis Ababa, Ethiopia. Regional reports filled the first four days of the Assembly, and regional working groups proposed a broad range of activities in education for the next four years. Asia called for further study of "education or miseducation"; Europe, for investigating education's dependence upon and perpetuation of a class society; Latin America, for student activity with the masses of people; Africa, for emphasis upon liberation in and through education; and North America, varied approaches including women's liberation. The education working group reflected increasing interest in the cultural effects of education, its irrevelance in many places to the local culture, the need for education to work more for social change, and the desire for greater participation of youth in deciding questions of policy in society.

Thus, reflecting student Christian movements on campuses all around the world, the WSCF during the last decade has become increasingly an arena for intense debate about the related topics of education and politics, of schooling and social change. An increasing political awareness about education was becoming evident in many student movements. A related tension has been in the theological interpretation of this development: has it reflected a move away from Christian faith or a move toward valid extension of it in new ways? Greater regional consciousness and structures contributed to the diversity of viewpoints and programs. Organizational strength shifted from Geneva to the regions, a move which symbolized the wider sharing of power in the Federation. Thus through the decade of the 1968 student explosions the WSCF maintained a Christian presence in and concern for education.

The World Alliance of Young Men's Christian Associations

Founded in the mid-nineteenth century, the YMCA counts at least 12 million participants in its programs, including seven hundred thousand volunteers and ten thousand professional leaders working in eighty-two countries. Leadership development therefore finds a high priority in YMCA programs. The YMCA has a tradition of emphasis on education as part of its work. A 1965 consultation at Addis Ababa which explored YMCA development in Africa recommended that "YMCAs should sponsor both formal and informal educational programmes . . . directed towards good citizenship . . . and future responsibilities." Health education and religious education were also emphasized.

At its World Council meeting in 1973, the YMCA recommended stronger programs in development education, including work by national movements toward an understanding of the needs and implications of global development, commitment to the struggle for social, economic, and political justice, and "internationalization" of local YMCAs. In the continuing search for ways to carry forward the "development thrust," a sharp challenge came from the National General Secretary of the Tanzania National YMCA, who pointed out that the YMCA has been a middle-class organization and asked, "To what extent is the YMCA prepared to become involved with the forgotten masses and to involve them in planning and conducting activities? Are YMCA projects really planned *with* the needy and *by them* or will the YMCA continue to plan for gymnasiums, swimming pools and hostels?" (*World Communiqué* [May-June, 1974], p. 17). Through such continuing dialogue, the YMCA searches for ways to develop citizenship participation through education.

Youth programs remain high YMCA priorities. The conflicts of the sixties intensified the generation gap, and YMCA efforts tried to analyze and deal with that problem, and with the unemployment and leisure-time problem related to the technological and urban world. Thrust therefore into political, economic, and social issues, the YMCA attempted to develop guidelines for statements and positions taken by different YMCAs on controversial matters. The 1969 Council recommended that the World Alliance take more definite stands on certain social issues and that the YMCA in general face more directly social and economic issues that need to be resolved according to Christian principles. Education was one of the issues of special importance, as were others affecting young people. Physical education continued to be an important program for youth. Family education, including communication skills, was emphasized also.

The meaning and importance of the letter *C* in YMCA became a major source of discussion during the early seventies. Many local YMCAs had long since opened their programs to non-Christians. From many sides came requests to reappraise the "basis" on which the YMCA had operated since 1855. Substitute statements were offered and studied, theological positions were developed, and throughout the world many local YMCAs worked on the problem in preparation for the Kampala World Council in 1973. At that meeting the original "Paris basis" was reaffirmed. Additional "Kampala principles" were also adopted. Along with the reaffirmation of the Christian basis came continuing emphasis on education by discipleship, Bible studies, Christian unity, and interfaith dialogue. Its most recent World Council therefore worked to re-establish the identity and mission of the YMCA, basing it on Christian principles and extending its work out into the troublesome educational, political, social, and economic issues of today.

The World Young Women's Christian Association

From its beginning as a Christian lay movement in the mid-nineteenth century, the YWCA has focused attention upon young persons and women. The report of its Executive Committee in 1963 began with these words: *"Education in a world of change.* If rapid social change is accepted as one of the most general characteristics of our day, it is true that the two groups of people most affected by it are youth and women. . . ." The report then described three main lines of YWCA education work: (1) understanding its own role and offerings in education; (2) examining educational questions from the Christian perspective; and (3) cooperating with other organizations to develop sound educational systems providing equal opportunity for all. Particular programs emphasized education for international understanding and ecumenical and religious education. Four years later, at the 1967 Council meeting, reports stated that increasing government education efforts should stimulate YWCA work with women and school-leavers, those often ignored by the developing systems. As formal education expanded, the YWCA stressed informal group activities and leadership training, and programs of international understanding. A continuing emphasis was on Christian education and ecumenical questions.

A major draft statement which the Council adopted affirmed the right to education for all and not just a few and the legal right to religious education. It urged that the YWCA should try to influence the development of education in society both by influence upon governments and by working with parents. It proposed establishing institutions of education, and especially developing out-of-school education. It stated that the YWCA needed "an abiding certainty that God is at work in education if we are to recognize the truly common cause we have with others in public education. . . ." With a growing concern for unemployed youth, the program stressed vocational training.

By 1971 the World YWCA had urged national associations to establish national committees on education to study problems and work to help find solutions. At the international level increased involvement in UNESCO activities as a nongovernmental organization opened up ways to affect educational policies. A 1970 consultation on vocational training brought YWCA educators from twenty-seven countries to study better ways of contributing in that field. YWCA librarians met to search for better ways of serving educational needs. Literacy programs were also surveyed and analyzed. An unusual form of training took place near Geneva when leaders from thirty-nine countries gathered for a ten-day live-and-work community study experience in five different local situations, as part of an International Training Institute. In 1972 the UNESCO Tokyo Conference on Adult Education stimulated YWCA activity regarding life-long education and provided motivation for a study of all its adult education work. At the same time, the YWCA reviewed its efforts in literacy programs. Vocational training continued to be a strong emphasis, as the number of unemployed school-leavers increased in many countries.

Thus in the mid-seventies the World YWCA was developing its educational work with women and young people through its own programs and through efforts to influence public systems.

The World Council of Churches

Education has always been an important part of world ecumenical activity. The 1910 Edinburgh Conference published a volume from its discussions on "Education and the Christianizing of the Nations." Although no formal department of education was established at the first WCC Assembly in 1948, the Theological Education Fund began work in the early sixties and programs of youth, laity, and women involved educational activities. In 1961 the WCC Assembly instructed its Division of Ecumenical Action to pay attention to "education in all its aspects." During the sixties increasing attention to education throughout the world called forth a Joint Study Commission on Education from the WCC and the World Council of Christian Education.

The WCCE traced its world ecumenical educational work back into the Sunday school movements of the eighteenth and nineteenth centuries—and specifically to the first World's Sunday School Convention in 1889. Tighter organization had made it an association in 1907, and the broader scope of its work led to its becoming the World Council of Christian Education in 1947. Joint youth work with the WCC and a move of its London office to Geneva in the sixties brought it more centrally into the converging world ecumenical activity in education.

At its assembly in 1968 the WCC established a new Office of Education to bring clearer focus to these activities. Immediately a Joint Negotiating Committee was formed with the WCCE, which led to integration of the two bodies in 1972. Soon a new subunit on education in the Program Unit III Education and Renewal included the former WCCE interests, along with those of the Office of Education and also family education, lay and adult education, and scholarships. The Theological Education Fund still worked in that field, from its London offices, and in the WCC in Geneva education for development, urban industrial missions, and education for mission also worked with education.

The new Office of Education held an initial consultation in 1970 in Bergen, Holland, on "The World Educational Crisis and the Church's Contribution" as a way of testing the results of the Joint Study Commission on Education and finding guidelines for its work.

Representative church leaders, educators, and journalists from eleven countries analyzed current educational planning with a UNESCO expert, studied significant innovations from their own experience, and asked the WCC to help the churches support and reappraise their educational work. The report, entitled *Seeing Education Whole,* suggested in its title and content the broader perspective needed for such rethinking and reconstruction of education.

A major emphasis in the ensuing years by the WCC has been support of consultations around the world for reappraising church strategies in education. All have been planned jointly with regional and national ecumenical agencies. In 1971 a North American meeting studied Silberman's book *Crisis in the Classroom* as a means of moving the churches toward deeper concern for general education. Studies of educational reforms like those in Chile and Peru led a Latin American conference into its analysis and proposals. National consultations in Asia focused on Christian education in the context of the troubled situations there. In Europe a special conference, held jointly with the Lutheran World Federation, concentrated on church education with children and helped educators there face the problems resulting from changes in their situations regarding education and religion. A series of meetings in Africa on "The Role of the Church in the Future of African Education" led to major proposals for Africanization of education, better adult education, and coordination of leadership training for both lay and clergy. In 1975 similar consultations for the Middle East and the Orthodox churches helped reappraisal efforts there.

In 1972 representatives of lay centers and centers of social concern from all around the world gathered in Crete to share their problems and possibilities for residential adult Christian education in their programs, and a world collaboration committee continues to encourage their interchange and leadership development. The following year, thirty family-education specialists in a meeting at Malta reassessed the WCC program of family ministries and proposed broader priorities for leadership development, study of the Christian dimensions of planned parenthood programs, and research into changing family patterns through national case studies. Through a task force the WCC scholarship program shifted its focus from traditional individual overseas academic study toward an emphasis on programs of leadership development within the same cultural area, where short-term group training may fit better the churches' needs for future leadership. In 1974 a major conference sponsored by the Women's Desk in the Renewal subunit on "Sexism in the 1970s" concentrated attention on the place of education in perpetuating sexist stereotypes. In the same year Familia '74, a congress on the family in Tanzania jointly sponsored by the WCC and the International Confederation of Christian Family Movements, immersed nearly three hundred persons from all around the world in experiences in Ujamaa villages, in a country where the tribal family pattern was providing a basis for development of a new society based on "African socialism."

Despite the wide variety of topics and regional and national differences, these consultations showed certain similarities regarding education. In most of them new social conditions were calling for radically new educational strategies on the part of the churches. In Africa the new government systems of education in many countries were "taking over" church day schools. In Latin America political and economic oppression was demanding of the churches new types of liberating education. In the North Atlantic countries the growing secularization of societies was forcing radical changes in traditional patterns of church education. In the face of such challenges, church educators who had for generations identified education with their schools and formal courses found themselves unable easily to free their energies and imaginations to develop new strategies, despite their increasing awareness that the old ones were less and less effective. Ironically, in many cases the churches were doing better educational work than ever before, with improved curricula and teacher training, but the larger and deeper changes were making their efforts less successful. In their growing uneasiness and search for better strategies, they welcomed interdisciplinary and intercultural exchange which could help them gain perspective and understanding and which could give them awareness of fresh options. Facilitating that exchange and meeting those needs therefore became the first major program emphasis of the Office of Education. In the past five years more than 500 church educators from most of the 267 member churches of the WCC have participated in these meetings.

Another major educational activity in the WCC was a prophetic challenge, based on a Christian vision of human beings and society, toward a reconstruction of educational goals and methods. The coming of Paulo Freire to the staff in 1970 helped make this aspect effective. A Brazilian educator famoús for developing a new adult education program in his country, Freire had put together the syllabic Portuguese language and the people's deepest concerns in a new way of literacy training in which they learned quickly not only how to read and write but how to articulate their needs and begin to work together to change society and give them more power over their own lives. His books, especially *Pedagogy of the Oppressed,* were translated into more than ten languages. His way of analyzing education became a stimulating challenge to those who were deeply worried about it and who were searching for clearer understanding and new ways ahead. His method appealed especially to those who were oppressed. They found his analysis a fresh and provocative way of challenging traditional education and the modern powerful social systems, on the basis of the Christian vision of human beings and society.

WCC educational activity therefore expanded into multiple contacts and involvements toward education for liberation. Staff participated in seminars in every continent, with government and intergovernmental agencies, church education and mission agencies and groups, minority groups, students, and liberation movements. In 1973 a seminar in Geneva brought representatives from various action groups to analyze together "education and theology in the context of the struggle for liberation." Later that year, in cooperation with the YMCA, the YWCA, and the WSCF, the education office prepared a reference paper for the International Conference on Education in Geneva, sponsored by the International Bureau of Education, a UNESCO agency, on the theme, "Education, Training and Employment, with particular reference to secondary education." The paper, entitled "Ongoing Social Education," challenged societies and the churches to deal with the causes of the problems, not just the symptoms, and cited various experiments where nongovernmental organizations were engaged in efforts toward that end.

Other major WCC programs also challenged traditional ways of educating. The Theological Education Fund in its Third Mandate, in addition to channeling support to theological colleges in Africa, Asia, Latin America, and the Middle East, developed awareness of contextuality as a way of lessening the dependence of their programs on European and North American patterns and resources. Regional associations began to bring innovative potential closer to the places where theological education and church life took place. The inherited Western style of doing theology as well as the Western patterns of training theologians came under fire from those who sought more authentic grounding of Christian faith and theological education in their own cultures. At the same time the Churches' Commission on Participation in Development was building its programs of education for development. One part tied the WCC to certain "counterpart" situations where innovative efforts were made by local groups to deepen the understanding of human development and to improve ways of bringing people into participation in development programs. Another part focused on Europe and North America, where a great need existed for the churches to help people and governments face up to their responsibility in regard to world trade, aid, and overseas investment. In addition, in the Commission on World Mission and Evangelism, urban industrial mission programs around the world with their community action methods brought an active dimension into the WCC's total work and thinking about education. In 1973 a new education for mission desk promised to bring more resources to the training of the people of God for their mission service. Through all these WCC programs thousands of educators and other church persons have sharpened their Christian critique of education and have been stimulated to work toward more humane education in their societies and their churches.

From 1970 to 1973 the Education Renewal Fund, begun jointly with the WCCE during the period of integration, channeled over one million dollars into more than seventy projects of educational innovation around the world. More than a dozen major curriculum development projects, many of them initiated through WCCE activities before integration, engaged church educators and leaders in rethinking the meaning of faith and the processes of education in the modern world. Other projects included imaginative experiments in training leaders, as with a mobile center in Uganda. Others supported youth secretaries in regional councils of churches. With the end of the ERF in 1973 educational projects continued to be channeled through interchurch aid. During these five years approximately 25 percent of its projects have been in education.

The early seventies have been exploratory years. The WCC now looks to the Fifth Assembly in Nairobi to focus priorities for its future educational work. Section IV of the Assembly on "Education for Liberation and Community" will bring together reports of church educational activity from around the world. Certain emphases already are emerging, such as the following, from which future priorities may develop:

1. Continuing reappraisal of educational strategies in some places, especially with mission agencies.
2. Significant innovations need to be identified and supported.
3. The distinctive Christian contribution needs to be more clearly articulated.
4. Conscientization needs to be further developed and tested more broadly.
5. Church educational work with children needs concentrated attention.
6. Family life education requires special activity in this time of changing family patterns and assumptions.

7. Lay education, or the "theological education of the whole people of God," needs strong development.
8. The provincialism of Christian consciousness and consciences calls for ecumenical global education.

In the next decade the particular forms of educational activity in society and in the churches will continue to change. Educational work in the ecumenical movement will therefore also be changing. The ecumenical organizations included in this article will continue to search for effective ways to work with their colleagues and partner agencies around the world. Education thus continues to be a major priority for the world ecumenical movement.

Bibliography

1. Histories of the ecumenical movement:
Ruth Rouse and Stephen Charles Neill, eds., *A History of the Ecumenical Movement, 1517-1948* (London, SPCK, 1967).
Harold E. Fey, ed., *The Ecumenical Advance: A History of the Ecumenical Movement, Volume 2, 1948-1968* (London, SPCK, 1970).
2. Appropriate chapters in *Orientation in Religious Education; Religious Education: A Comprehensive Survey;* and *An Introduction to Christian Education.*
3. Materials referred to in the article or other materials from the organizations listed may be ordered from:

World Council of Churches
150 Route de Ferney
1211 Geneva 20
Switzerland

WSCF, YMCA, or YWCA
37 Quai Wilson
1201 Geneva
Switzerland

Chapter 18

RELIGIOUS EDUCATION IN WESTERN EUROPE

Krister A. Ottosson

Introduction

In this chapter the assumption is made that we are concerned with all aspects of religious education as they affect the churches. Therefore, as well as considering provision made by the churches for the Christian formation of church members, both children and adults, we will also examine the provision of religious education in the day schools.

Historical Context of the Current Debate

A dominant characteristic of the religious education scene in Western Europe is that of confusion. Worry about the decline in institutional church membership and the desire to build up an informed laity have led people to be concerned about religious education to an unprecedented degree. But those expressing this concern come from widely different ecclesiastical and theological traditions and frequently hold divergent views about the ways people learn and are influenced to a greater or lesser degree by the debate about the relationships between religion and contemporary society.

So, at one extreme there is that group of people in all traditions which is concerned primarily with method. At the other extreme there is the group of people that wishes to raise fundamental questions about the whole operation. These two positions can be said to represent respectively the conservative and radical ends of a spectrum of views about religious education. There is also an infinite number of positions which can be held along this spectrum. The confusion about religious education in Western Europe arises precisely because there is no clear, agreed view about the purpose of the whole exercise.

How has this situation come about? During the nineteenth and early twentieth centuries it was generally assumed in Western Europe that the Christian faith represented the highest that man could attain in

Krister A. Ottosson is Education Secretary for the British Council of Churches, London, England.

terms of religious commitment and moral philosophy. Christianity was regarded as "the truth" to be rejected only by occasional intellectuals, cranks, unthinking heathens, and adherents of other faiths. It was therefore possible to make the following general identifications (recognizing that all generalizations have their exceptions):

a. Religious morality was the same as secular morality in the sense that the latter was seen simply to fall short of the former rather than being distinctively different from it.

b. Christianity was somehow identified with "high culture" and was therefore concerned with the preservation and transmission of inherited excellence. This applied to learning, to the arts, and to social convention and behavior, all of which affected what was generally thought to be "good" in society.

c. Secular socialization and religious socialization were two sides of the same attempt to instill into people basic loyalties to their societies and nations.

Sometime during the first half of the twentieth century a subtle change occurred in the relationship between Christianity and society. There was a subtle shift from the situation where the Christian faith and its institutional expressions were seen as the upholders of all that was good toward which the whole community, enshrined in "the state," should strive, to the situation where the churches were seen as supporters of the status quo in societies which were endeavoring to change.

This change occurred in different European countries at different times and to different degrees. The effect of this change, when it occurs, is radically to alter the fundamental presuppositions underlying the task of Christian education. Part of the problem in Western Europe is that although outside observers can see this process taking place, there are many within the established churches who do not recognize that it has occurred.

There are three essential ingredients underlying the new situation confronting the Western European churches as they seek to reach an understanding of the nature and purpose of Christian education.

a. Some of the formerly dominant social and religious values are regarded as self-evidently false by large sections of the population, in particular the young. For instance, increasing numbers of young Europeans would reject the view that war is a permissible weapon for ensuring peace. Traditional attitudes regarding authority are now criticized for having preserved privilege and untruth. Traditionally great institutions of society like the church and the monarchy are condemned for appearing to have little to do with justice in the affairs of men and much to do with the perpetuation of an unjust past. And the whole concept of "high culture" with its attendant elitism is rejected for its irrelevance to the majority in any society.

b. There has been a wholesale rejection of institutional Christianity. Generally the churches of Western Europe have been unable to cope with the radical social and theological questioning of the age. They remain strong only where they are identified with causes shared by the community (as in Northern Ireland) or where their constituency has shielded itself from the general critique made of the church by society (and this explains the continued Roman Catholic strength in many parts of Western Europe).

c. Christianity has become a minority activity. Within the churches, opinion ranges between those on the one hand who believe the church to be in a predominantly missionary situation in which a revealed religion has to be ever more strongly proclaimed, to those on the other hand who speak of dialogue, openness, the breaking down of institutional structures of the churches in response to many elements in the secular critique, taking seriously the reality of disclosures of the ultimate in secular models, and of education as participation in learning as opposed to the transmission of a body of truth.

An examination of the situation in England consequent upon these social, cultural, and theological changes will illustrate general tendencies in Western Europe as a whole.

The Situation in England

Attitudes toward religious education in England are considerably influenced by the Education Act of 1944. This act prescribed that every school day should begin with a communal act of worship and that every pupil below the minimum school leaving age should receive at least one period of religious instruction each week. A conscience clause was included for the benefit of the Jewish community. The religious instruction to be provided was to be in accordance with an agreed syllabus drawn up by the representatives of the churches and the education authorities.

Thus, laid upon the state was the obligation to provide religious instruction of a Christian nature for children in school. In order to avoid denominational confrontations, the only universally acceptable religious instruction was that which was biblical. It was assumed that the Bible was an acceptable and easily understood book for all Christians, and therefore it was appropriate that this should form the basis of the spiritual and moral development of English schoolchildren for a generation or more.

The religious instruction provided in schools was a means of reinforcing that which was provided in the churches and Sunday schools. All the non-Roman churches in England had large Sunday school systems which implicitly provided long-term denominational training, one of whose objectives was to elicit from teen-agers some form of adult profession of faith. In the Roman Catholic Church there was little in the way of programs of Christian education, and it was assumed that the church member received his instruction in the confessional and in attendance at Mass. In the Church of England, children would normally have been expected to attend Sunday school, followed, in due course, by a specific period of confirmation instruction. After confirmation there was usually no further provision. The Free Churches in England have always laid great store by learning, and a number of channels of religious education have been developed during this century. In the immediate postwar period, the Sunday school was still immensely popular, and in certain parts of the country, notably the industrial north, some form of instruction was available on Sunday afternoons for people whatever their age. In addition, particularly in Methodism, church members would be expected to attend for instruction during a weekday evening. Such instruction would usually consist of a biblical exposition set within the context of an act of worship.

The early sixties radically changed the situation: the "Honest to God" debate brought about for many people a fundamental reassessment of their religious beliefs; the findings of Harold Loukes *(Teenage Religion)* and the British Council of Churches *(Religion and the Secondary School)* caused many to reassess their assumptions about what was in fact achieved in schools in terms of religious education; and the work of Ronald Goldman stimulated a reassessment of church and state provision of religious education. The authors of these works did not themselves initiate a new debate and new thinking; they were the catalysts around which a great upsurge in new thinking could develop. And what was happening in England had its reflection in most parts of Western Europe. The seventies have introduced a new issue of major importance, and that is the emergence of a recognition of a pluralist society. The two kinds of pluralism which are significant are the religious (concerning the acceptance of denominationalism and the existence in society of faiths other than Christian) and the political and philosophical (concerning underlying ideologies conveyed by the schools). In England, the former is currently of greater significance, while in France it is the latter.

As a result of these changes there have been some major changes in religious education in some Western European societies. In England they can be indicated as follows:

Religious education in schools. In those schools which do not have religious foundations it is now regarded as unacceptable that religious education should consist in the presentation of one faith alone. The aims of the subject have been broadened so as to embrace the opening up of pupils' minds to an awareness of the religious dimension of life. In some situations this has resulted in an alliance between people of different religious convictions who have felt threatened by the secularization of society, thus the encouragement given to an organization like the World Congress of Faiths. In other situations there have emerged those who rejected as invalid the implied claim that a religious commitment was better than one which was not recognizable as religious in traditionally understood terms; this has led to a concern that religious education should help young people explore varieties of life-style and form their own commitments from a basis of knowledge rather than ignorance. Hence the encouragement given to organizations like the Religious Education Council (formed in 1973) and numbering representatives of the British Humanist Association among their membership.

As always, Christians themselves are divided. While many Christians are happy to engage in dialogue with adherents of other faiths, many who do so are frequently at the receiving end of attacks from fellow Christians accusing them of neglecting the missionary ingredient in their faith; and while many Christians feel committed to an openness of syllabus in the state school system, there are others in society including nonpracticing Christians who fear the erosion of basic Christian values at the hands of secular intrusion, hence the legal action taken against the Birmingham Education Committee for attempting in 1974 to introduce a syllabus which included a section on communism, and hence the relative strength of movements like the Festival of Light and the Order of Christian Unity which attribute a so-called lowering of the moral values of society partly to the failure of schools to provide adequate Christian education.

On the whole, informed educationists ignore the conservative right and concern themselves with providing an educationally credible base to religious education. The Christian Education Movement, the Education Department of the British Council of Churches, and denominational education divisions have encouraged the debate in this direction, aided by the government-backed Schools Council for Curriculum

Development. But while many church education departments may be in the vanguard of religious education thinking, many bishops, clergy, and ministers having influence on educational provision in restricted localities appear unaware of contemporary educational thinking and reinforce conservative attitudes.

Christian education of children in the churches. Although it is still regarded as acceptable to provide specifically Christian denominational education in the church sponsored day schools, nevertheless all the non-Roman Catholic churches proceed on the assumption that it is the function of the church to make available the resources for the Christian education of their younger members. But even in the Roman Catholic community attempts are being made to supplement the religious instruction provided in the church day school. This new departure for the Roman Catholic community takes the form of provision of some form of religious education in existing youth work programs such as the "chai ro" scheme available to Scouts in Roman Catholic Scout troops, and the introduction of an overtly religious ingredient in some youth-club programs. Additionally, teen-agers would be involved in discussion groups and religious services organized in the homes of certain parishioners where there is experimentation with house churches.

In the Church of England there exists a profusion of individually produced syllabuses and schemes of work designed both to cater for Sunday school members and confirmation instruction. The Church of England has no agreed policy about the age at which young people should be confirmed, and so there is a wide range of practice varying according to churchmanship, local tradition, and the predilection of particular incumbents. Much of the material currently available suggests that its authors may never have heard of Goldman and are unaware of the package of ideas lying behind a phrase like *readiness for religion.* There is also a more open and adventurous group representing a more radical view which is attempting to develop new approaches to the whole matter of Anglican religious education. One branch of this group includes parishes involved in the "Quest" program. Here, subscribing parishes receive regular mailing containing up-to-date program suggestions and ideas relating to contemporary issues. A number of schemes such as this have emerged recently. The implicit theology in many of these schemes is dynamic, open, and existential, and the educational objectives have more to do with nurture than with teaching—though there are even some people participating in these schemes who feel the concept of "nurture" to be too conservative and who adjust their educational aims accordingly.

The Free Churches have tended to be the most systematic of the English churches in their religious education programs. Following the writings of Goldman, these churches committed themselves to the "experiential approach" and established a completely new program for the seventies. The British Lessons Council published its syllabus, "Partners in Learning," which provided a complete set of lesson materials for every Sunday of the year for different age groups ranging from the under fives to the adults. In this program an attempt has been made to provide a relevant experientially based program for all age groups and which established its coherence in the family act of worship. The overall syllabus itself is profoundly biblical in base as opposed to some of the experiential Anglican material which is much less concerned to relate insights discovered in the educational process to a biblical origin. The major problem encountered by the producers of "Partners in Learning" has been the fact that it is much more demanding of the teacher than was the old-fashioned exposition of a biblical text. The traditional Protestant emphasis on knowledge possessed by the teacher to be transmitted to the pupil is here replaced with a joint search for knowledge arising out of experience. This demands an openness and an uncertainty alien to a dominant strand in Protestant culture. At this point, both the Free Churches and the Anglican schemes share an ingredient with radical secular educationists—the view that the integrity of the learning situation depends among other things, on whether or not the teacher as well as the pupil is open to new experiences, insights, and knowledge.

Adult Christian education. In the English churches it has until recently been assumed that the matter of adult Christian education concerned simply the way in which Christians advanced their understanding of the faith as a received body of truth. Thus, adult education was generally thought to occur during the sermon, or in weeknight Bible classes, or talks, e.g., to women's groups. In addition, some church communities have always sustained Bible study groups, which represent a form of self-learning.

The first major breakthrough in the churches' understanding of adult Christian education within the context of the local church communities was the People Next Door program provided by the British Council of Churches in 1967. This was a highly successful program of interdenominational locally based house groups which met, mainly to discuss different denominational approaches to the Christian faith, for a limited period. The success of People Next Door has encouraged experimentation in house group work as a means of educating the adult laity in the churches, and there exists a multiplicity of such programs.

Lay education tends to be highly intellectual, and during the late sixties, university extramural departments increasingly provided courses for Christians who wished to study some aspects of their faith—courses in contemporary theology, church history, biblical exegesis, and so forth. However, a report published by the British Council of Churches in 1974 drew attention to the academic and middle-class presuppositions which underlay lay training provision which church members were encouraged to use and argued that these presuppositions committed Christians to the reinforcement of the status quo in society. The report went on to argue that all education contains implicit political stand-points, and if the churches were committed to changing society, then their adult education provision must become rather less static and more dynamic. It encouraged the churches to involve themselves in com-munity action in which people could become aware of their rights, their needs, and the possibilities open to them to change their living environment. Thus the action/reflection process has begun to find its way slowly into adult education provision by the churches. Needless to say a predominantly middle-class group of churches finds such a development difficult to handle, particularly when its traditional in-volvement in "good works" has often been at the level of charity which reinforces the social structures that cause the needs that charity fre-quently seeks to alleviate.

Christian Education in Western Europe

Some attention will now be given to the European scene as a whole. First of all, *the situation in schools*. In 1958 there came into being an organization called the Inter-European Commission on Church and School (ICCS), with the aim of providing an ecumenical arena for the discussion of issues in religious education common to the various countries in membership. ICCS organizes conferences every three years, and the titles of the 1958 and 1973 gatherings indicate a develop-ment in attitudes toward the nature of religious education: the 1958 conference under the title "The Function of the Gospel in School Education" understood religious education in schools in missionary terms; the 1973 conference under the title "Education Between Gospel and Contemporary Society" analyzed the context within which religious education takes place, destroyed the myth of the neutrality of any educational system, and examined the tensions between religious and other values.

But even in the Europe of the seventies there are wide divergencies of views: In the predominantly Roman Catholic countries the religious education provided by schools is assumed to be overtly Roman Catholic —as in Spain, Italy, and Ireland. In Roman Catholic countries with a strong Protestant minority (Italy and Ireland), that teaching which is provided by Protestants frequently has more sympathy with that provided by non-Christians than that provided by Roman Catholics. This applies not only to countries as a whole, but often to specific regions of particular countries where a strong localized Catholic community is thought to present a threat to a Protestant minority in an otherwise strongly Protestant country; the west of Scotland around Glasgow is a particular example of this manifestation. In countries like Spain, Portugal, Ireland, Scotland, Italy, and Wales, where traditional religious understandings maintain a strong hold on the thinking of society, religious education in schools is invariably professedly Christian and frequently unapologetically denominational.

In most European countries the churches have maintained considerable legal power in matters of religious education, as in Norway, Holland, some regions of Germany, and in Belgium, where they have the power of inspection. But in these countries also the forces of secularization have made deep inroads into traditional religious understandings, and while in some rural areas religious education may be fairly conventional, in urban settings it can be profoundly radical, concerning itself with personality development, the interaction between religions and cultures, the making of choices and the establishment of relevant life-styles. Where the churches attempt to exercise their authority, they are generally unable to distinguish between evangelism and education, and it is usually lay teachers of religious education who are most able to help the subject to develop. Generally, the non-Roman churches are anxious to avoid pressing their claims too strongly out of a fear of evoking a backlash from strong sectors of the community who tolerate religious education up to certain limits. Countries like Sweden and Denmark, where the churches are regarded by many outside observers as subject to considerable state control, the religious education provision frequently claims to be neutral, i.e., teaching about religion.

On the whole, school religious education in Europe stands on Christian assumptions to the degree that the churches are able to exercise overt or implicit control over the curriculum. Where they are not able to do so, secularized values take over (as in many regions of France) and religious education is frequently omitted from the timetable. Where Christians have brought educational criteria to bear on the subject, they have enabled it to develop and, in multiracial areas, moved it on from simply being a liberal study of Christian versus secularized values to enabling it to embrace study of some of the great non-Christian religions as well.

As regards *church education programs for the Christian education of children,* the situation is highly complex. The 1973 consultation jointly organized by the World Council of Churches and the Lutheran World Federation at Glion in Switzerland on Church Education in Europe exposed a wide divergence of opinion, ranging from those who were concerned with more effectively organizing existing church programs and using up-to-date communications techniques to those who wished to be skeptical about the whole of the Christian education enterprise until such time as the churches indicated in their life that they truly were the church. On the whole it can be said that the Roman and Orthodox communities in Western Europe believe in the incorporation of children into the worshiping life of the church, while the Protestant communities concern themselves with knowledge and study leading to informed and responsible profession of faith.

It follows therefore that the more liturgically orientated churches of Western Europe do not concern themselves particularly with Christian education except in so far as they are concerned to resist the forces of secularization. The Protestant churches, on the other hand, have developed a profusion of syllabuses and church education programs, employed specialist education officers, devised modern techniques, published ever more attractive books, provided training programs for teachers, and generally devoted more and more of their budgets to Christian education. The often unmentioned aim lying behind these activities is the reversing of the trend of declining church attendance. On this basis, all these efforts can generally be adjudged as failures.

The most significant development is thought by some to be that which has been tried in Sweden where some city congregations belonging to the Church of Sweden abandon the aim of evangelizing children or teaching them about the Christian faith and, instead, simply set out to meet the needs of children and their mothers by providing weekday afternoon "Sunday schools" in which small children and their mothers learn together those things which they need in order to equip them for life—things like socialization, communication, awareness of and sensitivity to others, and general human relationships. This seems to be in the tradition of the earliest Sunday schools which also set out to do little more than provide children with basic tools that they lacked—like reading and writing. The significant dynamic of the Swedish experiment is that it involves the incorporation of children and their families into the liturgical life of congregations which express their faith in caring concern. The underlying philosophy is that people need to be loved before they are taught, and once they are loved into a community, children will happily share in that community's myths and stories without any problems. The task of Christian education is no longer one of educating (in the sense of imparting information about the faith) the children, but of educating the adults.

Many Christians in Western Europe set a great store by the development of *adult lay training*. There are three areas in which this is taking place: in the work of lay centers, urban industrial mission, and adult education.

The Ecumenical Association of Directors of Academies and Laity Centres in Europe is open to directors of academies and institutions "which endeavour to carry out the service of the Church to society mainly by means of conferences." In 1971 there were forty-nine such places affiliated representing West Germany (15), Netherlands (10), Switzerland (8), France (5), Sweden (3), Britain (3), Finland (2), Austria (2), and Crete (1). There is "corresponding" membership for persons doing society-related work without providing residential accommodation. Its annual budget is in the region of fifteen thousand dollars, half of which comes from the Protestant Church in West Germany. The kinds of issues with which these centers deal are industrial questions, agricultural questions, youth work, communications and the mass media, social and political questions, problems of development aid, organization of leisure, the role of women, legislation, church renewal, research and scientific knowledge, and law and order.

Urban industrial mission is being increasingly developed where groups of Christians become conscious of the dehumanization often endemic in advanced technological societies—the dehumanization of work and the dehumanization of urban living conditions. This work is most developed in Germany, France, and Holland, though with England and Belgium not far behind. Whereas the lay academies help persons to discuss and reach their own views about certain social questions, urban industrial mission attempts to help persons confront social problems in which they themselves are victims in order that they might change society.

Adult education may be defined as that which the churches have developed in the form of curricula, courses, audio-visual aids and sensitivity training, with the prime emphasis on the individual without much reference to his situation. Most of the churches in Europe are attempting some development of this work.

Conclusion

In the introduction to this chapter it was stated that the religious education scene in Western European Christendom was marked by a total lack of coherence and a total confusion of aims. More positively it can be said that this confusion indicates a profound turbulence. If there is one significant element emerging from the turbulence it is a vital concern for the deeply felt needs of people in Western society and a commitment by the churches to attempt to cater for those needs.

There appears to be an implied conviction that if the churches would commit themselves to providing the resources for the handling of human need in whatever form it appears, and if at the same time the churches would forget about any need to preserve ecclesiastical institutions, the religious communities themselves would adapt to contemporary circumstances and avoid the irrelevance of which static church communities are frequently accused.

Chapter 19

PATTERNS OF CHURCH EDUCATION IN THE THIRD WORLD

Gérson A. Meyer

The scope of this subject is obviously beyond the personal knowledge of any one person. Thus, it is necessary to rely upon a few reports published by regional and national leaders and also upon experiences which emerge from personal contacts in some areas of the world. Readers should be warned about this limitation and supplement the information given here with further readings on Christian education developments in different regions. This is just an introduction to a subject that deserves more thorough research.

Through these regional reports and visits, one immediately realizes how much the so-called Third World has in common and how very similar many of the educational problems are, perhaps because we inherited the same church structures transplanted from the same countries, usually the United States and Europe. Even today, as we shall see, the patterns of church education in the Third World are the ones the missionaries brought to Africa, Asia, Latin America, the Middle East, the Caribbean Islands, and the Pacific regions. What we have is what we got from them with all the weaknesses, strengths, and problems caused by the importation of programs which were prepared to fit another culture and social setting. In many cases, the implementation of these programs did violence to well-founded sociological and anthropological premises. Certainly we must pay our respects to dedicated missionaries who did their best and gave their utmost for the cause they were called to serve—not only pay respects, but recognize their pioneering work in difficult times. Many of them had great aspirations and visions for a better future in the country in which they came to minister. On the other hand, it is also important to see the negative points in this whole picture in order to understand what is going on in Christian education in the Third World. The problems we are facing today and the hopes we have for a relevant Christian education program require a study of our inherited patterns and an accurate analysis of the actual programs and plans.

Gérson A. Meyer is Secretary for Christian Education, Program Unit Education and Renewal, World Council of Churches, Geneva, Switzerland.

A meaningful teaching ministry of the church today in the Southern hemisphere should start with a serious analysis of the structures, content, and methodology which have been traditionally accepted by the churches.

Patterns Are Established

For example, one of the most important educational agencies we inherited is the Sunday school. In many places the local Protestant church started with a small Sunday school with a few children who later brought their parents to form the congregation. In the city of São Paulo, Brazil, one church had at one time eighteen branch Sunday schools sponsored by the central Sunday school, and all of them, except one, have today become flourishing churches. As with the first Sunday schools in England, children were collected from the streets and for the first time in their lives, they were cared for, feeling the interest and love of adults. That was primarily what brought their parents to church. The primary and secondary schools, as well as the literacy classes, were another aspect of the missionary concern for those who would otherwise never have had any opportunity of attending a private or state school at the time. At that time schools were established only for the higher classes and for those requiring education to serve colonial administrative purposes, especially in the Western-dominated parts of the Third World. In this respect we haven't changed very much. We still maintain with our church-sponsored day schools a classist system of education and certainly an elitist approach which today harms more than any other thing the neglected masses which are kept in ignorance.

Education was an important factor in the missionary enterprises in Africa, Asia, and Latin America. One could say that Protestant work in Chile started with the introduction of the Lancaster or monitorial system of education. James Thompson, an enthusiast of this system, was invited to start this kind of school in Chile. Thompson was also working for the Bible Society, and his interest thus went beyond establishing schools.[1]

In Christian and general education we had (and still have) in most of the Third World countries a carbon copy of the American and European educational systems. A report from Asia says: "As most of the Sunday Schools in East Asia were started by missionaries, who found little existing educational system at all, the one adopted by these schools is Western-oriented."[2] In Africa and Latin America we find the same situation. Everything was imported: structures, content with different materials, and methodology. Needless to say all this brought with it cultural elements, consciously or unconsciously imposed on the nationals, disregarding their social and cultural heritages. In primary and secondary education, for example, students in Africa were more familiar with the European geography than with their own. They had to know by heart the names of European rivers, and those who were subjects of the British Empire learned lists of the kings and queens of Great Britain.

In Sunday schools things were not different. The lessons were translated into the vernacular without too much concern for a really good adaptation. As a Latin American put it, "Even today some materials for the teaching mission of the Church just change John for Juan, and that is that." Stories and particular incidents all referred to another setting and culture, instead of being rooted in the social context in which the message was being proclaimed. In the fifties, church educators started asking the question about indigenous materials, and then we saw the All Africa Curriculum, the Latin American Course, and the South East Chinese Curriculum, among others, appear with a completely new approach, taking into account life involvement, age level characteristics, and, even to a small degree, the social reality in these regions.

In methodology, we had the same problems. It is true that in many countries planners of educational programs welcomed new methods' of teaching, especially where classroom lectures were the method. In spite of this new methodological approach in teaching in day and Sunday schools, the imported methodology never succeeded in adapting traditional indigenous ways of transmitting their cultural heritage, just because these were considered "pagan ways" or inferior in their sight. One example, in a culture such as the Peruvian, where drama was commonly used by the Incas to transmit their rich traditions, no special efforts were made to use what was familiar in that context for the proclamation of the gospel.[3] The emphasis was, and it is, very much on written and oral communication—the printed page and the classic sermon.

Reference has already been made to the Sunday school as the educational agency in the local church, but other educational agencies must also be mentioned to complete the picture. There were youth groups, women's associations, more recently vacation Bible schools, catechetical classes, Christian endeavor unions, and religious instruction in church-sponsored day schools where religion was part of the curricula and attendance at worship compulsory for everybody.

All these agencies were very important, but none had the prestige of the Sunday school which was, and is, more important than the church services in the rural areas of the Third World. In these areas Sunday schools are carried out by lay women and men, and it is the most important church gathering on Sundays where no pastor is regularly available. Today, there is a tremendous concern for reformulating the role of the Sunday school, especially in Africa and Latin America. "The arm of Christian education," as an African has defined the Sunday school, has certainly done a remarkable work in equipping children and new members, in teaching adults with denominational doctrines, but very little in preparing them for everyday life in a new complex world. As Mercy Oduyoye put it, "A greater part of our Sunday School teaching in Africa has been concentrated on providing answers to possible questions. Some teachers have successfully indoctrinated their students into an unquestioning conformity with law and practice." [4]

Women's associations have been another important arm of the church, but one may ask in certain contexts, whether they do not exist just for raising money and for sewing clothes for the poor. There is no doubt that these associations were important in some areas for evangelizing neighbors and relatives in an atmosphere of love and fellowship, but a real concern for nation-building was certainly not present in these groups in the past. We may laugh today at the kind of programs we had in youth groups some ten or fifteen years ago; the main purpose of these programs was geared toward keeping young people "out of the world," as an old pastor once said. Emile Leonard, a French sociologist, pointed out that youth manuals in one Latin American country used to give quite a lot of "detailed information on how to write a report to the central headquarters," but nothing else about the youth role in the society. Other departments of the local churches, such as men's groups and Boy Scouts, were not widespread in many areas, but Sunday schools, women's associations, and youth groups were well-accepted in the local situations and, as far as we know, they were very active in urban areas. Sunday school, however, is found both in rural and urban areas and there is no doubt of its importance in these regions.[5]

The Old Patterns

What has been said above gives us an idea of the situation. But we must characterize the old patterns in order to understand the present, and we especially need to see clearly what kind of educational programs are necessary in the future to change the present structure and content of materials required for a new and revolutionary world. The first characteristic is the participation of laymen in Christian education. With a lack of pastors, the work in Sunday schools was carried out by dedicated women and men with very little preparation in many cases. Many of them gave most of their free time to the work of the church. Their enthusiasm was certainly an inspiration. In contrast to Europe, Sunday school was (and is) for all ages. In many places, even in the urban areas, Sunday school is the only church activity on Sunday mornings. One may not agree with their motivation and programs, but their concern for what they believe is impressive. The only reason these educational agencies were so widely spread is the fact that lay persons were used, insufficiently prepared, but learning from their own mistakes and shortcomings.

On the other hand, some negative aspects of these patterns must be contrasted with these positive views because they hinder the equipment of all "God's people for the work in his service" (Eph. 4:12 NEB) in a time like this. Five characteristics of these patterns should be briefly mentioned here: the conservative approach to Bible and doctrine; the disassociation from the social reality; the ghetto mentality; the narrowness of the objectives for Christian education; and the fragmentation of the educational programs. All these together have been impediments to the development of a creative and realistic educational program meeting the needs of today.

In some areas of the Third World, Protestants have been called the "people of the Bible." Not only Pentecostals, who are new to these areas, but also members of the historical denominations have been identified in this way. They all emphasize Bible readings at home, they carry a Bible when they attend the local church, and they talk about it. However, we read it in our own way, and we use it for our own purposes, which makes a Third World member church not very much different from others. In general terms, our Christian education programs are Bible-centred, and most of the "teaching" is biblical information out of the social context in the assumption that "what you do not need today, you certainly need tomorrow." A Latin American leader writes: "Biblical and theological contents are far from being recommendable for a conscientious teaching task in the Church. We find isolated and unrelated Bible verses, untrue interpretations and material loaded with unhealthy doctrine. We then challenge our children to repeat and memorize disconnected and senseless stuff." [6] "Our Christian responsibility," said another Latin American leader, "is to save souls, not to solve their slum problems," referring to the emphasis some leaders were putting on social dimensions of the gospel for the neglected people in the slums. With this narrow approach to the Bible, Sunday schools and other agencies in the local churches missed the opportunity offered on Sundays to study the Bible in a relevant way and thus equip tens of millions attending church services.

Inevitably, this leads to the next point: Protestant people have been happy inside the four walls of the local church where they feel secure from the world around. A good church member is the one who doesn't do this and that (the record is long). The teaching ministry of the church is carried out with no connection whatsoever with social, cultural, and economic reality. For this reason today, we do not condemn classist societies where the rich are richer every day and the poor poorer by the control of many by a small elite, and we do not see anything wrong with people living in inhuman conditions. We do not, as a worldwide church, raise our voice to protest against torture and the denial of human rights. Groups related to problems of church and society were looked at with suspicion by many Protestant leaders, and the inclusion of these concerns in the texts for the educational agencies of the local church met always with opposition from these leaders. Such a disassociation places the church, for many, outside the world, because its members do not live in the world. They are in the world to earn a living, but they do not care for politics or social change of the structures. We were taught to look at the church as our refuge.

Thus, a ghetto mentality is evident in the attitudes, hymns, Christian festivals, sermons, and general programs. The only place where we feel at home is inside the local community and in our homes. We were not nurtured to be the salt of the earth in the real sense of the word. Evangelism becomes excursions into the world to bring some refugee back. As Hans-Reudi Weber put it:

> This gives the impression that Christ is only the centre of the life of the Church. The world becomes then exclusively the bad world and the realm of the devil. Through such a conception there grows, inevitably, a wide gulf between the Church and the world, between Sunday and working day, worship and work, and between our Christian faith and the day to day decisions in our family life, professional life and life as citizens.[7]

Such a concept is well reflected in our teaching materials, with some exceptions, and the programs are available for proof. The wrong interpretation of the Bible has created this ghetto mentality which has been responsible for many negative attitudes by Third

World people toward what the gospel means for the whole person, from womb to tomb in all his relationships.

For historical reasons, the main purpose for the Protestant church's ministry in education has always been "to make converts" among pagans and Roman Catholics. That was also the reason for opening schools or establishing literacy classes. What was wrong with this approach was not the dominant emphasis on evangelism, but the lack of nurturing concepts for educating children, young people, and adults in the contextual reality. They took the first part of the "Great Commandment" very seriously, but they neglected the second part.[8] In Africa, church schools were the source for church membership. Today when governments are taking over these schools, churches are reappraising their role in education, trying to find new ways of making a new contribution to education in nonformal and informal ways in order to respond to a new emerging issue for which the church must feel itself responsible.

For years and years we have been putting our educational programs in boxes. A good picture of this situation is given by William B. Kennedy:

> Theological education was separated from the parish programmes; church schools and colleges formed two other organizations separate from the rest; church work on university campuses still another; lay training and men's and women's groups engaged on other separate educational activities, and even within the parish the pastor carried on his traditional confirmation class independently from the Sunday School and youth activities.[9]

This picture characterizes very well the educational programs in the Third World. It has not been easy at all for church educators to find a holistic approach in planning for local churches. This fragmentation has caused a tremendous waste of time and resources which hinders an effective work, and it has isolated the educational program of the church from its context as already mentioned. This of course does not apply only to the Third World, but it is particularly harmful to developing countries where funds available for church education are very limited indeed.

Present Situation

There are hopes that things will change. From the crisis we are experiencing, where ferment is present, certainly a different pattern will emerge. Sunday schools are no more what they used to be in many parts of the world. "Today the Sunday School teacher in Africa is a potential force for revolutionizing many aspects of the Church and even the society." [10] Youth groups, as a special department in the local church, are being replaced by some other flexible kind of work regardless of age. Very few denominations in the Third World keep the traditional youth programs of the old days. Women's associations traditionally dealing with prayer meetings, sewing sessions, and fund-raising activities, are now discussing seriously a more active participation in church and society. Gone are the days when they passively accepted, without resistance, a secondary role. Lay centers for social concerns are also found in Africa, Asia, Latin America, and related areas, where adults are nurtured in different ways to be better equipped for their role in the life of the community.

Content and methodology in educational programs have been challenged "to make the study of the Christian faith dynamic . . . in order to find God's revelation in present history for the current problems, concerns and aspirations of the people living in communities and in a country plagued by troubles of a developing society." Reports from all parts of the world say more or less the same. Fed up with irrelevant materials and traditional authoritarian methodology, Christians in the Caribbean Islands go beyond, asking for major changes in the educational programs. What is called for now is a

> complete de-colonization represented by cutting dependence upon ex-Caribbean sources of support both in terms of finances, supply of media resources and personnel, content of written materials and conceptualising. De-colonization of the mind is an even greater and more urgent imperative and must be a priority in content and methodology at the institutions which prepare our leaders, ordained and not ordained.[11]

The old narrow objectives for Christian education must be changed to be bold, aggressive, and prophetic. From the 1971 World Council of Christian Education Assembly in Lima, Peru, comes a challenge:

> To educate is not so much to teach as it is to become committed to a reality in and with the people; it is to learn to live, to encourage creativity in ourselves and in others; and, under God and his power, to liberate mankind from the bonds that prevent the development of God's image. This will necessarily require radical change in the objectives, contents and methods of our educational task.[12]

In this statement, participants from eighty seven countries show that they are not simply interested in teaching "truth concerning God," but in what God is doing through us in order to liberate those who are under all kinds of oppression. The "Message to the Churches" called for "radical changes in the objectives, content and methods of our educational task." It is not easy to change the old patterns, but there are signs of willingness, and one can see these signs in action groups, innovations, and new experiments here and there. In some areas, due to a decline in Sunday school enrollment and attendance at other church activities, new options are being sought and new programs being undertaken. Among these are the New Life in Christ Course in Latin America for illiterates and semi-illiterates, which takes into account the particular situation of dispossessed people in rural and slum areas; the special programs for rural youth in Asia under the Christian Conference of Asia Youth Secretariat; and development issues built into the materials being prepared for the Caribbean churches and others.

Leaders in all the Third World countries are raising their voices these days against the traditional patterns kept through the years as "sacrosanct":

> The present structure of the Church institution is linked to the power structure and has ceased to be the assembly of the called people. In order to become the church, the church must be de-institutionalized. A church free from the temptation of power, free of its buildings, free of social influence, a *church of poverty*, may again become the "light of the world," "the salt of the earth" and the leaven of the nations.

> Education is the service of the Church for the salvation and liberation of man, the community and the nation. This mission determines its relations with the other institutions of society, including the State, both in struggle and cooperation. Society reproduces within its educational system the injustices which we find in its economic and social set-up. Furthermore, the Church has turned the system into the only means of promotion. Therefore, the Church must concentrate on these phenomena; one, to reform the system to make it more just, and to create other forms of education which would lead towards the liberation of man, the community and the nation.

> In order to assist lay people and clergy, women and men, young and old, to discover and perform their Christian life and action, our programmes of Christian, theological, laity education and leadership development must be renewed.[13]

These voices, from three continents, could be multiplied in order to show how wide is this concern for change in Christian and general education. The important factor is that such cries are louder today, and some leaders are becoming impatient with the resistance on the part of church leaders to undertake the radical changes necessary for the church to be *the Church*.

Conclusion

The task before us in the Third World is tremendous. How can churches equip people for this complex and revolutionary world? How can Third World churches be aware of the completely neglected masses? How can the church in these areas face its problems before it is too late? How can the church "confront the economic structure of society wherein the gap between the wealthy and the poor is widening and where new increasing affluence is making the gap increasingly more difficult to bear?"[14] How shall we understand that traditional educational agencies are collapsing and that new agencies, such as trade unions, political parties, clubs, peer groups, are far more effective? How should we prepare children, young people, and adults for their role in these new educational agencies? These and many other questions are before us, demanding urgent solutions.

The following are some of the important issues facing church educators and others in the Third World: an ecumenical education which leads to the unity of mankind, freeing people from race, class, and sex discrimination; programs to enable individuals and groups to denounce injustice and work for the establishment of a new relationship among all persons and nations; an educational system which will serve the majority of the people and not just an elite; educational programs in the churches to prepare men and women for their specific role in the society; and a kind of education to allow every person to participate fully in the transformation of church and society.

It is encouraging that today all the regional councils in the Third World have an educational department. This was not the case some fifteen years ago. They have been fully involved in finding solutions for the above questions, but also trying to find the distinctive role churches must play in education today.[15] They may not represent all the Christians in their areas, but they surely offer their services to all, and their influence extends beyond the affiliated member churches to governmental agencies dealing with education and development, liberation movements in the case of Africa, nongovernmental organizations, independent groups, and many other persons not connected with the church at all. Some of the most significant issues in education today are being raised and analyzed by these educational departments in cooperation with national and international organizations. As it was said, the ferment is acting there, and certainly the future will see some relevant changes in the old patterns of church and general education.

NOTES

1. R. C. Moore, "Los Evangélicos en Marcha . . en America Latina," in *Editoriales Evangelicas Bautistas* (Santiago, Chile, 1959), pp. 23-25.
2. J. Gamboa, Jr., "Sunday Schools in East Asia," *World Christian Education,* 26 (1971), 2.
3. Garcilaso Inca de la Vega, *Comentarios Reales de los Incas,* vol. 1, bk. 2 (Lima: University of San Marcos, 1960), pp. 206-10.
4. Erich F. Voehringer, "The Development of Religious Education in Other Countries," in *Orientation in Religious Education,* P. H. Lotz, ed. (Nashville & New York: Abingdon-Cokesbury Press, 1950); Oduyoye "The Role of Sunday School Teachers in Africa Today," *World Christian Education,* 26 (1971), 2.
5. Emile-G. Léonard, *O Protestantismo Brasileiro* (São Paulo, Brazil: Associação de Seminarios Teológicos Evangélicos do Brasil, 1963).
6. Luis F. Reinoso, "Sunday Schools in Latin America," *World Christian Education,* 26 (1971), 2.
7. Weber, *Salty Christians: A Handbook for Lay Training Courses* (Geneva: World Council of Churches, 1959).
8. Matthew 28: 19-20.
9. Kennedy, "Seeing Education Whole" (Address at the Strategy Workshop on Education, Freetown, Sierra Leone, 1972).
10. Oduyoye, "Sunday School Teachers, 26 (1971), 2.
11. F. Allan Kirton, "Christian Nurture and Caribbean Development," in *With Eyes Wide Open,* David I. Mitchell, ed. (Christian Action for Development in the Caribbean, 1973), p. 150.
12. "Message to the Churches," Assembly of the World Council of Christian Education at Lima, Peru, 1971. See "Encuentro: New Perspectives for Christian Education," *World Christian Education,* 26 (1971), 3-4.
13. Hugo Ortega, *Toward a New Perspective in Christian Education in Latin America* (Mexico, 1972); report from All Africa Conference of Churches Consultation on the Role of the Church in the Future of African Education, Limuru, Kenya, 1974; John England, "Asia: Priorities for Life and Action," *Education Newsletter,* 2 (World Council of Churches, 1973).
14. "Christian Education and Lay Training in Asia," a statement by the East Asia Christian Conference Consultation, Singapore, 1967. EACC changed to Christian Conference of Asia (CCA) summer of 1973.
15. All Africa Conference of Churches, Christian Conference of Asia, Caribbean Conference of Churches, Latin American Commission on Christian Education, Middle East Council of Churches, and the Pacific Council of Churches. These councils are all equipped with an educational department, as well as some of the national councils.

Chapter 20

ROMAN CATHOLIC
RELIGIOUS EDUCATION

James Michael Lee

Jesus' last commission to his friends on earth was a twofold one: to engage in the sacramental ministry and to teach religion (Matt. 28:16-20). Consequently, since the very beginning of its existence, the Roman Catholic Church has generally centered its activities around the sacramental ministry and religious education. Indeed, history plainly gives testimony to the sorry fact that when the Catholic Church has accorded heavy attention to so-called secular affairs, to the neglect of enriching and renewing its fundamental twofold mission of sacramental ministry and religious education, the church and its mission have tended to deteriorate.

One major point should be constantly kept in mind concerning Roman Catholicism in general and Roman Catholic religious education in particular: *There is more genuine pluralism and sharp divergence within Catholicism than most non-Catholics imagine.* This phenomenon is not of recent origin; it has been part and parcel of the church since the earliest centuries. Reviewing the history of Christianity, the present writer discovered that when Protestants have disagreed among themselves on some crucial religious or doctrinal point, they typically started a new denomination. But when Catholics have disagreed among themselves on some major religious or doctrinal point, they frequently founded a new religious order or a new school of spirituality. In contemporary American Catholic religious education, the religion teacher, the priest, the parish, the school, the diocese, and the region can, and often do, operate as a separate, basically uncontrolled entity. These persons, groups, and institutions do, of course, work within that defined but rather elastic framework called Catholicism; nevertheless, they do act with far more independence and with far less accountability than is imagined. Indeed, it can be legitimately argued that what is urgently needed in Roman Catholic religious education is not an abandonment of a monolithic structure (which never really existed in the United

James Michael Lee is Professor of Religious Education in the Department of Graduate Studies in Education, Notre Dame University, Notre Dame, Indiana.

States), but rather some unity and order. It would appear that the desire to introduce some semblance of unity and order into Roman Catholic religious education was one of the primary reasons why the Vatican's Sacred Congregation of the clergy issued the *General Catechetical Directory* in 1971 and urged every country to formulate its own *National Directory*.[1]

The Purpose of Religious Education

Throughout the history of the Roman Catholic Church in the United States, three purposes of religious education have been proposed at one time or another, namely the moralist, the intellectualist, and the integralist. The predominant one, historically speaking, has been the moralist purpose. The moralist viewpoint contends that the primary proximate purpose of religious education consists in making the learner more virtuous. Religious knowledge and understanding are of secondary importance and have their place in the religion lesson only to the extent that they promote virtue in the learner. The intellectualist position has always had its staunch adherents, especially in Catholic schools conducted by certain religious orders such as the Jesuits. The intellectualist position holds that the primary proximate purpose of religious education lies in the intellectual development of the learner in matters pertaining to religion. Moral or religious virtues are either impossible of being taught or are outside the purview of any formal agency of religious education.[2] The intellectualist position came to especial salience in American religious education during the late fifties and the sixties due to several factors, including the resurgent Catholic interest in high-level theology and biblical studies, the criticism made by such scholars as John Tracy Ellis and Thomas O'Dea that Catholic education in virtually all its forms was anti-intellectual, and finally, the writings of religious education theorists such as Gabriel Moran who hoped that religious education would become the basically intellectual endeavor of understanding revelation and theologizing "catechetically." [3] The integralist position maintains that the primary proximate purpose of religious education is an amalgam of understanding, love, and action, all coequally blended into a definite Christian life-style. There seems to be a trend in the seventies toward adopting the integralist position, a trend accelerated by at least two factors, namely a growing awareness on the part of Catholic religious educators that religion-teaching must be guided by holistic, life-style–oriented purposes, and second, by the impact of the books, articles, and speeches of the present writer who has consistently championed the integralist view.

The Locus of Religious Education

Religious education in the Roman Catholic Church in the United States is typically situated in two basic kinds of loci, the Catholic school and, for want of a better term, in milieux other than the Catholic school. Indeed, the very phraseology into which these two settings were just now cast reflects both the history of Roman Catholic religious education in America and its present dilemma.

The Catholic school. The Roman Catholic school system as it presently exists is unique in the church, both in the modern world and throughout all of ecclesiastical history. There does not seem to be any precedent in church history for the American Catholic endeavor of establishing a total system of church-related schools for the general education of *all* children and youth regardless of vocational destination.[4] Never before had the Roman Catholic Church in any country established such a *total* school enterprise, ranging from kindergarten all the way through graduate schools and professional schools (including dental schools, for example). Why did this exceptional phenomenon occur in, of all places, the New World? The answer to this question lies in the history of the nation and its public schools. The English colonists established basically a Protestant country, and this strong Protestant flavor lasted well up until recent times. At the time of the Revolutionary War, Catholics numbered less than 1 percent of the population. In 1820 their number had risen to 2 percent; in 1840 to 4 percent; in 1850 to 7 percent; in 1860 to 10 percent; in 1920 to 19 percent; in 1940 to 17 percent, and in 1970 to 24 percent.[5] The public schools tended to reflect and even to transmit this Protestant character of the United States as shown in the aforementioned population figures. It was during the two decades from 1840-60 that the Roman Catholic Church made the full and earnest psychological commitment to establish its own separate school system on a widespread scale.

This commitment by no means suggests a lack of formal, Catholic, pre-1840 ecclesiastical statements promoting the Catholic school or the nonexistence of a goodly number of Catholic schools before this time. Indeed the First Provincial Council of Baltimore (1829) urged the establishment of Catholic parochial schools because of what the council fathers perceived to be an anti-Catholic bias in the public school curricula and in American society at large. The Fourth Provincial Council of Baltimore (1840) warned Catholics that public schools constituted a danger to the faith of those Catholic children attending them. In 1840 there were over 450 Catholic churches with "at least two hundred parish schools in the country"—although it may be questioned whether these schools were truly parochial and whether they were schools in the full sense of the term *school*.[6] In addition, there did exist in various parts of the country some private, nonparochial elementary and secondary schools conducted under the auspices of various religious orders. Notwithstanding the facts adduced in this paragraph, the key point remains that prior to the 1840-60 period there was no firm, full, or irreversible commitment made by Roman Catholic officials to set up a separate, total Catholic school system on a nationwide scale.

That the period from 1840-60 saw the rise of a total commitment to a complete Catholic school system is not surprising in the light of the history of this era. Militant anti-Catholicism was at one of its most feverish pitches in the entire saga of the United States. Bible riots, burnings of Catholic churches and convents, publication of virulent anti-Catholic tracts, and mass anti-Catholic meetings were not uncommon occurrences. It was this social climate, compounded by the sudden tremendous increase in the Catholic population (a 250 percent increase during the 1840-60 period, from 4 to 10 percent of the total population) which served as fuel for the fire of intense "Catholic identity and separation" ignited by the Great School Controversy in New York in the early 1840s. This heated dispute involving the conservative and headstrong John Hughes, Catholic bishop of New York on one side and the Public School Society (a private, Protestant-oriented association) on the other side eventuated in the originating for the first time of a deliberate, full Catholic commitment to the organized, wholesale establishment of a separate and total Catholic school system.[7] It was Hughes who enunciated what was to become a guiding principle for American Catholicism, a principle which lasted well up until the Second Vatican Council: "Let parochial schools be established and maintained everywhere; the days have come, and the place, in which the school is more necessary than the church." And so it came to pass that from Hughes's day until Vatican II, Catholic schoolbuildings were often erected before the church edifice, with Mass and other liturgical services conducted in the school hall. The original underlying rationale for this predilection for Catholic schooling has consistently been that the public school was *de facto* a nonsectarian, Protestant school, and hence unsuited and injurious to the proper religious education of Catholic children. By the end of the 1840-60 period, however, the adjective *godless* began to be substituted for *Protestant* in Catholic characterizations of the public school. This change in Catholic perception, in effect, spelled the end of any viable possibility for Catholics, Protestants, and public schoolmen to effect a working rapprochement whereby a state-supported, multidenominational common school system could be brought into being.[8] During the twenty-year period from 1840-60, Catholic parishes, dioceses, and religious orders began a stepped-up organized program to erect Catholic schools at every educational level.

The First Plenary Council of Baltimore (1852) specifically urged that schools be established in connection with all churches in each and every diocese. But it was the Third Plenary Council of Baltimore (1884) which formally legislated the establishment of a diocesan school system by ordering that "near each church, where it does not exist, a parochial school is to be erected within two years . . . and it is to be maintained *in perpetuum* . . . . All Catholic parents are bound to send their children to the parochial schools." In 1918 the highest ecclesiastical authority in the worldwide Roman Catholic Church issued the *Code of Canon Law (Corpus Juris Canonici)*, a massive compilation which codified into one single volume all the decrees and laws issued by the church since apostolic times. Canon 1374 strictly prohibits Catholic children and youth to attend public schools or any other educational institutions which are not specifically Catholic. Attendance by Catholics at schools not under Catholic auspices can be approved only in exceptional cases. Canon 1379 requires that bishops establish and that the laity support Catholic elementary and secondary schools; this same canon also strongly urges that Catholic universities be erected. In 1929 Pope Pius XI issued his famous encyclical *Divini Illius Magistri* in which he authoritatively stated that since the very nature of any school is such that it is subsidiary and complementary to the family and to the Catholic Church, a public school or any other form of nonreligious school cannot exist either theoretically or practically. This encyclical further forbade Catholic children and youth to attend schools which were not Catholic in nature and curriculum, except by special permission from the local bishop.[9]

By the time the Second Vatican Council (1962-65) had come, there was some serious criticism being voiced among certain articulate Catholics about the necessity and effectiveness of a total Catholic school system as the optimal means for religious education. The first major salvo was fired by Mary Perkins Ryan who argued that the

Catholic school system did not provide the best kind of religious education because it often tended to be ghettoistic, anti-ecumenical, and not promotive of a family-centered religious education orientation. The second major tremor which received national attention was an article by the present writer which urged the abandonment of Catholic elementary schools on the grounds that the available empirical data suggest that deeper religious attitudes and values are not learned by children in the age range of six years to puberty.[10]

In the ten years which have elapsed since the last edition of this book of essays on religious education, edited by Marvin Taylor, there has been a critical examination of the necessity and role of Catholic schooling. This critical examination has been characterized by serious questioning of the wisdom of allocating such a disproportionately heavy amount of money and personnel on a school system which serves only a small segment of the Catholic population. Moreover, this critical examination of the Catholic school, accompanied by a sharp decrease in both the number of Catholic schools and the number of children and youth attending Catholic schools, has typically revolved around the following six points. *First,* American Catholics are starting to realize that their obligation to send their children to a Catholic school exists *only* if such a school is necessary for the child's overall religious education; a child might in fact be able to receive a well-rounded religious education without ever attending a Catholic school. Hence emphasis is shifting away from a preoccupation with the Catholic school system as such toward a stress on those educational means, institutional or otherwise, which can best promote religious growth and development in the learners. *Second,* both the available hard empirical data together with the average Catholic's experiential "hip-pocket data" have led to a serious questioning of the classical assumption that the survival and prosperity of the Catholic Church in America depends in large measure on the existence of a Catholic school system. *Third,* there seems to be some doubt as to the religious effectiveness of Catholic schooling. Thus, for example, a national research investigation comparing Catholic students attending Catholic schools with matched Catholic students attending public schools discovered that in terms of the practice of the virtue of charity (identified by the investigators as constituting "the essence of Christianity") there was no noticeable difference between the two groups of students. In various onsite consultation visitations made by the present writer, there appears to be scant evidence that religion permeates the entire Catholic school curriculum—or even that religion is a particularly distinguishing feature of the Catholic school experience. These data become particularly disquieting when it is recalled that the primary reason why parents send their children to Catholic schools is to deepen and enhance their offsprings' religious understanding and life-style.[11] *Fourth,* Catholics are asking themselves whether a separate school system is indeed religiously ghettoistic and thus corrosive of the most relevant, the most catholic, and the most Catholic kind of religious education. *Fifth,* there is increasing concern within the Catholic community as to whether the very existence of Catholic schooling actually encourages parents to evade their crucial responsibility as the chief religious educators of their children. *Sixth,* with the United States Supreme Court decisions since World War II ruling emphatically against federal and state subventions for denominational schools, coupled with the rapidly rising costs of operating a separate school system, Catholics are giving serious thought as to whether the substantial financial burden involved in maintaining a total Catholic school system is justified. This financial burden is exacerbated by two post-Vatican II developments. The sharp decline in vocations to the priesthood, brotherhood, and sisterhood has left the Catholic school system in short supply of relatively low-cost, dependable teaching personnel. Also, the increasing number of lay teachers staffing Catholic schools has added considerably to the fiscal problems of running a separate school system.

The present writer is firmly convinced that Catholic schools are useful and necessary for the church to the extent that they result in religious outcomes consistently superior to those of alternate forms of religious education. It seems obvious that any discussions and decisions as to whether to keep, abandon, alter, or enlarge the present Catholic school system must be made primarily but not exclusively on the basis of its effectiveness in developing religious outcomes in its students.

Nonschool Catholic milieux. Foremost among the nonschool Catholic milieux for religious education are those associated with the Confraternity of Christian Doctrine (CCD) which was founded near the beginning of the twentieth century. The purpose of the CCD has always been to encourage and assist the religious education of all those Catholics, regardless of age or circumstance, who were not enrolled in Catholic schools. However, until the sixties the major focus of the CCD was, in fact, on Catholic children and youth who did not attend Catholic elementary or secondary schools. For these children nearly every parish supplies a weekly religion lesson, usually lasting about one hour, and typically staffed by volunteer, untrained teachers.

Though it was erected as a general-purpose, nonschool agency, the CCD program for children and youth seems to have been based on a school model. Perhaps this factor, along with the use of untrained teachers and a very limited time and budget allotment, largely explains the empirical research evidence which indicates that the CCD has not adequately performed its task in terms of the achievement of its objectives.[12] Beginning with the mid-sixties there has been a renewal of CCD in terms of energizing, assisting, and actively engaging in all sorts of nonschool religious-education programs, such as those for adults, parents, preschool children, and so on.

Religious Education as a Distinct Field

One of the most significant developments in very recent American Catholic religious education is the emergence of religious education as a recognized field in its own right. The radicalness of this new development can be graphically demonstrated by comparing this chapter with the chapters on Roman Catholic religious education which appeared in the two previous editions of this Marvin Taylor handbook. In Taylor's 1960 edition, Gerard Sloyan, the author of the Catholic chapter, does not treat religious education as a field. Indeed, in that chapter nearly half the space is allotted to a treatment of Catholic schools while the remaining half deals with the European origins of the catechism, the use of the Bible in religious education, and key personnel in religious education. In Taylor's 1966 edition, Neil McCluskey, the Jesuit author of the Catholic chapter, devoted his entire essay to the Catholic school. In this current third edition of the Taylor handbook, we see for the first time about half the Catholic chapter devoted specifically to religious education as a separate field distinct from Catholic schooling. This cursory content analysis serves to indicate that by the seventies much of the American Catholic Church had come to the realization that religious education is not synonymous with Catholic schooling or with CCD. Religious education is perceived now to be a special work demanding focused scholarship, unique training programs, and personnel who are specifically prepared in a distinctive field of activity known as "religious education." In such a conceptualization, religious education is regarded as comprising the religion lessons in the Catholic school, the help which religious-education workers give to other subject-matter teachers in the Catholic school, released-time religious education, adult religious education situated in institutional or noninstitutional settings, preschool education offered in institutional or noninstitutional settings, and so forth. Religious education is beginning to come into its own and is gradually being regarded by Catholics as a single, unitary enterprise, irrespective of the setting in which it occurs. It is impossible to overemphasize the enormous theoretical and practical consequences which this emerging development has caused in the pastoral work of the Catholic Church in the United States at every level. Further, the growth of a distinct field of religious education within American Catholicism has enabled Catholic religious educationists and educators to engage in a depth of ecumenical dialogue and shared activities with Protestants which the very structure, rationale, and preservation orientation of a separate Catholic school system all but precluded.

Current Leitmotifs in Catholic Religious Education

The following ten leitmotifs tend to characterize the main current of present-day Catholic religious education.

Revelation. There is focused attention on religious education as fundamentally a personal, ongoing relationship between the learner and the triune God who is here and now disclosing himself to the learner in every facet of the world in which the learner lives.

Kerygma. Religious education is regarded as a joyous affair in which the learner understands the good news of salvation and lives in a celebrational world which has been made fresh by the cross/resurrection event.

Christocentric Personalism. Religious education is aimed toward enabling the learner to develop and live out his full human potential as this potential is illumined and empowered by the conscious awareness of Jesus as constituting the learner's enabler and his Point Omega.

Bible. The Scriptures are used in religious education not only as an indispensable norm for Catholic behavior, but also as an inexhaustibly rich wellspring from which the learner can draw in order to make his own life as religiously actualized and fruitful as possible.

Ecumenism. Catholic religious education is by and large committed to tapping the distinctive Christian perspectives of other Christian denominations in order to simultaneously deepen the religious lives of Catholics and to actively work side by side with non-Catholic Christians in together building a Christocentric world where all men can grow more fully in the love of Jesus.

Doctrine. There has been a decided shift away from a heavy (and sometimes exclusive) stress on doctrinal formulae and creedal state-ments to an awareness that authentic doctrine is one which is a living, loving, processing relationship with God and with all of God's creation.

Multimilieux. A firm commitment exists that religious education is a discrete enterprise which properly takes place in a wide variety of settings rather than some sort of overly general activity which is simply confined to the Catholic school or to CCD classes for elementary and secondary schoolchildren.

Multiclientele. Whereas religious education heretofore was con-centrated almost exclusively on children of school age, the religious education movement has broadened its clientele base to include large-scale new programs aimed at other populations, particularly at pre-school children, adults, and family groups.

Professionalism. In sharp contrast to the previously existing situa-tion, there is now a growing insistence on graduate training in religious education for all administrators and teachers of religious edu-cation, for curricula to be built by trained personnel, and for the development of special new administrative positions and organizational structures to manage the various mushrooming sectors of the religious education enterprise.

Social-Science Approach. There appears to be an emerging trend —sometimes explicitly stated, more often implicitly enacted—among religion teachers, curriculum developers, and administrators toward the social-science approach to religious education and away from the theological approach.[13]

Major Theorists in Catholic Religious Education

An educational practice is, at bottom, the enactment and partial enfleshment of some educational theory. Put in a homespun idiom, educational practice is basically educational theory on the hoof. More than anyone else, therefore, it is the theorist of religious education who ultimately and most profoundly shapes the teaching and ad-ministrative praxis of religious education.

Until the mid-fifties there had never been an American Catholic religious education theorist of outstanding calibre. Prior to this time, and indeed until the mid- to late sixties most American religious education practice was derived from European Catholic religious educa-tion theorists. For the first half of this century the Europeans who exerted the greatest influence on American Catholic religious educa-tion were Otto Willmann, Heinrich Stieglitz, and the other German and Austrian theoreticians who devised the so-called Munich Method first in articles in the Munich-based periodical *Katechetische Blätter* and then at the First International Catechetical Congress in Vienna (1912). The Munich Method was organized around the famous Herbartian steps of pedagogy and accorded significant attention not only to the product content of the religion lesson but also to instructional practice (albeit of a completely transmissionist genre). In 1936 Josef Andreas Jungmann, perhaps the most high-level and influential European religious education theorist of this century, published his book *Die Frohbotschaft und unsere Glaubensverkündigung* which triggered in postwar European and American Catholic circles an emphasis on the kerygmatic character of religious education. Johannes Hofinger (Jungmann's student at the University of Innsbruck) and Alfonso Nebreda further developed and elaborated the main themes originally set forth by Jungmann; these two Jesuits also lectured extensively throughout the United States from the fifties onward. Jungmann's fellow Jesuits at the theologically oriented International Center for Studies in Religious Education (founded 1946) in Brussels—most notably Marcel van Caster and Pierre Ranwez—highlighted the kerygmatic accent on salvation history and fidelity to the resurrection event.[14] Many leading American Catholic religious education leaders in the sixties either were trained at the International Center (often called *Lumen Vitae*) or were influenced by the theoretical treatises of the center's professors.

The first important figure in American Catholic religious education theory was Joseph Collins, a Sulpician priest who spanned the pre- and post-World War period. A prime force in bringing to America the latest European theoretical insights as well as a potent force in invigorating the CCD movement, Collins can probably be most accurately described as a "nuts-and-bolts man," a precursor to the major theorists who were to emerge toward the twilight of his career.[15]

In the mid-fifties Gerard Sloyan, a diocesan priest, made his appearance on the religious education scene. Sloyan, a man of erudition, established the highly influential Catholic University of America graduate program in religious education. While Sloyan's scholarly output in religious education was limited to a few edited books and some significant articles, his importance stems from the fact that he was the first American Catholic religious educationist to introduce high-level theoretical elements into the mainstream of the American Catholic religious education movement.[16] In 1967 Sloyan abandoned the field of religious education to become a professor and researcher of New Testament studies.

Like Gerard Sloyan (his teacher), Gabriel Moran opted to turn his theoretical searchlight on selected points of crucial importance for Catholic religious education rather than to erect any thoroughgoing systematic theory of religious education. A theologian specializing in revelation, Gabriel Moran's significance for the field of religious education came about by virtue of several well-received books which made religious education an area for serious and critical concern for Catholics both inside and outside the religious education field.[17] It was Moran more than anyone else who interested Catholics in adult religious education, in nonschool alternatives for religious education, and in exploring the theological underpinnings for the religious education enterprise. After writing a few books and several articles on religious education, Moran (who is a religious brother), announced that he was forsaking religious education in order to devote his research exclusively to scientific theology.

When the first book of James Michael Lee's trilogy on religious education appeared in 1971 a Protestant reviewer for the journal *Religious Education* termed it "a revolutionary work" in the field. Lee's work is regarded as revolutionary in several respects. As the founder and chief proponent of the social-science approach to religious education, he attempts to demonstrate that religious education is the process by which religious behavior is facilitated; consequently religious education is a mode of social science rather than a branch of theology. Second, Lee (a Catholic layman, and hence not a brother or a priest) is generally recognized as the first Catholic (or Protestant) who has attempted to build an overall, comprehensive, systematic theory of religious education from which effective practices can most fruitfully flow. Third, Lee is the first major Catholic (or Protestant) religious educationist who deals with the corpus of Protestant and Catholic religious education theory and practice as a unitary, overall ecumenical phenomenon. Fourth, he is the first Catholic (or Protestant) theorist to declare that religious education is an ontologically separate and distinct field in its own right and therefore must be emancipated from what he terms "theological imperialism." Finally, Lee is the first Catholic (or Protestant) religious education theorist to develop an overarching praxiological macrotheory for the actual *teaching* of religion.[18] The doctoral program in religious education which Lee established at the University of Notre Dame enfleshes his viewpoint.

Future historians might well be able to observe that just as the pre-1955 malaise in Catholic religious education can be largely traced to the lack of any major Catholic theorists of religious education, so now the emergence of a vigorous religious enterprise as a mighty force in the American Catholic Church came about through the appearance of several highly influential theorists.

Organizational Features of Roman Catholic Religious Education

Catholic schools at all levels are controlled by one of three groups: (1) dioceses, (2) religious orders, (3) lay persons. In virtually all cases, the control is very loose so that each school typically does whatever it wishes, within a very general diocesan, religious order or lay framework.

Religious education in the proper sense of the term takes place either under the auspices of the school or of the parish.[19] In the elementary school, each teacher generally teaches religion as well as other curricular offerings. At the secondary school level there is a special department of religion in which the teachers are either full time in the department or are teachers who teach religion in addition to either their other subject-matter areas or their regular nonschool pastoral duties.

In nonschool milieux, religious education is normally conducted under the direction of the individual parish. Most parishes conduct a weekly CCD program, typically lasting an hour. In many ways the CCD is the Catholic counterpart of the Protestant Sunday school. As is the case so often in the Sunday school, the teachers are usually nonsalaried volunteers and typically have little or no training in the theory or practice of religious education. Since the mid-sixties many alert parishes have inaugurated "total religious education programs" to facilitate the religious education needs of all segments of the parish. These programs tend to be the responsibility of a parish-financed religious education coordinator (sometimes called the director of religious education) who is more often than not specially trained in religious education or in theology.

School and nonschool full-time religion teachers, coordinators, and administrators are increasingly being trained at the master's degree level either in theology or in the more than sixty graduate programs in religious education which have sprung up in Catholic colleges and universities since the mid-sixties. Many of these programs are summer-only operations, have a visiting faculty, and concentrate more on the personal spiritual renewal of their students than on providing them with an organized, professional set of solid courses in religious education. Consequently, many of these programs are of dubious quality. Some advanced dioceses have inaugurated in-service training programs for their religious education personnel; the quality of these programs tends to vary directly in proportion to the calibre of those designing and implementing the program.

It might come as a surprise to Protestants that there is no set of official Roman Catholic curricular materials for religious education in the United States. The only official curricular material is the *Baltimore Catechism*. Curricular textbook series and other kinds of curricular packages are prepared by textbook companies of divers hues and marketed to dioceses and parishes. Each religion teacher is free to choose which textbook series is most appropriate for his instructional objectives. Some dioceses and parishes have prepared a list of "preferred" textbook series which they suggest but do not require their religion teachers to use. A few revanchist dioceses and parishes impose a particular textbook series on the religion teacher with a questionable degree of success. The *General Catechetical Directory,* issued in 1971 by the Vatican's Sacred Congregation for the Clergy, is intended to provide assistance to curriculum builders, textbook writers, catechism compilers, designers of national "catechetical" directories and bishops. The *General Catechetical Directory,* together with the national *United States Catechetical Directory* which was in preparation as of this writing will not be a norm or an imposed viewpoint, but rather a help and a sort of guideline for religious educationists and educators.

There are three major American Catholic journals devoted to religious education. The most significant is the semischolarly *The Living Light,* sponsored by the National Center of Religious Education, a division of the United States Catholic Conference.[20] Next comes *The Catechist,* a commercially-sponsored periodical which aims at combining significant religious education scholarship in popular form with practical suggestions for religion teachers and administrators. Finally there is *Religion Teacher's Journal,* another commercial venture which sets its sights at the basic "nuts-and-bolts" aspects of the religious education enterprise.

Toward the Future

If it is to achieve its Jesus-commissioned purpose, Catholic religious education should shape its own future history rather than waiting for future events to shape it. The following points represent some of the more important and fruitful ways in which this future can be beneficially shaped.

First, Catholic religious education must shed its high-sounding but meaningless (and therefore not teachable) instructional goals and frame these goals and objectives in behavioral performance terms. *Second,* Catholic religious education must professionalize itself to a greater degree than is currently the case, with all religion teachers, coordinators, and administrators receiving formal, full-time training in religious education appropriate to their level of service. *Third,* Catholic religious education must continue to develop its own autonomy as a distinct field of scholarship with a distinct field of work, thereby fully emancipating itself from its former role of messenger boy of theology. *Fourth,* Catholic religious education must attract to its rank scholars of the very highest calibre so as to produce the type of top-level theory and research so urgently needed. *Fifth,* Catholic religious education must design and implement graduate university training programs which are of the best theoretical and practical levels and which concentrate on religious education per se, rather than being programs which devote the bulk of their attention to laudable but inappropriate endeavors such as "catechetical theology" or personal renewal. *Sixth,* dioceses should initiate or augment their in-service–teacher-training efforts, employing the most appropriate and the most thoroughly researched teacher-training protocols and instrumentation. *Seventh,* religion teachers should be taught to constantly insert their pedagogy into a sound teaching theory, rather than to operate out of no explicit theory or to attempt to operate out of some pseudotheory such as the blow "theory," the witness "theory," or the authenticity "theory." [21] *Eighth,* parents, learners, and the entire parish community should be more intimately involved in planning and implementing the religious education program than has thus far been the case. *Ninth,* Catholic religious education should press forward in its total religious education program, offering religious education to persons of every age and circumstance, in school and out. *Tenth,* Catholic religious education should ultimately rely on the competence of its personnel rather than on pious invocations to the Holy Spirit in the hope that the Spirit will miraculously supply what has failed through the incompetence of its personnel; for after all, the Spirit does not blow capriciously or in the fashion of a magician, but rather blows in and through the normal antecedent-consequent relationships which exist in the world he has made and continues to make by his sustaining presence within it.

NOTES

1. Sacra Congregatio pro Clericis. *Directorium catechisticum generale* (Città del Vaticano: Libreria Editrice Vaticana, 1971).
2. For an expanded treatment of this subject, see James Michael Lee, *The Purpose of Catholic Schooling* (Dayton: National Catholic Education Association and Pflaum Press, 1968); for one advocate of the moralist

position, see Kevin O'Brien, *The Proximate Aim of Education* (Milwaukee: Bruce, 1958); for an extreme intellectualist view see Vincent Edward Smith, *The School Examined: Its Aims and Content* (Milwaukee: Bruce, 1960). For a moderate intellectualist perspective, see Neil G. McCluskey, *Catholic Viewpoint in Education* (Garden City, N. Y.: Doubleday & Co., 1962).

3. Ellis, "The American Catholic and the Intellectual Life", *Thought,* 30 (Autumn, 1955), 351-88; O'Dea, *American Catholic Dilemma: An Inquiry into the Intellectual Life* (New York: Sheed & Ward, 1958); see, for example, Moran, *Catechesis of Revelation* (New York: Herder and Herder, 1966).

4. Jerome Edward Diffley, "Catholic Reaction to American Public Education, 1792-1852" (Ph.D. diss., University of Notre Dame, 1959), p. 303.

5. Sources for these data come from recent U.S. census reports; from Bureau of the Census, *Historical Statistics of the United States: Colonial Times to 1957* (Washington, D. C.: U.S. Government Printing Office, 1960), and from Gerald Shaughnessy, *Has the Immigrant Kept the Faith?* (New York: The Macmillan Co., 1925).

6. Shaughnessy, *Has the Immigrant Kept the Faith?* p. 249; Marie Carolyn Klinkhamer, "Historical Reason for the Inception of Parochial School System," *Catholic Educational Review,* 102 (February, 1954), 85.

7. For a thorough treatment of this controversy, see Vincent P. Lannie, *Public Money and Parochial Education* (Cleveland, Ohio: Case Western Reserve University Press, 1968).

8. Quoted in J. A. Burns, *The Principles, Origin, and Establishment of the Catholic School System in the United States* (New York: Benziger, 1912), p. 375; see Lannie, "Alienation in America: The Immigrant Catholic and Public Education in Pre-Civil War America," *The Review of Politics,* 32 (October, 1970), 515-17.

9. *Corpus Juris Canonici* (Roma: Typis Polyglottis Vaticanis, 1918); Pius XI, *"Divini Illius Magistri," Acta Apostolicae Sedis,* 20 (February 22, 1930), 76-77.

10. Ryan, *Are Parochial Schools the Answer?* (New York: Holt, Rinehart, and Winston, 1964). There had been other criticisms of total Catholic schooling in the nineteenth and twentieth centuries, but none seems to have had the impact which Ryan's book enjoyed; Lee, "Catholic Education in the United States," in Lee, ed., *Catholic Education in the Western World* (Notre Dame, Ind.: University of Notre Dame Press, 1967), pp. 306-8. This article did not urge wholesale abandonment of the entire Catholic school system; indeed it argued for especial emphasis on the preschool, high school, and adult sectors inasmuch as these are the developmental periods of life when deeper religious values are best learned.

11. It is estimated that 70 percent of the average parish budget goes into the support of its parochial elementary school. See Andrew M. Greeley and Peter H. Rossi, *The Education of Catholic Americans* (Chicago: Aldine-Atherton, 1966), pp. 221, 66-67; Reginald A. Neuwien, *Catholic Schools in Action: A Report* (Notre Dame, Ind.: University of Notre Dame Press, 1966), pp. 261-66.

12. Greeley and Rossi, *Catholic Americans,* p. 191.

13. For a short summary of the social-science approach, see Lee, "The Teaching of Religion," in Lee and Patrick C. Rooney, *Toward a Future for Religious Education* (Dayton: Pflaum Press, 1970), pp. 55-92, 1-4.

14. Jungmann, *Die Frohbotschaft und unsere Glaubensverkündigung* (Regensburg: Pustet, 1936), and *Handing on the Faith,* trans. and rev. A. N. Fuerst (New York: Herder and Herder, 1959); Hofinger, *The Art of Teaching*

Christian Doctrine, rev. ed. (Notre Dame, Ind.: University of Notre Dame Press, 1962); Nebreda, *Kerygma in Crisis* (Chicago: Loyola University Press, 1965); see Marcel van Caster, *The Structure of Catechetics,* trans. Edward J. Dirkswager, Jr., et al. (New York: Herder and Herder, 1965).

15. His most significant book is *Teaching Religion* (Milwaukee: Bruce, 1953).

16. See especially Sloyan, ed., *Shaping the Christian Message* (New York: The Macmillan Co., 1958).

17. See, for example, Moran, *Theology of Revelation* (New York: Herder and Herder, 1966).

18. Lee, *The Shape of Religious Instruction* (Notre Dame, Ind.: Religious Education Press, 1971); this is the task of vol. 2 of Lee's trilogy. See Lee, *The Flow of Religious Instruction* (Notre Dame, Ind.: Religious Education Press, 1973).

19. In his own books and articles, the present writer distinguishes between *religious education* and *religious instruction;* however, in this chapter the two terms are used more or less interchangeably. See Lee. *The Shape of Religious Instruction,* pp. 6-9.

20. While being the "official publication" of the NCRE, the views expressed in the magazine's articles do not necessarily reflect the stance of the sponsoring agency. Since assuming its executive editorship in 1973, Berard Marthaler has made this journal much more scholarly than it had hitherto-fore been.

21. On this point, see Lee, *The Flow of Religious Instruction,* pp. 149-205.

Chapter 21

THE CHURCHES AND HIGHER EDUCATION

Charles S. McCoy

American colleges and universities are at the vortex of the crisis of change threatening to engulf our society and its religious institutions. In part, it is a crisis produced by rapid development of technology, and higher education has been a major source of new means of every kind which have extended human capabilities in marvelous and awesome ways. In part, it is a crisis of rising expectations among previously submerged and oppressed sectors of the human community, and the college and university have been among the most important vehicles of evoking hope for a better life. In part, it is a crisis of changing values and priorities, as the limits of growth and the necessity for recognizing the human stake in the natural environment have become apparent; and the campus has taken the lead in pointing both to the problem and to possible solutions. In part, it is a crisis of competing faiths as diverse human movements have been brought closer together in the global marketplace, and the academy has served as a primary place for the meeting of different patterns of commitment. As never before "the higher learning now addresses itself to the totality of . . . life, not just to its intellectual aspect."[1] And therefore higher education must be a focus of involvement for all groups concerned with the shaping of culture and the reshaping of society toward humane goals.

A Changing Scene

"We live in an age of transition," Adam is reported to have said to Eve as they left the Garden of Eden. And the same can be said of each era since the original change in the fortunes of humanity.

The relation of the churches to higher education has been a part of the changing scene. The founding of cathedral schools and the development of universities in medieval times was both an agent of the revival of learning and also a means for the emerging church to exercise some

Charles S. McCoy is the Robert Gordon Sproul Professor of Theological Ethics and Higher Education at Pacific School of Religion and the Graduate Theological Union, Berkeley, California.

control over culture and to cope with the incursion of ancient Greek learning through the Moslem universities of Spain. The resulting form of higher education can be called the scholastic university, with its emphasis on dialectical argument and authority.

What began as a small stream of classical learning became a torrent in the wake of the Renaissance. And the smaller movements of reform in the Middle Ages became a major revolt in the Lutheran Reformation. These changes produced what might be called the liberal university, with emphasis on languages, especially for the study of the Bible in its original tongues, and on the wisdom of ancient Greek, Hebrew, and Roman cultures. This new university became a prime weapon of the Reformation churches and in turn shaped them and the society around them. Jewish learning, largely underground in the Middle Ages, gained a place on the edges of these transformed academies and, subsequently, has made massive contributions at the center of higher education.

The venturesome spirit which changed Europe from a musty corner of a large world into a power reaching out around the globe could not be contained within the boundaries of inherited learning. Parallel to exploration on the high seas was an intellectual exploration which produced what Alfred North Whitehead has called "the century of genius." Discoveries based on an experimental approach to learning began outside the universities but in the eighteenth century infiltrated the academy. This explosive movement of the mind led in the nineteenth century to the emergence of the research university, based upon the impulse to expand the horizons of human knowledge and human control of the world.

Early colleges in the British colonies of America and in the United States were patterned after the liberal university of Renaissance and Reformation. But the research university gained increasing influence after the Civil War and, in conjunction with the intensely practical interests of American society, produced far-reaching changes in the colleges and universities of this country. Growth in curricular offerings, in number and variety of institutions, in size of faculties and enrollment, in research, in budget, and in plant are among the more obvious alterations. Equally important is expansion of public funding for higher education. Not only have innovations in industry and agriculture resulted, but also the discovery of new technology and sources of power has produced changes more sweeping than the industrial revolution. Once serving mainly as a finishing school to acquaint various social elites with their cultural heritage, higher education in the twentieth century has become a prime resource for every aspect of national life as well as a pluralistic forum of diverse faiths and multiple interests.

The expansion of the churches, however, has outstripped the campus. From having 5 percent of a population of 4 million as members in 1790, the churches in the early 1960s had membership amounting to more than 60 percent of a 200 million population. And the changes in the character of churches were no less significant. In the wake of growth in the nineteenth and twentieth centuries came a global missionary movement, expanding social concern, increasing scope of activities, organizations on a national scale with proliferating agencies, enlarging budgets, and enormous investment in buildings.

In the tumultuous decade of the sixties both university and church continued to be a part of the rapidly changing scene. The campus became a center of protest and demand for change. At times it seemed that an action university, perhaps to take its place alongside the research university, was seeking to be born. The churches also became oriented increasingly toward active participation in societal reform. But the end of the Vietnam war and the politicizing of the Civil Rights movement have been accompanied by less overt forms of activism on campus and by the churches.

Patterns of Relation

The impetus for involvement of the Judeo-Christian movement with higher education has been complex. It has derived in part from a commitment to express biblical faith in every sphere of human relation and to find in these encounters sources of renewal. In part this impetus emerges from the concern of persons for education dealing with meaning and purpose as well as knowledge and skills. But also the impulse comes from those who shape social policy and those who are its beneficiaries or victims to combine the resources of faith and learning, of commitment and expertise to develop a world more fit for human habitation.

It is clear that the Christian movement has been related closely to institutions of higher learning in the West from the inception of universities in the Middle Ages, and the relation has continued through the changes in higher education and throughout the rise of Western society to global dominance. Education and religion have been as intimately a part of this expansion as have political and economic forces. The involvement of churches with higher education in the British colonies and in the United States parallels and often replicates the relationships in Europe. And the founding of colleges and universities has been as much a part of the spread of the Judeo-Christian movement to every continent as it has been a prime agent of expansion and development in Europe and America. While the focus of this article is on the United States, the worldwide involvement of the churches and higher education should not be forgotten, as well as the intimate intertwining of the main forms of western religion and education with the emerging patterns of western society.

The relation of the churches to colleges and universities has been and remains a diverse one taking place on multiple levels. Helpful ways to view the relation are through the pluralism of denominations which has characterized society in the United States and by means of the differing patterns of American higher education. But a way which seems more illuminating is suggested by H. Richard Niebuhr in his discussion of theological education. He uses the terms *community* and *institution* in defining the church. "A social reality such as the Church," Niebuhr writes, "cannot be described by means of one of these categories only and much misconception of the Church results from such exclusive use."[2] Certainly the customary way of viewing the Judeo-Christian movement primarily as organization, doctrine, and ritual misses many important elements of its relation to society, including higher education. Religion also means communities of persons with similar commitments and faith who relate in various ways to diverse social patterns and institutions. Because neither perspective can be understood without the other, we shall look at the church in relation to higher education first as community and second as institution.

The Church Within Higher Education

When we regard Judaism and Christianity not only as institutions but also as communities of persons united, and divided, by biblical faith, it becomes clear that the relation of the Judeo-Christian movement to higher education is much more than one between various religious and educational agencies. This movement is and has long been *within* the patterns and functions of colleges and universities, intimately related to every part of them, participating at the core of their operations. Those who see the church primarily or exclusively in its institutional manifestation persistently overlook a crucial relation between the churches and every sector of society.

Thomas Aquinas was functioning in both church and university as he developed the synthesis of Augustinianism and Aristotelianism which shaped higher learning for centuries and still is widely influential. Erasmus was a part of the Christian movement as he shaped the patterns of liberal learning in the universities of Renaissance and Reformation, as also was Olevianus in his role as founding rector of the academy at Herborn, or Grotius in laying the foundations of international law, or Cocceius in contributing to the principles upon which biblical criticism would develop. Copernicus and Spinoza on the fringes of the academies of their times wrought their revolutions within the perspective of Judeo-Christian faith. Isaac Newton at Cambridge and Immanuel Kant at Königsberg shaped entire eras of Western thought yet lived and worked within a context of biblical faith. Can Louis Agassiz, Josiah Royce, and William Rainey Harper be identified as other than persons belonging to the Judeo-Christian movement as they made profound contributions within higher education? So also is the case with Martin Buber, Jacques Maritain, George Washington Carver, Michael Polanyi, Reinhold and H. Richard Niebuhr, Nathan Pusey, Clark Kerr, and Kenneth and Elise Boulding. But these illustrations suggest only a few better known names. The list could be extended into all fields and functions of higher education.

From one perspective this glimpse of the biblical movement of faith within the university can be regarded as the ministry of the laity. But such a view scarcely does justice to the quality and scope of this involvement. Persons highly trained and experienced are professionals, by contrast with whom others outside their specialty comprise a laity. Whether faculty or researchers, administrators or students, we are speaking of persons who are committing significant portions of their energies to work within higher education and who understand themselves, their companions, and their world through biblical faith, however variously conceived. Through such persons the churches are related internally to the widest possible range of activities within the campus; and higher education in its institutional forms, in its purposes, in its relations, and in its results shows their influence.

It is not a matter of developing institutional relations or of transporting the church for the first time onto the campus. The community of biblical faith is already at work in important ways. Issues may be raised about the quality of the various ministries being undertaken without benefit of clergy or ecclesiastical supervision, but it is going on and has been going on for centuries. Such ministry must be ranked among the most important ways in which churches have related to higher education.

Relations of this kind obviously are not limited to "church-related" colleges. Private and public institutions are also, in this perspective, related closely to the community of biblical faith. And the relation is not one-way. As higher education has been developed and enriched by the Judeo-Christian movement, so also churches, synagogues, and religious agencies cannot be understood apart from the contribution in many forms from colleges and universities. Increased recognition of the diversity of noninstitutional relationships and greater awareness of their potential could enrich the interaction of churches and higher education. Rather than thinking of the university "as an instrument of the Church for the carrying out of its *teaching* mission," Father John E. Walsh suggests, the more basic relation may be seen as "the Church *learning*."[3]

Institutional Relations of Church and Higher Education

When the Judeo-Christian movement is regarded primarily as institution rather than community another sector of relationship emerges. Important institutional relations include: the church-related college and university; campus ministries; theological seminaries; and instructional programs of religious studies on the undergraduate and graduate levels. Space allows consideration here only of the first two of these. As we do so, it becomes clear that the institutional and communal aspects of religious movements are distinguishable but not separable.

1. *Church-Related Higher Education.* No other institutional relation between the churches and higher education in the United States has been more extensive than the church-related college and university. These institutions have been numerous and have served as important instruments of the churches in taming the frontier, developing committed members, influencing culture, and training clergy. Difficulties have constantly beset most of these colleges, and recent decades have increased the complexities of maintaining them as church related. Certainly no one should derive the impression of a current upsurge in numbers because J. Edward Dirks reports the existence of 771 church-related colleges and universities in 1959 (486 Protestant, 280 Roman Catholic, and 5 Jewish) and Pattillo and Mackenzie report that in 1962-63 of over 2,100 institutions of higher education, there were 817 colleges and universities which could be considered church sponsored (339 Roman Catholic and 478 Protestant and others).[4] The overall increase occurs because of different criteria of church-relation.

Precise numbers vary as these criteria change, but, according to the U.S. Office of Education, of the 2,665 institutions of higher education existing in 1972 in the United States, 1,182 or 44 percent were public, 693 or 26 percent were private, and 790 or 30 percent were church related. Of these latter, 493 were classified as Protestant, 266 as Roman Catholic, and 31 as Jewish, Latter Day Saint, Greek Orthodox, Russian Orthodox, or Unitarian.[5] And, as has often been noted, over 80 percent of these church-related institutions are in the eastern half of the nation and in the southern states.

It seems probable that over the past two decades the institutional relations of churches to colleges and universities have become more attenuated. The primary reason is the greater access to federal funds for colleges without overt ecclesiastical control. This means in part that churches are placing less reliance on explicit institutional ties and more reliance on the presence of committed persons within college structures.

Though the proportion of public institutions is less than half, around 75 percent of the students are enrolled in them, an increase from around 20 percent of an enrollment of 237,000 in 1900. For example, in the fall of 1970, of a total enrollment of 8,498,117 in the United States, 6,371,008 were enrolled in public institutions, 1,213,073 were in private institutions, and 914,036 were in church-related institutions, with 478,604 in Protestant institutions, 392,912 in Roman Catholic institutions, and 42,520 in institutions under Jewish, Latter Day Saint, Greek Orthodox, Russian Orthodox, or Unitarian control.[6] The proportion of students in public institutions will probably go even higher over the next decade, carrying even further the tilt away from private and church-related higher education.

Higher education in the United States, it has been said, is the child of religion. This is undoubtedly true in the sense that "the Christian tradition was the foundation stone of the whole intellectual structure which was brought to the New World." The colleges of the colonial period, however, were not church colleges in the later meaning of the term but rather were "state-church colleges," or better still, public Christian colleges, which subsequently have become the core of the strong private sector of American higher education.[7] The church-related colleges of today are in continuity not so much with colonial colleges as with the sectarian colleges which proliferated in the nineteenth century. The mortality rate among colleges founded by churches has been very high. A substantial number has indeed survived, though the existence of many is precarious.

It would be a mistake, however, to assume that the dramatic shift toward public higher education in this century means that church-related colleges are faced with extinction and that their primary problem today is *survival*. Some are being forced to close, and others are severing ecclesiastical ties in order to secure public funds. But the more important problem for the larger number of them is adjusting to changes in their social environment, in problems of funding, in constituencies, and in purposes. "The church-related college today," I have suggested, "finds itself in a crisis of identity, caught between its sectarian past and its public present. It must act responsibly in terms of this public present if it is to fulfill its Christian heritage and survive as a meaningful part of American higher education."[8]

Church-related colleges can no longer be characterized as "sectarian" or even clearly "special-interest" institutions. They have become one sector of a national system of higher education. There is considerable diversity among institutions with reference to whether they have community, regional, or national constituencies, and in regard to their function as college, technical institute, professional school, or research university. But within these categories, church-related institutions are not sharply distinguished from those in the private and public sectors.

A major problem is that church-related colleges continue to seek a uniqueness based on some particular function such as the teaching of religion or personal concern for students which no longer set them apart. Rather than pursuing that "will o' the wisp," it would be better for church-related institutions to discover in the heritage of Judeo-Christian faith resources for serving responsibly the needs of the people, the institutions, and the society around them. In a time of emerging ecumenical relationship, church-related colleges of differing denominational backgrounds might develop cooperative programs which capitalize on religious diversity. In a time requiring more efficient operation, smaller institutions might form consortia to complement and strengthen their educational programs. In a time of growing interest in pluralism, church-related colleges might build on their diversity to enrich the pluralistic climate of higher education and to resist the isomorphic tendencies deriving from state educational bureaucracies.

While many difficulties face all sectors of higher education, churches and colleges have much to gain from continued cooperation. Indeed, the time is at hand to develop joint centers of policy research and action to inform the leadership and enhance the capabilities of colleges and religious agencies.

2. *Campus Ministries.* Related as they are to dynamic and colorful parts of American society, campus ministries constitute a vital, varied form of relationship between the churches and higher education. Though present also in church-related and private institutions, campus ministry in different forms has increased greatly in importance and in resources committed to it as the public sector of higher education has

expanded. The turmoil of the sixties affected these ministries deeply, frequently providing them an unaccustomed notoriety and often producing diminished financial support. Campus ministries have emerged in the seventies somewhat chastened by events and, among Protestants, with fewer professionals employed but with greater confidence and maturity.

Only over the past two decades has *campus ministry* displaced the term *student work* and come into general usage to designate, on the one hand, the professionals or campus ministers who provide the leadership for organized campus ministries and, on the other hand, the wider operation of activities which include the ministry of the laity as it carries out diverse tasks and functions within higher education and relates to the larger society. As the line between campus and community becomes blurred by the emergence of the learning society, *"campus ministry"* seems in its turn an increasingly inadequate name. It is clear also that the various ministries of the churches—campus, urban, parish, etc.—must cease to be seen as operating in isolated sectors and developed as cooperative efforts to perform the tasks of ministry in the human community.

The origins of campus ministry in this country go back to the beginnings of higher education in the British colonies. Because the college was intended to carry out religious and moral as well as intellectual education, campus ministry began as a function of the entire college community radiating from the president as "campus minister." This more generalized form was supplemented by student societies which emerged powerfully in the late nineteenth century through the Christian Associations, the Student Volunteer Movement, and the World Student Christian Federation. These groups produced clerical and lay professionals who gave leadership on campus and also to the missionary outreach, the social concern, and the ecumenical convergence of the churches. By 1900, the churches were supplementing these student Christian movements with denominational ministries which, by the fifties, had expanded enormously in personnel, organization, and buildings. The evangelical groups followed suit in the Inter-Varsity Christian Fellowship, Campus Crusade, and, more recently, such countercultural groups as the Christian World Liberation Front. During this same period, colleges and universities themselves—public, private, and church related—perceived the rising tide of religious commitment in American society and through chapel programs, chaplains, coordinators of religious activities, and instructional programs added to the variety of campus ministries.[9]

There are differing evaluations, obviously, of this upsurge of religion on campus. It occurred in part in response to the increasing pluralism in higher education, within which Christianity appeared as one evangelism among others in a campus marketplace of competing faiths.[10]

In the mid-sixties the Danforth Foundation sponsored the most extensive examination yet made of campus ministries.[11] The Danforth Study attempts to bring conceptual order to the diversity of campus ministries by positing four modes of ministry—priestly, pastoral, prophetic, and governing—suggesting that attention is too often focused on the first two modes at the expense of the latter two and that more attention must be given to prophetic inquiry and policy ministries aimed at shaping a more humane environment. But the protest movements of the sixties would not stand still to be researched, and the Danforth Study emphasized ideal types of ministry inadequately related to changing realities.

In the wake of protests for racial justice, educational reform, and peace in Vietnam, which many church members saw as encouraged by campus ministers, support from institutional church sources decreased.[12] There is, however, no evidence that campus ministry in any of its varied forms is in serious decline. Ministries supported cooperatively by mainline Protestant bodies have been hardest hit, but apparently no more than educational activities generally. Ministries supported by colleges and universities have suffered decreased budgets but not decreased personnel. YM and YWCA's have shifted in program and sources of support. And it appears that the number of Roman Catholic and Jewish campus clergy has increased. What has occurred is an overall leveling off after the dramatic upsurge in funding during the two decades after World War II, but not collapse as some exaggerated reports have nervously announced. Campus ministries continue to serve the entire spectrum of American higher education, with the institutions which are larger and more prestigious receiving greater attention.

Promising developments in church-related campus ministries include: growing ecumenical cooperation, greater attention to ministry within the structures of higher education, increasing work with parish and urban ministries, and some solid beginnings of interest in social policy. Recent reports by Parker Palmer and Robert McAfee Brown to the Danforth Foundation stress the continuing importance and potential of campus ministry.[13] Brown seems to suggest that campus ministry in the seventies is and should be taking up again the tasks of the early sixties. Palmer reflects more specifically the impact of the Danforth Study and sees developing interest in theological/ethical analysis and policy research.

Out of the turmoil of recent years has emerged increased maturity in all sectors of campus ministry. That factor, combined with the enhanced mutual support among ministries and the perspective provided by recent studies of campus ministry and of higher education, insures the continued strength of campus-related ministries as a crucial area of relation between the churches and higher education.

Conclusion

"There is an urgent need for campus and church to join in generating within America a new vision of its possibilities for human fulfillment," states a recent report.[14] Raise the sights to global rather than national perspective and the challenge is even clearer. Leaders in religious movements rely too heavily on intuition and charisma. Scholars rely too much on research data. Coping with the dilemmas confronting humanity today requires the uniting of commitment, knowledge, and the power of decision in social policy. To accomplish this difficult task, the relations of churches and higher education must be decisively extended and strengthened beyond the situation which now exists.

NOTES

1. John S. Brubacher and Willis Rudy, *Higher Education in Transition* (New York: Harper & Bros,. 1958), p. 374.
2. Niebuhr, *The Purpose of the Church and Its Ministry* (New York: Harper & Bros., 1956), p. 21.
3. Walsh, C.S.C., "The University and the Church," in Edward Manier and John W. Houck, eds., *Academic Freedom and the Catholic University* (Notre Dame: Fides Publishers, 1967), pp. 108, 109.
4. Dirks, "Religious Education in Church-Related Colleges and Universities," in Marvin J. Taylor, ed., *Religious Education: A Comprehensive Survey* (Nashville: Abingdon Press, 1960), p. 295n. That article provides an excellent brief account of certain aspects of church-related higher education and might well be read as complementary to this article, which is written in the perspective of theology and social ethics; Manning M. Pattillo, Jr., and Donald M. Mackenzie, *Church-Sponsored Higher Education in the United States: Report of the Danforth Commission* (Washington: American Council on Education, 1966).
5. *Digest of Education Statistics, 1973 Edition* (Washington, D. C.: U.S. Department of Health, Education, and Welfare, Office of Education), p. 93.
6. *Ibid.,* p. 72.
7. Brubacher and Rudy, *Education in Transition,* p. 6; Frederick Rudolph, *The American College: A History* (New York: Alfred A. Knopf, 1962), p. 13.
8. Charles S. McCoy, *The Responsible Campus: Toward a New Identity for the Church-Related College* (Nashville: Board of Education, The United Methodist Church, 1972), p. 19.
9. See Clarence Prouty Shedd, *Two Centuries of Student Christian Movements* (New York: Association Press, 1934); Shedd, *The Church Follows*

Its Student. (New Haven: Yale University Press, 1938); and Merrimon Cunninggim, *The College Seeks Religion* (New Haven: Yale University Press, 1947).

10. See Charles S. McCoy and Neely D. McCarter, *The Gospel on Campus: Rediscovering Evangelism in the Academic Community* (Richmond: John Knox Press, 1959).

11. Reported in Kenneth W. Underwood, *The Church, the University and Social Policy* (Middletown, Conn.: Wesleyan University Press, 1969), and in *New Wine: Report of the Danforth Commission on the Study of Campus Ministries* (St. Louis: Danforth Foundation, 1969).

12. Philip E. Hammond, *The Campus Clergy* (New York: Basic Books, 1966), and Jeffrey K. Hadden, *The Gathering Storm in the Churches* (Garden City, N. Y.: Doubleday and Co., 1969), suggest that campus ministers are more liberal and activist than parish clergy.

13. Brown, "Selections from a Review of Danforth Campus Ministry Grants," *CSCW,* (January, 1974), and Palmer, "Selections from a Review of Danforth Campus Ministry Fellowships," *CSCW Report,* (March, 1974). Note especially his comment: "Contrary to popular opinion, campus ministers do not generally engage in 'political activity, community organization, etc.'"

14. *The Church, the University and Urban Society* (Department of Higher Education, National Council of Churches, 1972). See also suggestions made in *The Responsible Campus.*

A SELECTED BIBLIOGRAPHY: SINCE 1966

Compiled by Marvin J. Taylor

This is the third successive bibliography which I have compiled for this series of symposia. Readers desiring access to pre-1966 publications should consult *Religious Education: A Comprehensive Survey* (1960) and *An Introduction to Christian Education* (1966) for suggestions. In the latter volume, which followed its predecessor after only six years, I indicated that more than six hundred volumes worthy of inclusion had been identified in that short time. This time almost a decade has passed, yet the list is shorter. It is still a "selected" bibliography. From among some four hundred possibilities, I have chosen a representative sample of materials which have been found to be of continuing usefulness.

Lest there be misunderstanding, it is probably well to identify the criteria used in the selections: (1) The outline of categories is a virtual duplication of that used in the two previous volumes. Combining the three will provide the interested reader with almost a thousand important references in the field since 1950. (2) This is a selection of *new* materials. With rare exceptions, few pre-1965 volumes appear. They can be obtained from the earlier lists. (3) The contributors of the several chapters were involved in these selections, since each was asked to provide a brief list. However, the final choices were mine, and contributors should not be held responsible for the presence or absence of any particular book in their subject field. (4) Once again, only rarely have denominational publications been included. While this undoubtedly has arbitrarily excluded many fine books, it has been simply impossible to include all. It seemed more appropriate to exclude all or most, under these circumstances.

The Nature, Principles, and History of Religious Education

1. *Nature, Philosophy, and Principles of Religious Education*

Belth, Marc. *Education as a Discipline.* Boston: Allyn and Bacon, 1965.

Bruner, Jerome S. *Beyond the Information Given.* New York: W. W. Norton & Co., 1973.

Butler, J. Donald. *Four Philosophies and Their Practice in Education and Religion.* 3rd ed. New York: Harper & Row, 1967.

Chamberlin, J. Gordon. *Toward a Phenomenology of Education.* Philadelphia: The Westminster Press, 1969.

Cully, Iris. V. *Change, Conflict, and Self-Determination.* Philadelphia: The Westminster Press, 1972.

DeGraaff, Arnold H. *The Educational Ministry of the Church.* Grand Rapids: Eerdmans Publishing Co., 1966.

Dittes, James E. *The Church in the Way.* New York: Charles Scribner's Sons, 1967.

Edge, Findley B. *The Greening of the Church.* Waco, Tex.: Word Books, 1971.

Evenson, C. Richard, ed. *Foundations for Educational Ministry.* Philadelphia: Fortress Press, 1971.

Ferré, Nels F. S. *A Theology for Christian Education.* Philadelphia: The Westminster Press, 1967.

Freire, Paulo. *Education for Critical Consciousness.* New York: The Seabury Press, 1973.

———. *Pedagogy of the Oppressed.* New York: Herder and Herder, 1970.

Haughton, Rosemary. *The Transformation of Man.* Springfield, Ill.: Templegate, 1967.

Hill, Brian V. *Called to Teach.* Sydney, Australia: Angus and Robertson, 1971.

Hurley, Mark J. *Declaration on Christian Education of Vatican Council II.* Glen Rock, N. J.: Paulist Press, 1966.

Illich, Ivan D. *Celebration of Awareness.* Garden City, N. Y.: Doubleday & Co., 1970.

———. *Deschooling Society.* New York: Harper & Row, 1971.

Jones, Richard M. *Fantasy and Feeling in Education.* New York: New York University Press, 1968.

Lee, James Michael. *The Content of Religious Instruction.* Dayton: Pflaum Press, 1975.

Leeper, Robert R., ed. *Humanizing Education: The Person in the Process.* Washington: Association for Supervision and Curriculum Development, The National Education Association, 1967.

Lentz, Richard E.; Vieth, Paul H.; and Henthorne, Ray L. *Our Teaching Ministry.* St. Louis: Christian Board of Publication, 1967.

Link, Mark J., ed. *Faith and Commitment: The Aim of Religious Education.* Chicago: Loyola University Press, 1964.

Lotz, Philip H., ed. *Orientation in Religious Education.* Nashville & New York: Abingdon-Cokesbury Press, 1950.

A SELECTED BIBLIOGRAPHY: SINCE 1966

Mason, Robert E. *Contemporary Educational Theory.* New York: David McKay Co., 1972.

Moran, Gabriel. *Catechesis of Revelation.* New York: Herder and Herder, 1966.

―――. *Design for Religion.* New York: Herder and Herder, 1970.

―――. *Theology of Revelation.* New York: Herder and Herder, 1966.

Nelson, C. Ellis. *Where Faith Begins.* Richmond: John Knox Press, 1967.

Oden, Thomas C. *The Structure of Awareness.* Nashville: Abingdon Press, 1969.

Phenix, Philip H. *Education and the Worship of God.* Philadelphia: The Westminster Press, 1966.

Rippa, S. Alexander, ed. *Educational Ideas in America.* New York: David McKay Co., 1969.

Rood, Wayne R. *Understanding Christian Education.* Nashville: Abingdon Press, 1970.

Russell, Letty M. *Christian Education in Mission.* Philadephia: The Westminster Press, 1967.

Sloyan, Gerard S. *Speaking of Religious Education.* New York: Herder and Herder, 1968.

Taylor, Marvin J., ed. *An Introduction to Christian Education.* Nashville: Abingdon Press, 1966.

―――. *Religious and Moral Education.* New York: The Center for Applied Research in Education, 1965.

―――, ed. *Religious Education: A Comprehensive Survey.* Nashville: Abingdon Press, 1960.

Toffler, Alvin, ed. *Learning for Tomorrow: The Role of the Future in Education.* New York: Random House, 1974.

van Caster, Marcel. *The Structure of Catechesis.* New York: Herder and Herder, 1965.

Vandenburg, Donald. *Being and Education: An Essay in Existential Phenomenology.* Englewood Cliffs, N. J.: Prentice-Hall, 1971.

Westerhoff, John H., III, ed. *A Colloquy on Christian Education.* Philadelphia: Pilgrim Press, 1972.

―――. *Values for Tomorrow's Children: An Alternative Future for Education in the Church.* Philadelphia: Pilgrim Press, 1970.

2. *The History of Religious Education*

Adamson, William R. *Bushnell Rediscovered.* Philadelphia: United Church Press, 1966.

Beutow, Harold O. *Of Singular Benefit: The Story of Catholic Education in the United States.* New York: The Macmillan Company, 1970.

Cremin, Lawrence A. *American Education: The Colonial Experience, 1607-1783.* New York: Harper & Row, 1970.

Gartner, Lloyd P., ed. *Jewish Education in the United States: A Documentary History.* New York: Teachers College Press, 1969.

Graham, Patricia Albjerg. *Progressive Education: From Arcady to Academe, A History of the Progressive Education Association.* New York: Teachers College Press, 1967.

Hilliard, F. H.; Lee, Desmond; Niblett, W. R.; and Rupp, Gordon. *Christianity in Education*. London: Allen & Unwin, 1966.

Jaeger, Werner. *Early Christianity and Greek Paideia*. New York; Oxford University Press, 1969.

Kliebard, Herbert M., ed. *Religion and Education in America: A Documentary History*. Scranton, Penn.: International Textbook Company, 1969.

Lynn, Robert W., and Wright, Elliott. *The Big Little School*. New York: Harper & Row, 1971.

Murphy, Francis X. *Moral Teaching in the Primitive Church*. Glen Rock, N. J.: Paulist Press, 1968.

Perkinson, Henry J. *The Imperfect Panacea: American Faith in Education, 1865-1965*. New York: Random House, 1968.

Pilch, Judah, ed. *A History of Jewish Education in the United States*. New York: American Association for Jewish Education, 1969.

Sherrill, Lewis J. *The Rise of Christian Education*. New York: The Macmillan Co., 1944.

Ulich, Robert. *A History of Religious Education*. New York: New York University Press, 1968.

Worley, Robert C. *Preaching and Teaching in the Earliest Church*. Philadelphia: The Westminster Press, 1967.

3. *Language, Religious Faith, and Communication*

DeWire, Harry. *Communication as Commitment*. Philadelphia: Fortress Press, 1972.

Fore, William F.; Ham, Howard M.; Jackson, B. F., Jr.; and Campbell, James C. *Communication—Learning for Churchmen*. Nashville: Abingdon Press, 1968.

Miller, George A., ed. *Communication, Language, and Meaning*. New York: Basic Books, 1973.

Miller, Randolph Crump. *The Language Gap and God: Religious Language and Christian Education*. Philadelphia: Pilgrim Press, 1970.

Williamson, William B. *Language and Concepts in Christian Education*. Philadelphia: The Westminster Press, 1970.

4. *Liberation Themes and Religious Education*

Cone, James H. *Black Theology and Black Power*. New York: The Seabury Press, 1969.

———. *A Black Theology of Liberation*. Philadelphia: J. B. Lippincott Co., 1970.

Daly, Mary. *Beyond God the Father: Toward a Philosophy of Women's Liberation*. Boston: Beacon Press, 1973.

Gutierrez, Gustavo. *A Theology of Liberation*. New York: Orbis, 1971.

Jones, William R. *Is God a White Racist? A Preamble to Black Theology*. Garden City, N. Y.: Doubleday & Co., 1973.

Reuther, Rosemary. *Liberation Theology*. Paramus, N. J.: Paulist Press, 1972.

Roberts, J. Deotis. *Liberation and Reconciliation: A Black Theology*. Philadelphia: The Westminster Press, 1971.

Tavard, George H. *Woman in Christian Tradition.* Notre Dame: University of Notre Dame Press, 1973.

Thomas, George B. *Young Black Adults: Liberation and Family Attitudes.* New York: Friendship Press, 1974.

Wilmore, Gayraud S. *Black Religion and Black Radicalism.* Garden City, N. Y.: Doubleday & Co., 1972.

Religious Growth and the Learning-Teaching Process

1. *Moral and Religious Growth*

Almy, Millie, with Chittenden, Edward; and Miller, Paula. *Young Children's Thinking: Studies of Some Aspects of Piaget's Theory.* New York: Teachers College Press, 1966.

Babin, Pierre. *Crisis of Faith: The Religious Psychology of Adolescence.* New York: Herder and Herder, 1969.

————. *Faith and the Adolescent.* New York: Herder and Herder, 1965.

Beck, C. M.; Crittenden, B. S; and Sullivan, E. V., eds. *Moral Education: Interdisciplinary Approaches.* New York: Newman Press, 1971.

Bull, Norman J. *Moral Education.* Beverly Hills, Calif.: Sage Publications, 1969.

————. *Moral Judgment from Childhood to Adolescence.* Beverly Hills, Calif.: Sage Publications, 1969.

Chazan, Barry I., and Soltis, Jonas F., eds. *Moral Education.* New York: Teachers College Press, 1973.

Elkind, David. *Children and Adolescents: Interpretive Essays on Jean Piaget.* New York: Oxford University Press, 1970.

Erikson, Erik H. *Identity: Youth and Crisis.* New York: W. W. Norton & Co., 1968.

Furth, Hans G. *Piaget for Teachers.* Englewood Cliffs, N. J.: Prentice-Hall, 1970.

Ginsburg, Herbert, and Opper, Sylvia. *Piaget's Theory of Intellectual Development.* Englewood Cliffs, N. J.: Prentice-Hall, 1969.

Gleason, John J., Jr. *Growing Up to God.* Nashville: Abingdon Press, 1975.

Goldman, Ronald. *Readiness for Religion.* New York: The Seabury Press, 1968.

Koppe, William A. *How Persons Grow in Christian Community.* Philadelphia: Fortress Press, 1973.

Loder, James E. *Religious Pathology and Christian Faith.* Philadelphia: The Westminster Press, 1966.

Mental Health: From Infancy Through Adolescence. New York: Harper & Row, 1973.

Nelson, C. Ellis, ed. *Conscience: Theological and Psychological Perspectives.* New York: Newman Press, 1973.

Oates, Wayne E. *On Becoming Children of God.* Philadelphia: The Westminster Press, 1969.

Piaget, Jean. *The Child and Reality.* New York: Grossman Publishers, 1973.

————, and Inhelder, Bärbel. *The Psychology of the Child.* New York: Basic Books, 1969.

Pruyser, Paul W. *A Dynamic Psychology of Religion.* New York: Harper & Row, 1968.

Schwebel, Milton, and Raph, Jane, eds. *Piaget in the Classroom.* New York: Basic Books, 1973.

Snyder, Ross. *On Becoming Human.* Nashville: Abingdon Press, 1968.

Stewart, Charles W. *Adolescent Religion.* Nashville: Abingdon Press, 1967.

Strommen, Merton P., ed. *Research on Religious Development,* New York: Hawthorn Books, 1971.

Westerhoff, John H., III, and Neville, Gwen K. *Generation to Generation.* Philadelphia: Pilgrim Press, 1974.

Wilson, John. *Education in Religion and the Emotions.* London: Heinemann Educational Books, 1971.

————. *Practical Methods of Moral Education.* New York: Crane, Russak, and Co., 1972.

————, Williams, Norman; and Sugarman, Barry. *Introduction to Moral Education.* Baltimore: Penguin Books, 1967.

2. *The Learning Process*

Foster, Virgil E. *Christian Education Where the Learning Is.* Englewood Cliffs, N. J.: Prentice-Hall, 1968.

Gagne, Robert M. *The Conditions of Learning.* New York: Holt, Rinehart and Winston, 1965.

Handley, George D. *Personality, Learning and Teaching.* Boston: Routledge & Kegan Paul, 1973.

Henthorne, Ray L., ed. *A Design for Teaching-Learning.* St. Louis: Bethany Press, 1967.

Holt, John. *How Children Learn.* New York: G. P. Putnam's Sons, 1967.

Kibler, Robert J.; Barker, Larry L.; and Miles, David T. *Behavioral Objectives and Instruction.* Boston: Allyn and Bacon, 1970.

Lembo, John M. *When Learning Happens.* New York: Schocken Books, 1972.

Rogers, Carl R. *Freedom to Learn.* Columbus, Ohio: Charles E. Merrill, 1969.

3. *The Teaching Process*

Allstrom, Elizabeth. *You Can Teach Creatively.* Nashville: Abingdon Press, 1970.

Belth, Marc. *The New World of Education: A Philosophical Analysis of Concepts of Teaching.* Boston: Allyn and Bacon, 1970.

Bowman, Locke E., Jr. *Straight Talk About Teaching in Today's Church.* Philadelphia: The Westminster Press, 1967.

Brenton, Myron. *What's Happened to Teacher.* New York: Coward, McCann & Geoghegan, 1970.

Bruner, Jerome S. *Toward a Theory of Instruction.* Cambridge, Mass.: Belknap Press, 1966.

A SELECTED BIBLIOGRAPHY: SINCE 1966

Cully, Kendig Brubacher, ed. *Does the Church Know How to Teach?* New York: The Macmillan Co., 1970.

Duane, James E., ed. *Individualized Instruction—Programs and Materials.* Englewood Cliffs, N. J.: Educational Technology Publications, 1973.

Green, Thomas F. *The Activities of Teaching.* New York: McGraw-Hill Book Co., 1971.

Haskew, Laurence D., and McLendon, Jonathon C. *This Is Teaching.* Glenview, Ill.: Scott, Foresman and Co., 1968.

Hofinger, Johannes, and Buckley, Frances J. *The Good News and Its Proclamation.* Notre Dame: University of Notre Dame Press, 1968.

Joyce, Bruce, and Weil, Marsha. *Models for Teaching.* Englewood Cliffs, N. J.: Prentice-Hall, 1972.

Langdon, Danny G. *Interactive Instructional Designs for Individualized Learning.* Englewood Cliffs, N. J.: Educational Technology Publications, 1973.

Lee, James Michael. *The Flow of Religious Instruction.* Notre Dame, Ind.: Religious Education Press, 1973.

————. *The Shape of Religious Instruction.* Notre Dame, Ind.: Religious Education Press, 1971.

Rood, Wayne R. *The Art of Teaching Christianity.* Nashville: Abingdon Press, 1968.

————. *On Nurturing Christians.* Nashville: Abingdon Press, 1972.

Skinner, B. F. *The Technology of Teaching.* New York: Appleton-Century-Crofts, 1968.

Thatcher, David A. *Teaching, Loving, and Self-Directed Learning.* Pacific Palisades, California: Goodyear Publishing Company, 1973.

4. Group Work and Group Dynamics

Casteel, John L. *The Creative Role of Interpersonal Groups in the Church Today.* New York: Association Press, 1968.

Rogers, Carl. *Carl Rogers on Encounter Groups.* New York: Harper & Row, 1970.

5. Simulation Gaming and the Teaching-Learning Process

Abt, Clark C. *Serious Games.* New York: Viking Press, 1970.

Benson, Dennis. *Gaming.* Nashville: Abingdon Press, 1971.

Boocock, Sarane S., and Schild, E. O. *Simulation Games in Learning.* Beverly Hills, California: Sage Publications, 1968.

Gillispie, Philip H. *Learning Through Simulation Games.* New York: Paulist Press, 1973.

Gordon, Alice Kaplan. *Games for Growth.* Palo Alto, California: Science Research Associates, 1970.

Inbar, Michael, and Stoll, Clarice S. *Simulation and Gaming in Social Science.* New York: The Free Press, 1972.

Raser, John R. *Simulation and Society.* Boston: Allyn and Bacon, 1966.

Zuckerman, David W., and Horn, Robert E. *The Guide to Simulations/Games for Education and Training.* Lexington: Information Resources, Inc., 1973.

Simulation/Gaming/News. A newspaper published five times yearly by S/G/N, Box 3039, University Station, Moscow, Idaho 83843. The March 1974 issue was devoted to simulation gaming and religion.

Organization and Administration of Religious Education

1. Organization in the Local Church

Edwards, Mary Alice Douty. *Leadership Development and the Workers' Conference.* Nashville: Abingdon Press, 1967.

Ernsberger, David J. *Reviving the Local Church.* Philadelphia: Fortress Press, 1969.

Judy, Marvin T. *The Parish Development Process.* Nashville: Abingdon Press, 1973.

Kilinski, Kenneth K., and Wofford, Jerry C. *Organization and Leadership in the Local Church.* Grand Rapids: Zondervan Publishing House, 1973.

Sandt, Eleanor E., ed. *Variations on the Sunday Church School.* New York: The Seabury Press, 1967.

Tower, Grace S. *Growing Up in Mission.* New York: Friendship Press, 1966.

2. Organizational Development Theory and the Church

Etzioni, Amitai. *A Comparative Analysis of Complex Organizations.* New York: The Free Press, 1961.

Havelock, Ronald G. *The Change Agent's Guide to Innovation in Education.* Englewood Cliffs, N. J.: Educational Technology Publications, 1973.

Kaufman, Roger A. *Educational System Planning.* Englewood Cliffs, N. J.: Prentice-Hall, 1972.

Litwin, George H., and Stringer, Robert A., Jr. *Motivation and Organizational Climate.* Cambridge: Harvard University Press, 1968.

Maurer, John G. *Readings in Organizational Theory: Open Systems Approaches.* New York: Random House, 1971.

Perrow, Charles. *Organizational Analysis: A Sociological View.* Belmont, California: Brooks/Cole Publishing Co., 1970.

Thompson, James D. *Organizations in Action.* New York: McGraw-Hill, 1967.

Worley, Robert C. *Change in the Church: A Source of Hope.* Philadelphia: The Westminster Press, 1971.

3. Religion in Public Education

Alves, Colin. *Religion and the Secondary School.* London: SCM Press, 1968.

Beggs, David W., III, and McQuigg, R. Bruce, eds. *America's School and Churches: Partners in Conflict.* Bloomington: Indiana University Press, 1965.

A SELECTED BIBLIOGRAPHY: SINCE 1966

Boles, Donald. *The Two Swords: Commentaries and Cases in Religion.* Ames: Iowa State University Press, 1967.

Boyd, William, and Rawson, Wyatt. *The Story of the New Education.* London: Heinemann Educational Books, 1965.

Clayton, A. Stafford. *Religion and Schooling.* Waltham, Mass.: Blaisdell Publishing Company, 1969.

Costanzo, Joseph. *This Nation Under God: Church, State, and Schools in America.* New York: Herder and Herder, 1964.

Cox, Claire. *The Fourth R: What Can Be Taught About Religion in the Public Schools.* New York: Hawthorn Books, Inc., 1969.

Dolbeare, Kenneth M., and Hammond, Phillip E. *The School Prayer Decisions: From Court Policy to Local Practice.* Chicago: University of Chicago Press, 1971.

Duker, Sam. *The Public Schools and Religion: The Legal Context.* New York: Harper & Row, 1966.

Engel, David E., ed. *Religion in Public Education.* New York: Paulist Press, 1974.

Fellinan, David, ed. *The Supreme Court and Education.* New York: Teachers College Press, 1969.

Freund, Paul A., and Ulich, Robert. *Religion and the Public Schools: The Legal Issue, The Educational Issue.* Cambridge: Harvard University Press, 1965.

Katz, Wilbur G. *Religion and American Constitutions.* Evanston, Ill.: Northwestern University Press, 1964.

La Noue, George R., ed. *Educational Vouchers: Concepts and Controversies.* New York: Teachers College Press, 1972.

Loukes, Harold. *New Ground in Christian Education.* London: SCM Press, 1965.

Mathews, H. F. *Revolution in Religious Education: A Commentary.* Wellington, Surrey, England: The Religious Education Press, 1966.

Michaelsen, Robert. *Piety in the Public Schools: Trends and Issues in the Relationship Between Religion and the Public School in the United States.* New York: The Macmillan Co., 1970.

Morgan, Richard E. *The Supreme Court and Religion.* New York: The Free Press, 1972.

Muir, William K., Jr. *Prayer in the Public Schools: Law and Attitude Change.* Chicago: University of Chicago Press, 1967.

Nielsen, Niels C., Jr. *God in Education.* New York: Sheed & Ward, 1966.

Panoch, James V., and Barr, David L. *Religion Goes to School.* New York: Harper & Row, 1968.

Pfeffer, Leo. *This Honorable Court.* Boston: Beacon Press, 1965.

Sizer, Theodore R., ed. *Religion and Public Education.* Boston: Houghton Mifflin, 1967.

Smith, J. W. D. *Religious Education in a Secular Setting.* London: SCM Press, 1969.

Swomley, John M., Jr. *Religion, the State, and the Schools.* New York: Pegasus, 1968.

4. Roman Catholic Religious Education

Brown, William E., and Greeley, Andrew. *Can Catholic Schools Survive?* New York: Sheed & Ward, 1970.

Donahue, John W. *Catholicism and Education.* New York: Harper & Row, 1973.

Greeley, Andrew M., and Rossi, Peter H. *The Education of Catholic Americans.* Chicago: Aldine, 1966.

Koob, C. Albert, and Shaw, Russell. *S. O. S. for Catholic Schools: A Strategy for Future Service to Church and Nation.* New York: Holt, Rinehart and Winston, 1970.

Lannie, Vincent P. *Public Money and Parochial Education.* Cleveland: The Press of Case Western Reserve University, 1968.

Lee, James Michael, ed. *Catholic Education in the Western World.* Notre Dame: University of Notre Dame Press, 1967.

McCluskey, Neil G. *Catholic Education Faces Its Future.* Garden City, N. Y.: Doubleday, 1968.

Marthaler, Berard L. *Catechetics in Context.* Huntington, Ind.: Our Sunday Visitor, Inc., 1973.

Neiman, Joseph. *Coordinators.* Winona, Minnesota: St. Mary's College Press, 1971.

Pawlikowski, John T. *Catechetics and Prejudice.* New York: Paulist Press, 1973.

Ryan, Mary Perkins, and Neighbor, Russell. *There's More Than One Way to Teach Religion.* Glen Rock, N. J.: Newman/Paulist Press, 1970.

Ryan, Mary Perkins. *We're All in This Together.* New York: Holt, Rinehart and Winston, 1972.

Shaw, Russell, and Hurley, Richard J., eds. *Trends and Issues in Catholic Education.* New York: Citation Press, 1969.

5. Religion and Higher Education

Cantelon, John E. *College Education and the Campus Revolution.* Philadelphia: The Westminster Press, 1969.

Hartt, Julian N. *Theology and the Church in the University.* Philadelphia: The Westminster Press, 1969.

Hassenger, Robert, ed. *The Shape of Catholic Higher Education.* Chicago: The University of Chicago Press, 1967.

Hoge, Dean R. *Commitment on Campus: Changes in Religion and Values over Five Decades.* Philadelphia: The Westminster Press, 1974.

Holmes, Robert Merrill. *The Academic Mysteryhouse: The Man, The Campus, and Their New Search for Meaning.* Nashville: Abingdon Press, 1970.

Martin, Warren Bryan. *Alternative to Irrelevance: A Strategy for Reform in Higher Education.* Nashville: Abingdon Press, 1968.

Michaelson, Robert. *The Study of Religion in American Universities.* New Haven: The Society for Religion in Higher Education, 1965.

Minneman, Charles E., ed. *Students, Religion, and the Contemporary University.* Ypsilanti, Mich.: Eastern Michigan University Press, 1970.

Pattillo, Manning M., Jr., and Mackenzie, Donald M. *Church-Sponsored Higher Education in the United States*. Washington: American Council on Education, 1966.

Ramsey, Paul, and Wilson, John F., eds. *The Study of Religion in Colleges and Universities*. Princeton: Princeton University Press, 1970.

Underwood, Kenneth. *The Church, The University, and Social Policy*. 2 Vols. Middletown, Conn.: Wesleyan University Press, 1969.

6. Building and Equipment for Religious Education

Lynn, Edwin Charles. *Tired Dragons: Adapting Church Architecture to Changing Needs*. Boston: Beacon Press, 1972.

Widber, Mildred C., and Ritenour, Scott T. *Focus: Building for Christian Education*. Philadelphia: Pilgrim Press, 1969.

Curriculum for Religious Education

Doll, Ronald C. *Curriculum Improvement: Decision-Making and Process*. 2d. ed. Boston: Allyn and Bacon, 1970.

Specialized Resources for National Curriculum Developers in the Church's Educational Ministry. New York: Division of Christian Education, the National Council of Churches, 1967.

Tools of Curriculum Development for the Church's Educational Ministry. Anderson, Ind.: Warner Press, 1967.

Methods in Religious Education

1. General Considerations of Method

Armsey, James W., and Dahl, Norman C. *An Inquiry into the Uses of Instructional Technology*. New York: The Ford Foundation, 1973.

Babin, Pierre. *Methods: Approaches for the Catechesis of Adolescents*. New York: Herder and Herder, 1967.

Houle, Cyril O. *The Design of Education*. San Francisco: Jossey-Bass Publishers, 1973.

LeBar, Lois. *Focus on People in Church Education*. Westwood, N. J.: Fleming H. Revell, 1968.

Lee, James Michael, and Rooner, Patrick C. *Toward a Future for Religious Education*. Dayton: Pflaum Press, 1970.

Leypoldt, Martha M. *Forty Ways to Teach in Groups*. Valley Forge, Pa.: Judson Press, 1967.

McManus, Lester W. *Handbook on Christian Education in the Inner City*. New York: The Seabury Press, 1966.

van Caster, Marcel, and Le Du, Jean. *Experiential Catechetics*. New York: Newman Press, 1969.

Voight, Ralph Claude. *Invitation to Learning: The Learning Center Handbook*. Washington: Acropolis Books, 1971.

2. Age-Group Methods

a. Children

Brearley, Molly, ed. *The Teaching of Young Children: Some Applications of Piaget's Learning Theory.* New York: Schocken Books, 1969.

Brusselmans, Christiane. *A Parent's Guide: Religion for Little Children.* Huntington, Ind.: Our Sunday Visitor Publications, 1970.

Cully, Iris V. *Ways to Teach Children.* rev. ed. Philadelphia: Fortress Press, 1966.

Evely, Louis. *Training Children for Maturity.* Paramus, N. J.: Paulist/Newman Press, 1968.

Hemphill, Martha Locke. *Weekday Ministry with Young Children.* Valley Forge, Pa.: Judson Press, 1973.

Jones, Mary Alice. *The Christian Faith Speaks to Children.* Nashville: Abingdon Press, 1965.

Keith-Lucas, Alan. *Christian Education for Emotionally Disturbed Children.* New York: National Council of Churches, 1967.

Klink, Johanna L. *Your Child and Religion.* Richmond: John Knox Press, 1972.

Lytton, Hugh. *Creativity and Education.* New York: Schocken Books, 1972.

Taylor, Florence M. *Your Children's Faith: A Guide to Parents.* Garden City, N. Y.: Doubleday & Co., 1967.

b. Youth

Audinet, Jacques. *Forming the Faith of Adolescents.* New York: Herder and Herder, 1968.

Babin, Pierre. *Options: Approaches for the Religious Education of Adolescents.* New York: Herder and Herder, 1967.

Browning, Robert L. *Communicating with Junior Highs.* Nashville: Graded Press, 1968.

Gilbert, Kent, ed. *Confirmation and Education.* Philadelphia: Lutheran Church in America, 1969.

Irving, Roy G., and Zuck, Roy B., eds. *Youth and the Church.* Chicago: Moody Press, 1968.

Little, Sara. *Youth, World, and Church.* Richmond: John Knox Press, 1968.

Marvin, Ernest. *Odds Against Evens: Young People and the Church.* Philadelphia: The Westminster Press, 1968.

Richards, Lawrence O. *Youth Ministry: Its Renewal in the Church.* Grand Rapids: Zondervan Publishing House, 1972.

Seely, Edward D. *Teaching Early Adolescents Creatively: A Manual for Church School Teachers.* Philadelphia: The Westminster Press, 1971.

Snyder, Ross. *Young People and Their Culture.* Nashville: Abingdon Press, 1969.

vanden Heuvel, Albert H. *The Humiliation of the Church.* Philadelphia: The Westminster Press, 1966.

Zuck, Roy B., and Getz, Gene A. *Christian Youth: An In-Depth Study.* Chicago: Moody Press, 1968.

c. *Adults*

Bergevin, Paul. *A Philosophy for Adult Education.* New York: The Seabury Press, 1967.

Knowles, Malcolm S. *The Modern Practice of Adult Education.* New York: Association Press, 1970.

Moore, Allen J. *The Young Adult Generation.* Nashville: Abingdon Press, 1969.

Moran, Gabriel. *Vision and Tactics: Toward An Adult Church.* New York: Herder and Herder, 1968.

Ramsey, William. *Cycles and Renewal.* Nashville: Abingdon Press, 1969.

Schaefer, James R. *Program Planning for Adult Christian Education.* New York: Newman Press, 1972.

Zuck, Roy B., and Getz, Gene A., eds. *Adult Education in the Church.* Chicago: Moody Press, 1970.

3. *Art and Christian Education*

Dillenberger, Jane. *Secular Art with Sacred Themes.* Nashville: Abingdon Press, 1969.

Wright, Kathryn S. *Let Children Paint: Art in Religious Education.* New York: The Seabury Press, 1966.

Prayer and Worship

1. *The Nature of Prayer and Worship*

Hoon, Paul W. *The Integrity of Worship.* Nashville: Abingdon Press, 1971.

Sloyan, Gerard S. *Worship in a New Key.* New York: Herder and Herder, 1965.

Snyder, Ross. *Contemporary Celebration.* Nashville: Abingdon Press, 1971.

White, James F. *New Forms of Worship.* Nashville: Abingdon Press, 1971.

2. *Prayer and Worship in Religious Education*

Cully, Iris V. *Christian Worship and Church Education.* Philadelphia: The Westminster Press, 1967.

Randolph, David J., ed. *Ventures in Worship.* Nashville: Abingdon Press, 1973.

Vieth, Paul H. *Worship in Christian Education.* Boston: United Church Press, 1965.

INDEX

INDEX

media and religious education, 16-18
Mesthene, Emmanuel, 142
Michigan and religion studies, 189, 190
Miller, Randolph Crump, 30, 32, 82, 92
missionary education, 231-41
Moltmann, Jürgen, 36, 48-49
monitorial education, 232
Moran, Gabriel, 14, 15, 133, 134, 243, 253
Murray, Henry A., 56
music education, 114

National Association of Evangelicals, 198-99, 206
National Sunday School Association, 203, 206
Nebraska and religion studies, 188
Nebreda, Alfonso, 252
neo-orthodoxy, 15, 21
Newton, Isaac, 263
Niebuhr, H. Richard, 81, 262, 263
Niebuhr, Reinhold, 81, 263
Notre Dame, University of, 253

objectives, 26, 108-9, 146-48
O'Dea, Thomas, 243
Oduyoye, Mercy, 234
Ogden, Schubert, 34
Ohio and religion studies, 188, 189, 190
Olevianus, 263
ordination of women, 98-99
organizing for religious education, 109-10, 117-26, 138-51

Palmer, Parker, 268
Pannenburg, Wolfhart, 34, 36, 48
Parsons, Talcott, 65
Pattison, E. Mannsell, 76
Peck, Robert F., 74
Peerman, Dean, 38, 39
Pennsylvania and religion studies, 187, 188
Pennsylvania, University of, 17
Phenix, Phillip H., 192
Piaget, Jean, 60-65, 74, 139, 142-45, 154
Plumb, J. H., 7
Polanyi, Michael, 117, 263
Powers, Edward A., 132
private schools, 205
process theology, 34
Progressive Education Movement, 14-15

public education, 9-14
public education religion studies, 186-97; Center, 190-97
Pusey, Nathan, 263

racism, 18, 80-95
Ramm, Bernard, 34
Ranwez, Pierre, 252
Rapaport, David, 56
Religious Education Association, 128, 202
Ruether, Rosemary R., 81
Roberts, J. Deotis, 88
Rogers, Carl, 89
Roman Catholics and women, 99
Roman Catholic religious education, 9, 242-58; curriculum, 132-33; history, 244-49; in Europe, 222, 224, 227-28; parochial schools, 11-12, 15, 16, 242, 244-50, 254-56; purposes, 243-44; theory, 249-53
Royce, Josiah, 263
Ryan, Mary Perkins, 246-47

Sawin, Margaret, 77
Schaefer, James R., 133
Schempp decision, 186, 188
Scott, Nathan, 35, 38
Scripture Press, 206
seminaries, 10, 98, 183, 184-85, 195, 205, 213, 216
seminaries and women, 98
sexism, 18, 96-106, 214-15
Shelley, Bruce L., 199
Shinn, Roger L., 129
Simmel, Georg, 154
simulation games, 152-70
Singer, Benjamin, 147
Skinner, B. F., 55
Sloyan, Gerard, 249, 252, 253
Smart, James D., 30, 107
socialization process, 72-73, 141
Spinoza, 263
Spivey, Robert A., 193
Sprague, Hall T., 156
Stieglitz, Heinrich, 251
Student Volunteer Movement, 267
Sugarman, Barry, 78
Sullivan, H. S., 56
Supreme Court, 83, 186-87, 194, 248; 1962 and 1963 decisions, 16, 186-87

Theological Education Fund, 213, 216
theology and religious education, 30-40; alternatives, 31-33, 35-39